Hey!
Be Bald!

"This book captures the essence of how to consistently grow an enterprise through relentless customer focus . . . Tiffani Bova is the quintessential storyteller . . . leading us through a framework that gives structure to our growth strategy. As a founder, some of these things are innate . . . but this book is a valuable tool to inspire my leaders throughout each of our businesses. It made me giggle, too. I remember my CFO asking as we hit our growth stride, "What is it that worked?" The answer, of course, is everything. We are in the 1 percent game now, looking and seeking growth of 1 percent from each of our initiatives—combined they deliver double digit growth annually. Thanks, Tiffani, for writing this down . . . a guide book for all leaders to inspire those around them."

—Naomi Simson, shark on *Shark Tank Australia*,
founder of RedBalloon, cofounder of Big Red Group

"Whether you're planning to disrupt an industry or protect your company from competitors, *Growth IQ* shows how urgent it is to choose the right path. This choice can be overwhelming but Tiffani simplifies your options into ten proven paths and empowers you to embark upon the right one for you with confidence . . . and results. Our love affair with comfort zones can be our downfall; Tiffani reminds us that almost all the good stuff happens when we venture off the well-trodden trail into uncharted—and therefore uncertain—territory. With her guidance, we discover that the uncertainty need not be so daunting—through examples, savvy, deeply-experienced analysis and synthesis, and valuable checklists, Tiffani will provide a bump to anyone's Growth IQ."

—Whitney Johnson, Thinkers50 management thinker,
author of *Build an A-Team* and *Disrupt Yourself*

"A worthy successor to Michael Porter, Bova's book is that rare gift: It opens doors for new ideas and new actions. No glib answers here, simply hard-won wisdom that will provoke big changes for organizations large and small."

—Seth Godin, author of *Linchpin*

"Too many companies foster cultures of burnout in the pursuit of short-term growth as an end in itself. Smart growth is sustainable growth and Tiffani Bova shows us how to maintain it by building a purpose-led culture and leveraging, instead of sacrificing, the dedication of your people."

—Arianna Huffington, founder and CEO
of Thrive Global, and founder of *The Huffington Post*

"We all want our business to grow, but how can we make that happen? Fortunately, Tiffani Bova is here with answers. In this smart book, she reveals ten growth paths—from creating an inspiring customer experience to disrupting business as usual. And she backs her findings with solid data and examples from thriving companies. You've got a choice: Tread the old paths or follow Bova into the future."

—Daniel H. Pink, author of *When* and *Drive*

"Tiffani Bova has a knack for rendering complex insights in clear, elegant prose. *Growth IQ* tackles the biggest question in business."

—Martin Lindstrom, author of *Buyology* and *Small Data*

"Look, I LOVE this book. PERIOD. *Growth IQ* has a crisp, clean, and invaluable superstructure. And it is well written. Those things are great, but not the basis for my love affair. The love comes from: Stories. Stories. Stories. Ten sound strategies, thirty compelling, memorable stories—from Starbucks and McDonald's to Under Armour and Red Bull. If these stories don't inspire you and add a ton to your stockpile of personal intellectual capital, I don't know what will. Bravo, Tiffani Bova!"

—Tom Peters, author of *In Search of Excellence*

"Growth is top of mind for every company, but the path to achieving sustained growth can be elusive. In *Growth IQ*, Tiffani applies her deep expertise from working with the world's top brands to light a path to growth in this era of rapid digital transformation."

—Keith Block, vice chairman, president, and COO of Salesforce

GROWTH IQ

GET SMARTER ABOUT THE CHOICES THAT WILL MAKE OR BREAK YOUR BUSINESS

TIFFANI BOVA

PORTFOLIO / PENGUIN

Portfolio/Penguin
An imprint of Penguin Random House LLC
375 Hudson Street
New York, New York 10014

Most Portfolio books are available at a discount when purchased in quantity for sales promotions or corporate use. Special editions, which include personalized covers, excerpts, and corporate imprints, can be created when purchased in large quantities. For more information, please call (212) 572-2232 or email specialmarkets@penguinrandomhouse.com. Your local bookstore can also assist with discounted bulk purchases using the Penguin Random House corporate Business-to-Business program. For assistance in locating a participating retailer, email B2B@penguinrandomhouse.com.

Library of Congress Cataloging-in-Publication Data

Names: Bova, Tiffani, author.
Title: Growth IQ : get smarter about building your company's future / Tiffani Bova.
Description: New York, New York : Portfolio/Penguin, [2018] | Includes bibliographical references.
Identifiers: LCCN 2018018219 (print) | LCCN 2018035210 (ebook) | ISBN 9780525534419 (ebook) | ISBN 9780525534402 (hardcover) |
Subjects: LCSH: Business planning. | Strategic planning. | Corporations—Growth. | Success in business.
Classification: LCC HD30.28 (ebook) | LCC HD30.28 .B6845 2018 (print) | DDC 658.4/06—dc23
LC record available at https://lccn.loc.gov/2018018219

Printed in the United States of America
10 9 8 7 6 5 4

Book design by Pauline Neuwirth

While the author has made every effort to provide accurate telephone numbers, internet addresses, and other contact information at the time of publication, neither the publisher nor the author assumes any responsibility for errors, or for changes that occur after publication. Further, the publisher does not have any control over and does not assume any responsibility for author or third-party websites or their content.

This book is dedicated to my tribe, my Ohana, who have been on this journey with me since day one. Without your support, none of this would have been possible.
I am forever grateful to each of you.

CONTENTS

MARKET
ACCELERATION

PRODUCT
EXPANSION

CUSTOMER/
PRODUCT
DIVERSIFICATION

CONTENTS

PATH 6
OPTIMIZE SALES

OPTIMIZE
SALES

PATH 7
CHURN

CUSTOMERS

CHURN

PATH 8
PARTNERSHIPS

PARTNERSHIPS

PATH 9
CO-OPETITION

PATH 10
UNCONVENTIONAL STRATEGIES

x

FOREWORD

Geoffrey A. Moore

I HAVE HAD THE PLEASURE OF working with Tiffani Bova over the past few years. I remember when she told me she was in the midst of writing her debut book and asked for any advice. I paused for a moment to reflect on how much the world had changed over the past three decades since I wrote *Crossing the Chasm* in 1991. Despite the changes, were there still some universal, fundamental ideas and wisdom—"the Force," if you will—that continue to be relevant? And if so, how would they apply to meeting the growth challenges of today?

Growth IQ provides great answers to these questions. As a former distinguished analyst and research fellow for Gartner, and now as the growth and innovation evangelist at Salesforce, a company on the cutting edge, reshaping the way the world does business, Tiffani has had numerous inside looks at successful growth strategies from a wide variety of companies. She has seen what has worked and what has not, and in *Growth IQ*, she shares a wealth of valuable lessons learned.

The book is organized around ten growth paths—each presented through a wealth of stories of both successes and failures, each making clear what things to focus on and what factors are critical for future success. She illuminates her core concepts with insightful stories and distills theoretical models with real-world examples that are relatable, accessible, and applicable. While a number of these growth paths may be familiar, Bova's conceptual model of applying market context, the combination of initiatives, and the sequence in which various paths are deployed goes above and beyond to establish a new paradigm for strategic business thinking.

It is true that every business must grow to stay healthy and relevant, and all the successful ones have proven formulas for so doing. Some of these strategic playbooks have become so powerful that executives are recruited away specifically to help another company re-create a similar growth trajectory. How does Amazon do what they do? How does Salesforce? Red Bull? Starbucks? Sephora? What can these companies teach you that you can apply to your business? Being able to draw on insights like these can be truly game changing.

Growth is good for everyone in the value chain, and it should always be top of mind for business leaders. However, the truth is that finding sustainable and repeatable growth is getting harder. Sometimes we hold on to our old growth "playbook" for too long, or our world is disrupted by a more agile start-up in ways we could have never imagined.

Either way, if you are looking to accelerate growth, recover from a slowdown in top-line sales, or expand to new markets or customer segments, I recommend that you read *Growth IQ*. It will reveal the landscape of opportunities you may not even realize you have at your fingertips. It will empower you and your team to navigate the realities of business today. And it will give you a framework that you can revisit over and over again.

GEOFFREY MOORE
a.k.a. "The Chasm Guy"
Author of *Crossing the Chasm* and *Zone to Win*

GROWTH IQ

THE ONE THING IS—IT'S NEVER JUST ONE THING

How do you stay ahead of ever-rising customer expectations? There's no single way to do it—it's a combination of many things.

—JEFF BEZOS

OVER THE THOUSANDS OF INTERACTIONS I've had with some of the world's biggest companies, I've found that one of *the most persistent and vexing challenges faced by executives is determining how best to grow their business*. Unless you're a small family business determined to stay small, or you are unable to take on more financial risk and workload along with their associated hiring demands, the quest for growth is never ending. While there is always a balance of high-sales and low-sales periods, an extended stall or slowdown in growth is often a cause for great concern among investors and employees.

Why? Because every company faces the same pressures—to keep the lights on, pay its people, get products out the door, and support its customers even when experiencing a low-sales period. *There is no way to reduce those pressures and keep the business going without top-line growth and bottom-line profitability*. Finding ways to grow the business, the top line, can become all consuming, especially for start-ups, small businesses, or even a new division of a Fortune 500 company. Every business has room for improvement, but not every business leader knows where to look for that improvement or how to course-correct and rally the company to change when times get tough.

Repeatable and reliable growth for established companies and new ventures alike is hard and seems to be getting harder. That's true even for one of the largest and most celebrated brands in the world. In its third quarter in 2017, IBM found itself with twenty-two straight quarters of declining revenue. Ginni Rometty, chairman and CEO of IBM, noted: "Be prepared to spot growth opportunities when they present themselves— because they are the key learning opportunities. You'll know because they make you uncomfortable, and your initial impulse may be that you're not ready. But remember: *Growth and comfort never co-exist.*"

So, what can executives do? Where do they go looking for that next 10 percent of growth—in revenue, in market share, in active users, or all of the above?

I have found that most executives—armed with reams of data, consultant white papers, and market trend reports—are looking for the *one* new product offering, new market, or sales and marketing tactic to fix their problems quickly. They may say: "We should try to sell more [product name] to our existing customers," or, "We should expand our distribution/sales overseas," or, "We should increase our marketing spend"—and they may be right. But that is only part of the story.

After years of watching companies make the same mistakes over and over again, or miss golden opportunities to accelerate growth, I realized that too many companies seek *the one right move*—which, by the way, rarely exists—in order to improve or sustain their performance, respond to a competitive threat, or recover from a growth stall. The reality is, when it comes to growth . . . *the one thing is it's never just one thing.*

RESPONDING TO CHANGE

Why do companies look for the one right move? Maybe it's because they do what seems doable: look for the one problem area to fix, the one big initiative they can take to boost the numbers quickly, or even repeat the one growth strategy that worked in the past. This last tactic is particularly insidious. *Companies often rely on strategies that worked for them once but may have outlived their purpose and no longer have the desired impact in current market conditions and context.* Companies that reach into a bag of old tricks without careful consideration of the changing market dynamics risk getting trapped in a vicious downward cycle, repeating the same actions and yielding ever worse results over time.

The cost of misalignment between perception and reality can be enormous, and keeping a business-as-usual attitude under such circumstances is bound to only make responding to change more difficult. The perception may be: "We got this . . . it's just a temporary setback," when the reality is that customers change, industries change, technology changes—heck, the world changes—and companies that don't constantly evolve, sometimes in the smallest ways, risk being left behind. Let this bring you comfort—you are not alone.

> *Success is a lousy teacher.*
> *It seduces smart people*
> *into thinking they can't*
> *lose.*
>
> **—BILL GATES**

While it is true that many companies struggle to keep up with the pace of change or the rate of disruption caused by innovative technology and new business models, these are not the only reasons why companies struggle to find and maintain growth and revenue streams. Sometimes, the biggest threat to a company can be its own success or, worse, complacency.

Why? Because for companies that are currently growing, and not yet aware of an impending growth stall, it reinforces the status quo, it rewards (at least for a time) resistance to change, and ultimately it makes company leaders terrified to pursue a new direction for fear they will mess up a good thing that it's got going. What had been, in the early days, an entrepreneurial spirit that embraced new opportunities (and risks) often shifts to one that fends them off . . . especially when things start to go wrong. The fact is, 87 percent of all companies go through

FOR THE PURPOSES OF GROWTH IQ

Growth refers to top-line sales organic growth, not cost cutting, mergers and acquisitions (M&A), or other means to grow profitability or the bottom line.

Growth strategy is defined as "a plan of action or policy designed to achieve a major or overall aim."

Growth path is HOW—initiatives that can focus the company on the task at hand and achieve the strategic growth goal.

THE ONE THING IS—IT'S NEVER JUST ONE THING

a growth stall at some point, and only a small percentage of them ever recover.

When asked what slows growth, it might surprise you to learn that most executives actually cite internal factors. In a Bain & Company study, 85 percent of the executives surveyed, and a full 94 percent of those running companies with more than $5 billion in revenue, said that internal, not external, obstacles keep their companies from growing profitably. What a shame; after all, it is the internal factors over which you are supposed to have control—as opposed to moves by your competitors, market shifts, and even "Black Swan" events.

TEN PATHS TO GROWTH

The more conversations I had on the subject and the more deeply I studied the ways in which companies have grown successfully, the more I came to realize that:

1. It wasn't just about what *growth strategies companies chose to pursue* that determined the likelihood of success but rather the context *in which a strategy was deployed and the combination and sequence of initiatives.*
2. Growth is far less complicated than most people make it out to be. You might be surprised to learn that you can categorize most growth efforts taken by a business into one of **ten growth paths.** *Deciding which path(s) are liable to have the greatest (positive) consequence will—and in fact should—change over time. No growth path should be written in stone.*

These ten paths are established routes that have been used by countless companies to successfully grow top-line revenues. They can help guide huge multinationals, small start-ups, and medium-size businesses, regardless of product, region, or industry.

THE TEN GROWTH PATHS

1. **CUSTOMER EXPERIENCE:** *Inspire additional purchases and advocacy*

2. **CUSTOMER BASE PENETRATION:** *Sell more existing products to existing customers*

3. **MARKET ACCELERATION:** *Expand into new markets with existing products*

4. **PRODUCT EXPANSION:** *Sell new products to existing markets*

5. **CUSTOMER AND PRODUCT DIVERSIFICATION:** *Sell new products to new customers*

6. **OPTIMIZE SALES:** *Streamline sales efforts to increase productivity*

7. **CHURN (MINIMIZE DEFECTION):** *Retain more customers*

8. **PARTNERSHIPS:** *Leverage third-party alliances, channels, and ecosystems (Sales, Go-to-Market)*

9. **CO-OPETITION:** *Cooperate with market or industry competitor (Product Development, IP Sharing)*

10. **UNCONVENTIONAL STRATEGIES:** *Disrupt current thinking*

THE ONE THING IS—IT'S NEVER JUST ONE THING

WHAT'S OLD IS NEW AGAIN

We'll soon look at each of these ten paths in depth—for now, just take a step back and look at them as a whole. Some of them may seem familiar, or somewhat obvious, and they should. This list is built on the back of long-standing management thinking and frameworks, including the Ansoff Matrix (a practical framework developed in 1957 by Igor Ansoff for thinking about how growth can be achieved through a *product* strategy), plus newer sales and marketing concepts used by companies today to stimulate growth.

Let me be clear: these ten growth paths recognize that many of the classics haven't gone away; paths like **Product Expansion** and **Customer Base Penetration** remain as valid as ever; but as the business world has become more complicated, with the rise of e-commerce, software-as-a-service, and other technological and business-model innovations, and the consumer has become more empowered and educated, the application of these requires a more modernized approach.

These various technological advances have provided companies new means to pursue growth alongside tried-and-true classics. Until recently the absence of detailed consumer, product, and market data meant that companies left a lot to chance, gut instinct, and previous experience. What worked in the past, such as increased marketing spends and price reductions/promotions, would simply be repeated. It isn't that companies didn't know anything about what was driving growth in the past; it's more the fact that today companies, in real time, can gain meaningful insights to make the right decisions, at the right time, with the right growth path.

CONTEXT + COMBINATION + SEQUENCE

It isn't enough to have the "right" new growth strategy. You must fully understand what the current market context is prior to making any moves; otherwise, even the right decision, or the right growth path, can put you in the wrong place at the wrong time. Let me be clear—*choosing the right growth path for your company should always start with* **context**, *the circumstances or events that form the environment within which your company competes.* When companies base growth decisions upon an intelligent appraisal of the product, market, and customer context, and the threat or opportunity those contexts bring, along with the *combination* and *sequence* necessary to support the chosen growth paths, it can make the difference between success and failure.

CONTEXT includes current social and economic conditions, existing product portfolio, competitive landscape, and corporate culture.

COMBINATION is the act of selecting key actions that can positively influence outcomes, when done together.

SEQUENCE is the act of establishing a priority, order, and timing to those actions.

Growth IQ is a holistic approach to finding the right path, in the right market context, in the right combination and sequence—*creating a multiplier effect that is far more powerful than just focusing on one or two efforts in isolation.*

A key thing to remember as you set out to reenergize your growth efforts: a company can attempt to duplicate a growth strategy from an industry rival, but rarely is it able to re-create a particular growth path (how a company grew), along with the exact same combination or sequence of efforts, within a particular market context, that led to that rival's success:

- Don't try to copy what you think your competitors are doing. Imitation is not the path to success, especially in the overcrowded industries most companies confront today.
- Don't get distracted by what landed you in this current situation—good or bad.
- Don't make the common mistake of believing that what you've always done will continue to deliver.
- Keep your mind—and your options—open.

THE ONE THING IS—IT'S NEVER JUST ONE THING

WHAT'S IN IT FOR YOU

While merely duplicating the efforts of other companies is unlikely to work for you, it's crucial to understand what decisions other companies made when they faced a fork in the road, and which growth paths, combinations, and sequences they chose. By reading the case studies of companies such as Under Armour, Sephora, Shake Shack, The Honest Company, Walmart, Mattel, Marvel, and others I cover in *Growth IQ*, you'll learn how some of the most successful companies were able to achieve growth, providing you with perspective on how to apply the Growth IQ framework to your own business as you push to increase top-line revenue. You'll also read notable examples of growth strategies that failed or backfired and learn how to avoid those pitfalls as you navigate the pursuit of growth for your business. *While all of the companies in this book followed their own decision-making process to take the steps they did, Growth IQ gives us a framework to deconstruct and understand their growth efforts within a single model.*

> *Follow effective action with quiet reflection.*
>
> *From the quiet reflection will come even more effective action.*
>
> **—PETER DRUCKER, author of** *The Effective Executive*

Each chapter of *Growth IQ* looks in depth at one of the ten Growth IQ paths, initially defining the path itself, what it is, and why it was chosen. We **Set the Scene**, highlighting the overall market context impacting a particular growth path, and then feature stories of a number of companies, spanning various industries and sizes—showcasing how they were able to leverage a particular growth path successfully over time or combine certain growth paths in just the right sequence to maximize their return on investment.

Each **Story** highlights companies that followed a particular growth path (or paths) to accelerate their current (growth) success or to recover from a growth stall or an unexpected slowdown after multiple quarters of strong performance. You will also see stories of **"How It Can Go Wrong,"** because failures can be one of the greatest teachers. Chapters conclude with: **Putting It All Together, What Works—and Potential Pitfalls,** and

Suggested Next Steps—how to apply the lessons learned to your own business.

My goal is to help you Get Smarter About the Choices That Will Make or Break Your Business—to develop a keen understanding of the ten growth paths and the importance of context, combination, and sequence, so you can deconstruct your own growth initiatives and become a "Growth Navigator"—capable of steering your company, your division, your sales team through even the harshest of market conditions with ease.

PATH 1

**CUSTOMER
EXPERIENCE**

CUSTOMER EXPERIENCE

You've got to start with the customer experience and work backwards for the technology. . . . What incredible benefits can we give to the customer? . . . Not starting with "Let's sit down with the engineers and figure out what awesome technology we have."

—STEVE JOBS

WHY CUSTOMER EXPERIENCE MATTERS

- Three-fourths of three thousand business-to-business (B2B) companies surveyed ranked customer experience as a major factor in supplier choice.
- Sixty-eight percent of C-suite executives expect organizations to emphasize customer experience over products in the future.
- Eighty-six percent of customers are willing to spend more for a better customer experience.
- Seventy percent of buying experiences are based on how customers feel they are being treated.
- Analysis shows that companies that excel in the customer experience grow revenues 4–8 percent above their market.
- Seven in ten Americans (70 percent) are willing to spend an average of 13 percent more with companies they believe provide excellent customer service.
- The promise of better customer service is a draw for shoppers: three in five Americans (59 percent) would try a new brand or company for a better service experience.

CUSTOMER EXPERIENCE IS THE NEW BLACK

How much did your last Uber ride, hotel room, airline ticket, or Starbucks coffee cost? (No cheating—if you had to submit it on an expense report, that doesn't count.) Now, what company have you recently engaged with that left you sitting on hold for customer service, or didn't get back to you quickly, or shipped the wrong product and the return process was a nightmare?

I'm betting you remember the brand names of the latter ones, those "experiences," much more vividly than the previous—and you aren't afraid to share them, either.

Recent snafus caused by subpar customer experience (CX) have made national, and in some cases international, news, including, for example, United Airlines (which dragged a passenger off one of its airplanes) and Wells Fargo (which signed up people for additional accounts without their consent), which erased, quite quickly, I might add,

> *The reputation of a thousand years may be undermined by the conduct of one hour.*
>
> **—JAPANESE PROVERB**

much of the goodwill that these well-respected brands and their CX efforts had built up over many decades.

Current research shows that more than 70 percent of customers look to (customer) "reviews" as the number one source when they are deciding among different brands and products. *That is why this growth path can be so unforgiving.* We will forever have those "negative" (customer experience) images burned in our memory and our conversations and memorialized on the Web—which means that those companies have to spend much more to "win" us back than they did to acquire us in the first place.

CUSTOMERS REMEMBER
THE EXPERIENCE THEY HAVE
WITH A BRAND LONGER THAN
THEY REMEMBER THE PRICE THEY PAID.

> Customer experience is the sum of all of a brand's touch points, both online and off-line, through both human representatives and now technology (such as bots, artificial intelligence (AI), and "things").

What is customer experience? For the purposes of *Growth IQ*, customer experience is centered on the interactions between companies and their customers. A *brand promise* is what *you* say about your company, customer experiences will impact what *they*—customers—say about your company. In principle, *customer experience is based on the feelings that arise once customers engage with your products, employees, and various sales, service, and marketing channels.*

Don't make the mistake of thinking that because you have a focus on improving CX, you are actually "on the **Customer Experience** path." Using CX as a catalyst for growth is very different from focusing solely on improving specific metrics, within a few groups. More than any other "revolution" in the last century, the shift in customer expectations is proving to upend everything we think we know about business growth.

The true source of competitive differentiation in the twenty-first century is: Customer Experience.

Unfortunately, many companies lose sight of CX and still have a narrow view of the drivers in delivering a compelling CX—mostly because: (1) they don't agree on what a "compelling" CX actually is, (2) they don't have a formal key performance indicator (KPI) to manage and track performance against, and (3) there is no "one" owner of CX but rather many roles or people or functions responsible for pieces and parts of it. I'm sure you are familiar with the saying, "If you can't measure it, you can't improve it," and

> Gillette has lost U.S. market share for six straight years. Its share of the men's-razors business fell to 54 percent in 2016, down from 59 percent in 2015 and more than 70 percent in 2010. This was driven by low cost subscription services Dollar Shave Club, Harry's Razors, and others. Cost plays an important role in this shift, and quality remains a key element, *but experience is a major driver*.

if you agree with that statement, the focus on CX should therefore result in a push toward ways in which CX efforts can be measured for the purposes of improvement—in the eyes of the customer, not the business itself.

Companies that adopt the **Customer Experience** path need to start by answering the question: Who is the customer? This has grown to be an increasingly difficult question to answer because *the definition of what a "customer" is . . . is blurring.* It is usually a person, of course, but of late, some companies need to consider that a customer could also be a thing (refrigerator, piece of machinery, a chatbot, etc.) or even a place (household, automobile, hotel). Gartner predicts that by 2018, six billion connected things will be requesting support. Think about it this way: soon your automobile will not only be able to let you know it needs its oil changed, but it could drive itself to the local auto mechanic to get it done—while you are working. Today, your smart appliances can reorder supplies when needed, like your washing machine knowing it has done twenty-five loads and needs more laundry detergent, or it has been ninety days since you replaced your air conditioner filter so the manufacturer just sends you a new one when it's time. While in all of these examples the machines are still serving people and operating to serve their needs, this changes the business-customer relationship in a profound way.

Furthermore, you have to consider: Are customers the same as buyers? Not necessarily. Keeping with the above examples, who or what is the customer—and who or what is the buyer—and who or what will be requesting support or service? Bottom line: *the level of complexity between a company and its "customer" is actually getting worse,* not better, especially when it comes to closely monitoring and managing the experience someone has with your brand.

WHAT'S GOOD FOR THE GOOSE IS GOOD FOR THE GANDER

The Japanese proverb *Omotenashi* (おもてなし) can be translated to "The customer is always right," but many in Japan will prefer the literal translation of "The customer is god."

With the advent of social media, smartphones, and the Internet, consumers are more informed and demanding than ever of the business-to-consumer (B2C) brands they interact with. Many B2B brands make the mistake in thinking that all the hype around CX is only applicable or valuable to B2C companies. That couldn't be further from the truth. You must remember that B2C customers, the ones who are more demanding and informed, bring the same expectations and purchasing habits into their workplace. Because of this, there is a lot that companies can learn from B2C companies and apply in a B2B environment.

Being on the **Customer Experience** path, and using it as a differentiator and an engine for growth, has proven to be a successful strategy for brands like Zappos, Nordstrom, Virgin Airlines, and Starbucks. Yes, each of them is a B2C company, but it doesn't mean that thousands of B2B companies haven't shown up in Las Vegas at the Zappos campus to attend the "School of WOW Customer Service Training." They don't care that Zappos is a B2C company. What they care about is upleveling the way they deliver customer service to improve overall CX.

> *Whatever you do, do it well. Do it so well that when people see you do it they will want to come back and see you do it again and they will want to bring others and show them how well you do what you do.*
>
> **—WALT DISNEY**

Today, some companies simply consider themselves "B2E" or "business to everything/everyone" to get out from under this long-standing B2B versus B2C distinction and focus on what really matters: *the customer.*

Make no mistake: regardless of what industry you are in or what segment you serve, there is no way around this. Becoming a customer-led company, one that is obsessively focused on customers and their experiences with a brand, isn't just one of the ten growth paths, *it is the growth path that must become the foundation for each subsequent path.* That is exactly why I made it the first one in *Growth IQ.* Think of it like this: in order for a company to use the **Customer Experience** path as a growth enabler, *CX must become the "nucleus" that sits at the intersection of all business units, all functions, all decisions, all employees. Everything.*

While the **Customer Experience** path may ultimately be the most rewarding of the ten growth paths, especially for the customer (after all, who wouldn't want to have the loyal customer bases of Southwest Airlines, Shake Shack, Starbucks, Disney, Amazon, Apple, or Sephora?), it is also often one of the most difficult to pull off. *Transforming customer experience requires complete company buy-in.* Each employee must understand his or her role in delivering the product or service to the customer. From the accountant to the cleaning crew, everyone plays a part. **Everyone.**

For some companies, transforming CX requires modest adjustments. For others, the aspiration may mean, at least in the short term, that they need to reevaluate all aspects of the business. Either way, it must first start with the willingness to make the shift. Then, and only then, will it translate into an overall mission—a "true north" for the company to rally around.

PATH 1 CUSTOMER EXPERIENCE

STORY

1

SEPHORA
A BEAUTIFUL EXPERIENCE

In today's retail environment, where very little is constant and clients' expectations are ever-evolving, one thing has remained true for SEPHORA: there is no better way to create meaningful connections with clients than through personalized experiences and a customized approach to beauty.

**—CALVIN MCDONALD,
president and CEO of Sephora Americas**

THERE SHOULD BE NO QUESTION that there has been a distinct shift in buyer behavior over the past decade. We only need to look at our own shopping habits to confirm that. Smaller-format and more experience-oriented retailers are beginning to hold their own against the larger stores.

One of those companies redefining retail is Sephora, which has been a trailblazer in the beauty (retail) industry for decades. In 2016, it gained market share across all regions and recorded double-digit growth in both revenue and profits. More than a hundred stores were opened in 2016 and it has opened seventy new stores in the United States in 2017 alone.

From its early days, Sephora has been focused on inventing new ways to make the beauty shopping experience fun and engaging for its customers. Originally, it didn't sell anything but other companies' products. So, what made them so unique? Many would say it wasn't *what* they sold but *how* they sold it—and how their customers felt when they engaged with the brand and its employees. There should be no question that Sephora has been on, and continues to be on, the **Customer Experience** path as it pursues additional growth opportunities.

Sephora was among the first beauty retailers to organize stores by product instead of brand, launch an e-commerce platform, launch native mobile apps, utilize data from its Beauty Insider (loyalty) program to send personalized communications and recommendations, integrate with Pinterest, use advanced technology such as beacons in stores, introduce mobile point-of-sale (POS) systems . . . the list is long.

Its newest concept, the Sephora Studio, a smaller store concept with high-tech beauty upgrades, pushes the CX envelope even farther. Research found that 43 percent of consumers would pay up to 10 percent more for a personalized shopping experience, and brands that create personalized experiences by integrating advanced digital technologies and proprietary data for customers are seeing revenue increase by 6–10 percent—two to three times faster than those that don't. That's great news for Sephora, which, according to the Sailthru first annual Retail Personalization Index, provides the most *personalized customer experience in the beauty business*. It's therefore no surprise that between 2010 and 2017, Sephora's U.S. revenue was expected to grow at 10 percent per year, far outpacing industry average.

EXPERIENTIAL RETAIL

Consumers haven't disappeared, and they are not spending less: their tastes (the market context) have changed. The always-on economy allows consumers to vote not only with their dollars but with their ongoing loyalty. Sephora does not want to be another store where customers go to just buy something. *Instead, it aspires to be more like a community of like-minded people where anyone can learn, try, and play with its vast array of products.*

When you think of innovation in cosmetics and beauty products, you typically picture clever new brand names, creative packaging, arresting point-of-sale images, and celebrity endorsements. But Sephora, founded in Paris in 1969 and now owned by luxury conglomerate LVMH, is a very different company.

Named after the most beautiful wife of Moses, the company has leveraged its masterful ability to expand into new markets (**Market Acceleration**), innovate new beauty products (**Customer and Product Diversification**), and develop both digital and mobile platforms (**Op-**

timize Sales), all with a comprehensive and pervasive focus on CX to become one of the world's largest beauty retailers. This willingness to innovate with products and the way it engages with its customers has defined the company from the beginning.

In its early days, Sephora, and its entrepreneur CEO, Dominique Mandonnaud, recognized that the context of the beauty business was changing from boutiques to large, multiproduct stores and from small lot production of a finite number of items to vast catalogs of increasingly consumer-defined product lines.

Mandonnaud also was one of the first to recognize the increasing interconnectedness of discrete industries, such as cosmetics and perfumes, into a more monolithic "solutions"-oriented industry called "beauty." Thus, the history of Sephora is the story of how Mandonnaud and those who followed him combined these different businesses and turned them into interactive (and eventually digital) customer experiences.

Sephora's ascent has a great deal to do with its unique approach to merchandising and the experience it wants its customers to have while shopping. The store's fluid layout allows shoppers to bounce from brand to brand and product to product with little effort.

One of Mandonnaud's first product innovations was what he called "assisted self-service"—essentially meaning that, unlike the rule at other cosmetics stores of the era, he let customers actually try products before they bought them. He used it to sell more products to existing customers (**Customer Base Penetration**), attract new customers (**Market Acceleration**), and further **Optimize Sales**. Needless to say, this concept was copied and has since swept the world of beauty retailing. Sephora led the charge on changing the brand loyalty paradigm away from the old model toward a "try-more-buy-more" proposition.

The first sign that Sephora was going to do something new came in 1999, right at the peak of the e-commerce boom, when the company announced its first online store (**Market Acceleration**), targeted at the U.S. market. As the Internet matured, a new kind of retailing emerged, one in which consumers were increasingly interested in the experience they had with brands online.

In an era when almost every other beauty product company was still selling its products in supermarkets, drugstores, and pharmacies, such a move was unorthodox, even somewhat shocking. Indeed, many of Sephora's competitors didn't take the same step for another decade—giving it a *big* head start. Beyond the significant first-mover advantage it may have had in the market with many of these things, you have to remember that just because a company copies something another company—maybe even a competitor—does, it doesn't mean that company will enjoy the same results. It was the combination and sequence of multiple things— growth paths—that made Sephora successful.

In 2006, the ever-innovative Sephora once again was pushing the envelope when pursuing the **Customer Experience** path. It wanted to get closer to an entirely new set of customers—those who weren't interested in patronizing an exclusive beauty and cosmetic store. It began by opening small—typically fifteen hundred square feet—"pop-up" stores inside JCPenneys in the United States. By the end of 2017, there were nearly 650 of them in operation, covering 75 percent of all JCPenney stores.

This combination of the **Customer Experience** path and the **Partnership** path provided the ability for customers to purchase Sephora online and pick up their order at a JCPenney store the same day—ultimately meeting the customer's expectations for accessibility and convenience. Since its initial launch, JCPenney has "significantly expanded" the assortment of Sephora products it carries online. The department store also revealed that it would soon add a feature that would enable customers to book makeovers with Sephora beauty consultants in its stores. This partnership went against the standard view that the era of brick-and-mortar

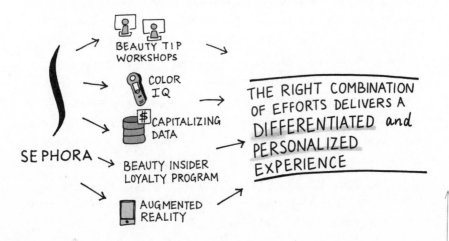

PATH 1 CUSTOMER EXPERIENCE

retailing was over, or even that competitive retailers could lean into the **Co-opetition** path to serve a common customer. Was this successful? During the November–December (2017) period, JCPenney posted a 3.4 percent sales increase as home, beauty, and fine jewelry led the store.

Crucial to Sephora's success was *the sequence in which it struck these partnerships, launched its own initiatives, and worked with previous competitors.* A large part of what allows Sephora to continue to find growth opportunities while others may struggle is the usage of the data it collects. From point-of-sale machines, loyalty programs, online purchases, and social media campaigns, *Sephora's ability to learn what its customers want and what they may want in the future helps it stay ahead in delivering a compelling customer experience over time*, resulting in repeat and loyal customers. It isn't just about personalizing the shopping experience, both online and off-line, that gives Sephora a significant CX advantage; it goes way beyond that. From its Beauty Tip Workshops, Color IQ, data collection and analysis, and augmented reality, Sephora isn't afraid to try progressive, unproven ways to continue to drive repeat purchases, loyalty, and growth.

> *We constantly challenge ourselves to discover new and better ways to make the customer experience even more inspiring.*
>
> **—CHRISTOPHER DE LAPUENTE,**
> **chairman and CEO of Sephora**

Don't let current success cloud your judgment and make you complacent. *Finding strong success in one market or customer base doesn't mean it's the only one.* Case in point, Sephora learned that there are two different types of beauty products customers: those who know what they want and those who want to try the items first, which meant that even as Sephora was showing strong growth on its own and through its partnership with JCPenney, it began selling its products on Amazon, once again using the **Co-opetition** path to serve its common customers better. Whether it is in its own branded retail storefront, in a pop-up in JCPenney, or via (an online) partnership with Amazon, when it comes to growth, nothing is off the table if it meets customer expectations and satisfies pent-up demand—and most definitely if it helps deliver an even more compelling CX, Sephora is in.

SEPHORA:
KEY TAKEAWAYS

- A company that is founded with a deep commitment to CX, has executive support, and has the required investments in place has a much easier time pursuing, even doubling down on, the **Customer Experience** path as a growth engine—especially over those companies that approach CX as an ad hoc nice-to-have. The former may find themselves having to make minor adjustments along the way, whereas the latter will need to make significant changes in people, systems, processes, and culture regarding the **Customer Experience** growth path.

- Keeping the human and technical investments in balance is what makes Sephora's pursuit of CX so effective, especially for younger shoppers who are increasingly seeking a compelling and different CX.

- Take advantage of big data, analytics, and CRM systems to identify and engage with your most loyal customers. Those most-valued shoppers can be engaged at a deeper level with relevant educational content, personalized promotional offers, and other messages that nourish positive brand sentiment.

STORY

2

SHAKE SHACK
RADICAL HOSPITALITY

We're not in the hamburger business; we're in show business.

—RAY KROC, "Founder" of McDonald's

SINCE 1919, WHEN A&W HIT the scene, and then White Castle (1921) and then McDonald's (1940) and then Kentucky Fried Chicken (1952 . . . known as KFC since 1991), there has been no slowdown in the number of fast-food restaurants opening around the globe, nor in the intensity with which they compete with one another. After all these years, one could surmise that fast-food restaurants continue to compete on product (what food they sell) and price. However, the traditional fast food many of us (over the age of forty, anyway) grew up with is evolving—due in large part to the context of the market changing.

There are two notable shifts to consider: One, consumers becoming more conscious of what they're eating and demanding food that is healthier, less processed, locally sourced, and better tasting; and Two, as well as customers wanting a "restaurant-like experience" at a more reasonable price point. Those two things have opened the door for new competitors to enter the fray and battle for fast-food dollars. Enter "fast casual," a new genre of restaurant that emerged with Panda Express in 1983, which was worth $47 billion in 2016, and is leading the restaurant sector when it comes to growth in 2017.

One of the brands taking advantage of new *market context* and customer demands is Shake Shack, the brainchild of Danny Meyer. Shake Shack had humble beginnings. It started in 2004 as a hot dog cart in Madison Square Park in New York City—part of a community art project. It quickly became so popular that it received a permit to open a permanent kiosk, expanded its menu, and consistently drew a line of customers forty-five minutes long.

Meyer set out to combine the leading CX and product quality of his other higher-end restaurants (especially the meticulous way it produces its beef and sources its products locally), all while serving its food in the fast-casual concept. Similar to Dominique Mandonnaud, the founder of Sephora, everything Meyer did was rooted in the CX above all else, which puts the company squarely on the **Customer Experience** path—CX has been part of the company's DNA—its **true north** for success since its inception.

You may think, as I once did, that I'm primarily in the business of serving good food. Actually, though, food is secondary to something that matters even more. In the end, what's most meaningful is creating positive, uplifting outcomes for human experiences and human relationships. Business, like life, is all about how you make people feel. It's that simple, and it's that hard.

—DANNY MEYER, CEO of the Union Square Hospitality Group

SHAKE SHACK'S PHILOSOPHY RUNS DEEP

Meyer believes that 49 percent of CX comes down to food, "which is more or less service." But the other 51 percent is made up of thoughtful things you do—*the customer service and enlightened guest hospitality.* In other words, it's people. To ensure Shake Shack stays on track, it uses real-time feedback (providing comment cards, roundtable discussions, and monthly dining vouchers for its staff) to deliver a consistent dining (customer) experience. Nothing is off-limits, and no detail is too small to consider improving.

Shake Shack's entire philosophy with CX is centered on putting its employees first as a way of providing both great service and acts of thought-

SHAKE SHACK → customer service ↘ guest hospitality → CUSTOMER EXPERIENCE CENTERED AROUND PUTTING EMPLOYEES first

fulness. Meyer, in his book *Setting the Table*, said he believes that he can guess what type of experience he will have, in any restaurant or business, solely based on how the staff members "appear to be focused on their work, supportive of one another, and enjoying one another's company." Too many companies believe that improving CX requires being hyper-focused on the customer, but Meyer demonstrates that CX can be improved by focusing on the employees as well. John DiJulius, author of *The Customer Service Revolution*, has said: *"Your customers will never be happier than your employees."* Tom Peters (a.k.a. the "Red Bull" of management thinking) tweeted DiJulius's quote, with the setup: "Says it all."

Shake Shack might have started out as a Manhattan hot dog cart, but now it has more than 136 locations across the globe, with overseas franchises in cities such as Moscow, Dubai, Istanbul, and London. As it expanded both domestically and internationally (**Market Acceleration** path), the fact it had a loyal and vocal (via social media) customer base validated its strong brand commitment to CX and inspired people to give Shake Shack a try. Its *dedication to quality and customer service bucked stereotypes of traditional fast food,* the notion that fast food had to be precooked or even prepared quickly in favor of quality ingredients and CX. Shake Shack spends barely any money on marketing, instead focusing on the quality of food and the hospitality of its employees to create "raving fans" of the brand. This focus has helped Shake Shack stay popular in an era where diners have far more "fast-casual" choices.

Randy Garutti, Shake Shack CEO, said to a roomful of its employees at the opening of its sixty-sixth Shake Shack in Boston, Massachusetts, in 2015: *"Put us out of business because you are so damn generous with what you give the people who walk in this door. If there's a kid crying, who's going to walk over with a free cup of custard? I challenge you to put us out of business with how generous you are. Go do it. Give away free stuff."*

I go back to what I said at the beginning of this chapter: *customer experience isn't a "nice to have," an afterthought, something you occasionally do—it must become part of your company's DNA,* its true north, especially if you want to pursue the **Customer Experience** path as a way to grow your top-line revenue. For Shake Shack, this isn't merely about the occasional things its employees do—*it's who they are.*

SHAKE SHACK
KEY TAKEAWAYS

- Be open to suggestions from anywhere. Shake Shack is a firm believer in customer feedback, providing comment cards, round-table discussions, and monthly dining vouchers for its staff, to use real-time feedback to ensure a consistent dining (customer) experience.

- If you are going to pursue the **Customer Experience** path, you must ensure your employees are part of the equation. It is no coincidence that many companies who excel at CX also top "Best Places to Work" lists. Happy employees give you a much better chance to have happy customers.

- A compelling customer experience isn't about just one thing— it's a combination of many things. You have to have great, or at least good enough, products. You have to have happy employees. You must be able to track and respond to customer sentiment. You must be consistent. And if you don't get it right, own up to it, fix it, and move on!

STORY
3

STARBUCKS
LOSING THE SOUL OF THE PAST

The damage was slow and quiet, incremental, like a
single loose thread that unravels a sweater inch by inch.
—HOWARD SCHULTZ, former CEO of Starbucks

STARBUCKS IS NOT ONLY ONE of the biggest and best-known brands in the world and a worldwide leader in coffee, but it also has an industry-leading Net Promoter Score (NPS) of 77 against an industry average of 40 in the fast-food category where it competes. So you might be surprised that I've picked it as a case study in *"how things can go wrong"* in **Customer Experience**. But suspend your disbelief for a moment and just stay with me here for a minute.

Consider the story of Starbucks Coffee in its darkest days. When you think about Starbucks, you usually look at either its explosive beginnings—from a tiny "second-generation" coffee pioneer emerging out of Pike Place Market in 1976, to leading the artisanal era of adult beverage drinking in the twenty-first century; or its current world dominance—with twenty-five thousand cafés around the world and nearly $20 billion in annual revenues.

What is often forgotten is that, beginning in 2007, Starbucks was a company in trouble, its stock tumbling, competitors challenging on every front, and both customers and employees exhibiting declining loyalty and morale. The cause? Ironically, the greatest success story of the coffee age had lost, well . . . *its soul*. It had actually grown too fast and, in doing so, put a tremendous strain on the entire organization. It failed to understand its customers' relationships with its coffee and the experience they had come to expect with the brand.

Every day, coffee drinkers around the world make a decision on whether they are going to make their own at home or stop someplace and spend their hard-earned money. It's not very likely that Starbucks is going to be your least expensive option, *so keeping customers coming back again and again even while spending more money requires a highly differentiated and unique experience*—and losing sight of that can be reason enough for a growth stall.

A TRIFECTA: NOT ALL GROWTH IS GOOD GROWTH

Between 1987 and 2007, Starbucks opened an average of two locations each day, an increasing percentage of which (currently one-third) were outside the United States. In time it was hard *not* to find a city or large town anywhere in the developed world that didn't have at least one Starbucks location. As for the stores themselves, part of the appeal was that they were uniform in decor and designed to offer a warm haven both for people on the road and locals looking for a comfortable place to enjoy a cup of coffee, socialize . . . and enjoy free Wi-Fi.

When Howard Schultz stepped down in 2000 after a thirteen-year run as CEO, he assumed the role of chairman, with the mission of focusing on the company's global growth strategy. At that time, Starbucks had only twenty-eight hundred stores, including 350 Starbucks locations outside the United States, and earned roughly $2 billion in annual revenue. Under Schultz's replacements, Orin Smith and then Jim Donald, Starbucks embarked on a trifecta of efforts. Business exploded, and there was no question Starbucks was in hyper-growth mode.

It pursued the **Market Acceleration** path with store count tripling to nine thousand locations. It more than doubled its revenue to more than $5 billion in fiscal 2004. By 2007, the company had roughly thirteen thousand locations worldwide. In combination with **Market Acceleration**, Starbucks also pursued the **Product Expansion** and **Customer and Product Diversification** growth paths—adding snacks, healthy food, CDs, gifts, and other retail items designed to further monetize its customers.

Isn't that amazing? Isn't all growth good growth? Well, not really. Unfortunately, although Starbucks was seeing top-line growth, all that growth came with an unexpected price tag. The rapid pace of change, explosion of product offerings, and store openings (with little consideration for letting the employees absorb all the changes and analyzing the impact of those changes to CX) managed to alienate just about everyone . . . existing loyalists and new customers alike.

> **GROWTH STALL:** when companies find themselves in a revenue slowdown, resulting in flat to no growth or, worse yet, negative growth. A company may be entering a growth stall when it has two consecutive quarters of lower revenue or profit compared to the prior year.

RETURN TO THE SOURCE

Starbucks found itself in a full-blown growth stall. Howard Schultz saw a disaster coming and wrote a memo to then CEO Jim Donald, predicting that if the situation didn't improve, Starbucks would eventually disappear. When the media got hold of the memo, Starbucks' stock, already falling, slumped even further—until by the end of the year it had lost nearly half of its value. The board fired Donald and asked Schultz to once again take over the role of CEO.

For most companies, the timing of this disaster would have been the worst possible news, as the entire world economy was itself tipping over into the Great Recession. But for troubled Starbucks, it was the perfect moment to stop and then hit the reset switch. That's exactly what Schultz did. It helped that the day he returned to Starbucks the stock market showed its confidence in him, boosting Starbucks stock by 8 percent.

Schultz returned as Starbucks CEO in 2008, saying: *"The most serious challenge we face is of our own doing,"* and, *"We became less passionate about customer relationships and the coffee experience. We spent time on efficiency rather than the experience."*

Within a week of Schultz returning as CEO, he became laser focused on shifting Starbucks away from bureaucracy and back to its customers. He wanted all employees to put themselves in the shoes of their customers. The battle cry became: *"Live and breathe Starbucks the way our customers do."*

Schultz set out to determine the cause of the growth stall. His approach was similar to Danny Meyer's, who believed in a strong feedback loop with customers and employees. Schultz's first step was to ask Starbucks customers and employees to e-mail and tell him what was wrong with the company, how it had lost its way. Within days he had received more than five thousand e-mails—and he took in all the complaints. He also called individual Starbucks stores across the United States and queried them about their problems.

Two of the biggest complaints Schultz heard were that the quality of Starbucks coffee was uneven and that many of the company's baristas didn't seem sufficiently competent to brew a good cup of coffee. It's important to note here that Starbucks charges a premium for its coffee, so if you get a subpar cup of coffee for that premium, you aren't only failing yourself and your employees—you are failing your customers.

In response, in an extraordinary moment in modern business history, in February 2008 Schultz closed more than seven thousand Starbucks stores—in a single shot—all across America for three and a half hours to retrain its baristas in the "art of espresso." The company lost an estimated $6 million that day—but the blanket coverage of the event by the media perfectly conveyed Starbucks' newfound commitment to quality and experience. And, thanks to the training, the company's product did improve markedly, giving it a chance to regain its former glory, one customer at a time.

Your premium brand had better be delivering something wonderful, or it's not going to get the business.

—WARREN BUFFETT

PATH 1 CUSTOMER EXPERIENCE

THE SMALLEST DETAILS COUNT

As I've said a few times the experience customers have isn't one thing—it's the combination of many things. But sometimes it's the smallest things that can make the biggest impact. Starbucks had unknowingly abandoned its focus on CX. Had they consciously kept CX as a key part of their growth strategy, it might have restrained them from the overzealous acceleration/expansion that ultimately diluted their brand. In all, *Business Insider* listed nineteen different actions Schulz made in turning Starbucks back around (a sample of which is below).

There was no quick fix—no single thing that could help Starbucks course-correct. It took Starbucks two years to reset itself and find its true north again. In 2010, Starbucks had more than $10 billion in revenue and employed 150,000 people. Starbucks came out of its hard times, its growth stall, stronger than ever. From January 8, 2008—the day Howard Schultz took back the corner-office duties and decided to double down on CX and not compromise on the soul of its business—through April 2017, when he became executive chairman, the stock's total return was 551 percent. Does focusing on the customer pay off? I would say, in this case, yes!

Key Actions Spearheaded by Howard Schultz

- **Starbucks closed seventy-one hundred U.S. stores for three and a half hours to retrain its baristas on how to make the perfect espresso. It lost $6 million that day.**
- **Schultz invited people to e-mail him directly—he received five thousand e-mails.**
- **The company replaced all of its outdated cash registers and computers for faster service.**
- **The company replaced all of its espresso machines with the Mastrena, a sophisticated Swiss-made machine.**
- **The company created a customer rewards card. In five months, customers had loaded $150 million onto the cards.**
- **The company rolled out a new design for all of its stores.**

- The company nixed heated breakfast sandwiches from the menu because the smell was overpowering the smell of the coffee.
- The company required baristas to grind the beans in the stores. Any coffee that had been sitting more than thirty minutes was to be tossed.
- The company launched "My Starbucks Idea" to help increase its focus on customers and what they wanted. By 2013, it had generated more than 150,000 ideas and had implemented 277 of them.

STARBUCKS
KEY TAKEAWAYS

- _You must combine growth paths in the right sequence and pace so as not to damage the momentum you've been able to achieve from other path(s)._ If you jump from one path to the other too quickly, you aren't able to pause and reflect on the results. Were they what you expected? Did they provide the boost you were looking for? Similarly, doubling down on a path too quickly—or worse, killing a path too quickly when all it needed was a bit more time to take hold—can damage growth.
- There is an interconnectedness among the growth paths chosen, and sometimes the unintended consequences of decisions made in isolation can negate all of the momentum other growth paths provide. _The company pursuing the most growth paths is not automatically the winner._
- Even if you have historically been extremely effective in maximizing performance on a particular growth path, that doesn't guarantee future success.
- No growth decisions should damage the most important sources of sustainable, profitable growth: _loyal and satisfied customers and happy and inspired employees._

PUTTING IT ALL TOGETHER

It is not the employer who pays the wages. Employers only handle the money.

It is the customer who pays the wages.

—HENRY FORD

CUSTOMER EXPERIENCE CAN BECOME A vital part of almost every successful company, which is why it is such a powerful path when pursuing growth. But navigating a successful **Customer Experience** growth path can be a long, often confusing endeavor: long, because your relationship with customers can evolve over years, and confusing, because it is constantly changing and evolving and on some occasions counterintuitive—most of it now controlled *by the customer and not you*. In other words, you have the most control over your destiny by having the least control over what your customers actually do with you.

WHAT WORKS—AND POTENTIAL PITFALLS

Often, I think of companies experiencing a growth stall as a massive *Undercover Boss* experiment. If you haven't watched the show, *Undercover Boss* is a reality television series in which each episode follows a person who has an upper-management position at a major business going undercover as an entry-level employee to discover what's really going on in a company—both good and bad. There rarely is an issue uncovered on the episode that isn't painfully obvious once the CEO or other executive actually experiences (sees it with their own two eyes) what their employees and customers must deal with on a day-to-day basis.

Suddenly everything becomes crystal clear—and long-overdue changes suddenly bubble to the top of the corporate to-do list. Why does it take *Undercover Boss* to highlight the somewhat obvious? I believe it is because *those making the big decisions have gotten too far away from the customer, and its frontline employees, those who play a huge role in delivering the customer's experience*. They make management decisions sometimes without the right context, with spreadsheets and reports that turn customers, and their people, into numbers, instead of the valuable assets which they are.

So far, there is something of a consensus on using Net Promoter Score (NPS) as an additional metric alongside traditional customer satisfaction (CSAT) scores and voice of the customer (VOC) research to help you zero in on what your customers really think—and how to make your products consistently exceed their expectations. If you haven't begun at least tracking those three things (NPS, CSAT, and VOC), that would be a place to start prior to embarking on this particular growth path.

Well-intended decisions sometimes have unintended consequences, and a vicious cycle of mediocrity, or worse, becomes the new normal. If you haven't figured it out yet, let me be clear: *CX is not an either-or decision; it must be a philosophy embedded into your company's DNA*. The reward? Loyal advocates who are willing to pay you more money for similar products, stay longer with you than a fly-by-night customer, and are much more likely to purchase from you again and again.

Using a customer-centric approach to achieve growth is to drive customer obsession throughout the entire organization. Today, you need an exceptional sales team. You need to have a strong marketing team. You need a responsive customer service team. By comparison, you may only need a "good enough" product. But those things alone aren't enough to sustain growth. It is the combination of all of those things that are required if you choose to pursue this path—**this is the path that must be combined with all of the others.**

There's no way to fake your way through this path; no amount of money, advertising, or vast product portfolio will make up for subpar experiences.

USING A CUSTOMER-CENTRIC APPROACH TO ACHIEVE GROWTH IS TO DRIVE CUSTOMER OBSESSION THROUGHOUT THE ORGANIZATION

Now don't get me wrong: you can't just have the best customer experience in town and serve terrible food or a subpar cup of coffee—or sell a product that doesn't work. Remember: *this path is a combination play supporting all of the other nine paths in some way.* And if you don't use it as a combination play when pursuing one or more (additional) growth paths, you actually risk finding yourself in a similar situation as Starbucks—diluting the value of your brand to your customers.

Furthermore, if you do make changes to your products or services that are not immediately embraced (think Apple removing the headphone jack or Twitter increasing its character counts), don't panic—sometimes short-term customer discomfort is needed to make way for longer-term improvement to customer experience.

PATH 2

CUSTOMER BASE
PENETRATION

CUSTOMER BASE PENETRATION

Make new friends, but keep the old. One is silver, the other gold.

—UNKNOWN

WHY CUSTOMER BASE PENETRATION MATTERS

- Acquiring a new customer is anywhere from five to twenty-five times more expensive than retaining an existing one.
- It costs six to seven times more to acquire a new customer than to retain an existing one.
- Seventy percent of companies say it's cheaper to retain a customer than acquire one.
- The probability of selling to an existing customer is 60–70 percent. The probability of selling to a new prospect is 5–20 percent.
- Repeat customers, on average, spend 67 percent more.
- Loyal customers are five times as likely to repurchase, five times as likely to forgive, four times as likely to refer, and seven times as likely to try a new offering.

THERE'S GOLD IN THEM THERE HILLS

It was all too common of a question: "How can I grow my business?" I remember flying back from meeting with the head of a division of a Fortune 500 company, where I sat next to a CEO of a small textile company in Los Angeles, California. He had successfully built a $3 million business when opportunity came knocking. He ended up selling his business but has remained CEO. The new "owner" wanted him to be 100 percent focused on acquiring new customers and driving top-line growth. He tasked the CEO to become an authorized (online) vendor for both Walmart and Amazon, which he did, while they worked on updating their website. That was its short-term growth strategy.

I wanted to learn more. I started with the basics, asking how many customers they had (i.e., how many have purchased from him at least once). He answered with, "Over one hundred thousand." I tried to dig deeper. I asked how often these customers made purchases, what the average order size was, what the top source of new customers was, and what it cost him to acquire a new customer. He was a bit perplexed by all the questions about his existing base of customers—he thought that the fact that they were available on two of the largest online marketplaces in the world was far more compelling of a conversation to have . . . but he couldn't have been more off the mark.

There may have been a time when "build it and they will come" would have been applicable to online businesses. Today, it is no longer so. Build a website, build a product, build a mobile app—you pick—whatever it is, I'm guessing there are hundreds or even thousands of alternatives to choose from. *The context of the market has shifted.* With the increased level of competition across countless industries and product categories, _businesses in every sector are struggling with ways to attract and acquire new consumers._ Complicating matters is the fact that many are finding that increasing customer acquisition costs (CAC) are making it difficult for companies to compete against others with larger advertising and marketing budgets—or even maintain the pace of new customer acquisition they have seen in the past.

Start-ups, small businesses, or large enterprises, it doesn't matter—nobody is immune to these new realities. For example, in 2013, it cost Netflix around $45 to acquire a customer in the United States, roughly what it costs to acquire an international customer today. But that number steadily rose throughout 2014 and 2015, followed by an explosive increase over the past year and a half. Over the trailing twelve months (2016–17), Netflix spent more than twice as much to acquire a U.S. customer as it did four years ago.

Over the past five to ten years, CAC has become an important metric to track, especially in the "as-a-service" business model or a start-up looking to attract investors, but many get so fixated on it that they forget the value of a customer once the customer actually buys from them. Rather than thinking only about how you can acquire a lot of customers, and how cheaply you can do it, you should be thinking about the lifetime value (LTV) or customer lifetime value (CLV) across all of the customers you already have. The change in market context means that companies should be thinking more broadly when it comes to uncovering new growth opportunities.

That brings me to a hidden tension within this growth path. *All too often, sales and marketing executives are trapped by management's mandate to grow the (net new) customer base, with little concern for the potential imbalance of focus that brings for existing customers.* Where companies allocate sales resources and marketing dollars can be a contentious process. And if you over-allocate toward acquisition programs, and not up-sell, cross-sell, or loyalty programs, you may actually end up alienating your existing customer base.

If you're not careful, ignoring your customer base will lead to a growth stall. If you gain a customer through your marketing efforts but lose one you already have—because you weren't paying enough attention to the customer—then you end up with the same number of customers but with lower profitability. Why? Because it costs far more to gain a new customer than to keep an existing one. With the ease of "switching" for customers (both in cost and time), spending money to acquire a customer (CAC) may never be recovered.

Winning a customer (once) and keeping a customer buying from you again and again are two very different things. According to a Bain & Company study, 60–80 percent of customers who describe themselves as satisfied do not go back to do more business with the company that initially satisfied them. This translates into the fact that although companies are spending more and working extremely hard to acquire customers, even satisfy them, they fail to capture any repurchase opportunities after the fact. What a shame.

The likelihood of success is exponentially higher when selling into the base than capturing new customers altogether, especially if it is for the same or similar products. The typical probability of selling to an existing customer is 60–70 percent. The probability of selling to a new prospect is 5–20 percent. While it may be a no-brainer, it also makes it a safe choice because it provides a potentially quick fix to what is often a more complex problem hidden behind the safety of current success.

One of the biggest untapped opportunities is understanding CLV (what customers are likely to spend with you in the future) and leveraging its additional revenue potential to fast-track your business growth, especially when facing a growth stall. *Strategies to increase sales from customers you already have are as important as what you do to acquire new customers in the first place.* In fact, these strategies may prove to be *more critical* for your long-term success. Why? Repeat customers, *on average, spend 67 percent more than new customers* and it's easier and cheaper to sell more to current customers than to try to gain completely new customers.

That is why if you choose to pursue the **Customer Base Penetration** path with a focused and orchestrated effort, you can find additional growth opportunities with a reduced acquisition cost, further establish customer loyalty, and keep your competitors from stealing them away. *Acquiring or "landing" a new customer is one way to grow—but landing them and then "expanding" how much they spend with you going forward is another.* That is the heart of the **Customer Base Penetration** path.

This path happens to be one of the least risky of the ten, because at its core it is about working with the customers you already have. While it brings less risk and has a higher likelihood of success, that doesn't mean you stop everything else you're doing and double down on the **Customer Base Penetration** path.

The Achilles' heel for maximizing the growth potential with this path is twofold: one part is *having enough data* and the other *is actually having a good-size customer base to penetrate.* In the previous story of the textile company, he had more than enough customers to pursue this growth path, but what he *didn't have* was clean and accessible data on those customers, which is why he was forced to go after net new prospects instead of mining what he already had acquired.

With the advances in technology, specifically customer relationship management (CRM) software (such as Salesforce.com and others), companies are now able to capture vast amounts of customer data. You have to know your customers (potentially more than one contact in an account), know their purchasing habits, identify products or services customers could buy but don't, and be able to share that data with the appropriate resources (i.e., sales, customer service, and marketing) to further sell into the existing base. This information can also help define what the ideal customer for net new acquisition may look like, which could help reduce CAC.

This is also about knowing who your customers are so that you can find more like them, especially if you want to pursue **Market Acceleration** in combination with **Customer Base Penetration**. This path makes the assumption that you actually have a *viable and sizable customer base* to penetrate and grow from, either because you are creating it (first mover) or you are attempting to take share from someone else. *Without a set of customers to work from, or a product category, industry, or customer base that is growing, this path is a nonstarter for you.* You must ensure that you are not wasting your time or spending too much money to acquire customers if there isn't enough growth to be had. If that is the case, you may want to consider waiting to pursue this path until you have the right elements in place for success.

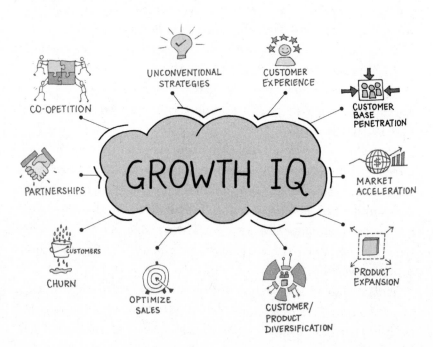

RED BULL
A THAI PHARMACIST AND AN AUSTRIAN ENTREPRENEUR WALK INTO A BAR

We don't bring the product to the consumer, we bring consumers to the product.

—DIETRICH MATESCHITZ,
cofounder and CEO of Red Bull

THAI PHARMACIST AND AN AUSTRIAN entrepreneur did meet one day back in 1984 (just not in a bar) in Thailand, when the Austrian toothpaste salesman Dietrich Mateschitz was searching for a remedy for his jet lag. As luck would have it, pharmacist Chaleo Yoovidhya suggested a local sweetened energy drink called Krating Daeng, Thai for Red Bull, which had been invented in the 1970s.

People have been using various beverages to feel that extra burst of energy for centuries. Over time, trends have changed from tea, to coffee, on to soft drinks, and back again. But just as people throughout time have sought something more powerful than caffeine, they now seek soft drinks with additional energy-boosting chemicals. Enter Red Bull. From 2008 until 2012, the energy drink market grew 60 percent, totaling $12.5 billion in U.S. sales by 2012. As founder Mateschitz has said, "If we don't create the market, it doesn't exist." That's a good place to be.

It was originally developed as a non-carbonated refreshment for factory workers and truck drivers to keep them awake through long shifts, and it had become a huge success in Thailand thanks to its careful sponsorship of boxing matches and sports events. But it wasn't until Mateschitz tried it and realized that if he transformed Krating Daeng from an obscure local remedy for sluggishness into a more universal concept, he could create an entirely new beverage category. He wrapped the drink in a blue and silver can, slightly modified the logo, and then wrapped that can with an eccentric and highly effective marketing campaign.

Despite its huge popularity today, Red Bull was not an instant success. It sold fairly slowly in Eastern European markets after its launch, but it wasn't until the company expanded (**Customer and Product Diversification** and **Market Acceleration**) into the United States in 1997 that the drink became a runaway success. It's now a leading name in energy beverages, with over sixty-two billion cans sold annually worldwide.

Red Bull GmbH launched in Austria in 1987. The company reworked the original Thai drink's recipe (**Product Expansion**), reducing the ultra-sweet taste of the original and carbonating it to better suit the taste of the Western audience it was going to be marketed to. Since then, Red Bull has become synonymous with energy drinks, a category it (in fact) created, and is one of the biggest names in the soft drink industry today. Just as some people refer to colas as "Cokes" or copying a piece of paper as "Xeroxing," or searching on the Internet as "Googling," many refer to all energy drinks as just "Red Bull."

ATTACK FROM THE EDGE

The rivalry between Coca-Cola and Pepsi is legendary, so much so that the decades-long battle has been dubbed the "cola wars" for its never-ending jockeying for market leadership. The battle began in 1886, when John S. Pemberton developed the original recipe for Coke. Twelve years later Pepsi-Cola was created by another pharmacist named Caleb Bradham. Throughout the years both drink titans have fought against each other using celebrities in their marketing campaigns, adding new flavors and recipes, new packaging, and exclusive partnerships—to name a few.

People who drink either Coke or Pepsi are loyal customers to a fault—they wouldn't think of switching, especially to the "other guys"—until a newcomer entered the carbonated drink market, shunning all traditional advertising tactics and using word of mouth to attract new customers. Unlike the age-old PepsiCo versus Coca-Cola competitions, Red Bull created an "energy drink" and, by extension, an "uncontested market" where no one else offered a similar product. This meant that it didn't need to concern itself with adjusting what it was doing to meet the changing needs and budget of current customers, or expand its product line one iota to compete with someone else, or deal with a growth stall—all it needed to do was to keep doing what it did best. In this case, it was the mixture of attracting customers to its brand via unorthodox means (student brand managers, consumer educators, attaching itself to sporting events and teams), coupled with a keen understanding of its likely buyer, which created the perfect storm for growth. This allowed Red Bull to dominate the category it created between 1984 and 2002 and capture the majority share, globally, that both Coke and Pepsi continue to chase with their own energy drink brands.

During this time, no one else was fighting for Red Bull's customers so it enjoyed explosive growth because it pursued **Customer Base Penetration** in its home market for its first five years. It followed up with the **Market Acceleration** path when it expanded outside its home market (Austria) in 1992. *The sequence of growing close to home, learning and developing a strong brand awareness, and gathering an extremely loyal customer base prior to branching out helped it accelerate its growth in new (regional) markets quickly.* Had it attempted to go global right out of the gate, I suspect it would have had very different results; it might have overextended itself, resulting in supply-chain issues (sales but no products to ship), and alerted (future) competitors of the high growth opportunity that energy drinks would bring. Remember, for all intents and purposes, other "carbonated soda brands" weren't even paying attention to what Red Bull was doing.

As I've mentioned before, it is often the case that big incumbent brands get so caught up in their own success or focusing on competitors that they don't pay attention to impending customer and market (context) shifts. The result? They ignore small, unknown companies that play on the "edges" of their product category and sometimes, as in this case, end up in a fight they weren't expecting or even anticipating. Even though in 2011 Red Bull only had a market share of 1 percent in the U.S. carbonated soft drink segment, it controlled 44 percent of the exploding energy drink market and was selling 4.6 billion cans a year.

Red Bull is now focused on **Customer and Product Diversification**, in combination with the other paths it has been pursuing. Had it diversified its products too early, it may have alienated its loyal customer base. Still to this day, the newly introduced Red Bull flavors are secondary to its original. The combination of unconventional marketing, strategic partnerships, simple product lineup, clear brand distinction, and significant customer engagement has proven to be too compelling for its competitors to replace it as the global leader in the energy drink category.

KNOWING YOUR CUSTOMERS

Remember, if you are going to pursue the **Customer Base Penetration** path, _you must know and understand your customers intimately—what they like as well as what they expect from you._ There is no question that the success Red Bull has achieved has been a direct result of the deep understanding it has of its customer base. From the beginning, Red Bull leveraged its eccentric advertising and marketing campaigns to target the action- and adventure-oriented customer and Generation Y males, age range of eighteen to thirty-four. It did so by being extremely focused on those "buyers," meeting them in the places they frequent, such as school campuses and extreme sporting events. Over the years it has become the premier title sponsor of action sports such as Formula racing—even owning its own Formula One racing team—snowboarding, cliff diving, and dirt bike racing, and has formed big alliances with NASCAR, to name a few.

Without spending millions on one-to-one customer acquisition campaigns, Red Bull's marketing and emotional branding strategies have created meaningful and enduring bonds between consumers and the brand—it's in their DNA, and it's what its customers expect. Red Bull's success has come not through convincing customers to drink it but through creating a reality in which the customer wants to be part of the "_Red Bull lifestyle._"

BRING CONSUMERS TO THE PRODUCT

It would be fair to say that _Red Bull never sold a product. They still don't. They sell an image,_ with lifestyle-oriented branding and social media input, and just casually make the product part of that image. For over two decades

KRATING DAENG

CREATING A REALITY
IN WHICH THE CUSTOMER
WANTS TO BE A PART OF
THE RED BULL LIFESTYLE

adrenaline junkies

"Red Bull gives you wings" has been its slogan, but after it settled a $13 million lawsuit, we all learned that Red Bull does not, it turns out, actually give you wings, even in the figurative sense. Regardless of the lack of scientific proof of its claims, its image remains and has allowed Red Bull to charge a premium over regular "cola," sometimes even twice the price.

Red Bull had first-mover advantage, building an uncontested "beachhead" that others would have to displace if they wanted to "steal" its customers. It wasn't until Rockstar Energy Drink came on the scene in 1999 and Hansen Natural Corporation launched Monster Energy in 2002 that Red Bull found itself facing any serious threats. PepsiCo didn't get into the energy drink market until 2013, when it launched Mountain Dew Amp. Coke waited until 2014 to launch Full Throttle, which in 2015 was purchased by Monster Beverage Corporation. Let's put those dates into context: Red Bull launched in 1987, which means PepsiCo and Coke gave, yes, gave, Red Bull a twenty-plus-year head start.

Which is why, with its leading market share and deep brand loyalty, Red Bull stayed on the **Customer Base Penetration** path for well over a decade as it dominated Europe, before it decided to jump to its next path, **Market Acceleration**, as it expanded geographically.

With the market for energy drinks growing, it took almost another decade before it moved on to the **Product Expansion** path, when it added additional flavors plus low calorie and low sugar alternatives. Adding new flavors was a natural next step for the Red Bull brand, Amy Taylor, vice president of marketing, told *USA Today*. "Taste is a barrier for the category, and taste is a barrier for Red Bull. After 12 years in the U.S.,

47

we can now introduce flavors without confusion. It's about expanding the consumer base." Red Bull chose the right sequence—by not initially over-diversifying or diluting its brand, or what its customers appreciated about it—all in the name of chasing new customers with too many new products. Remember, when considering if **Customer Base Penetration** is right for you, the market you are pursuing must be growing; otherwise you risk wasting time, money, and resources on the wrong growth path. In this case, Red Bull is in the driver's seat of a growing segment. The global energy drinks market is expected to reach $84.8 billion by 2025.

RED BULL
KEY TAKEAWAYS

- If you choose to create a new category, you must have patience and stay focused early on. Getting distracted trying to compete with larger incumbents who play in similar product categories (soda and energy drinks) can sidetrack you.
- The **Customer Base Penetration** path is more than "up-selling" existing customers. You can also expand "customer" to mean capturing share of similar buyers who are currently spending money with another brand. The former is the norm; the latter proves to be a bit more difficult because you don't have actual customer data from which to mine. However, what you do know is what they like—so you can capture them with targeted marketing and advertising campaigns versus direct selling.
- **Market Acceleration** becomes much easier if your current customers are creating new demand for you. Red Bull went straight to its target audience at college parties, libraries, coffee shops, bars, and other places they hung out. It got customers talking about it and spreading the word about its product for free. If prospective customers are awaiting your arrival to their city, country, or neighborhood, all the better for you.
- Don't be afraid to use unorthodox means to create (market) buzz around your products. It doesn't mean you have to sponsor and

then own a Formula One racing team or generate hype by having someone set a world record with a 120,000-foot skydive from the edge of space (Red Bull Stratos Jump). But what you can do is learn from Red Bull. It has always used events to reach consumers. *It put the audience of its marketing efforts first and selling its product second.*

- Red Bull uses content and events as its sales team. Everything revolves around one concept: creating content around what its audience loves and experiences people would be interested in *even if they don't care about energy drink brands.*

STORY

2

MCDONALD'S
READY, SET, BREAKFAST

LIKE MANY OTHER MAJOR CORPORATIONS, McDonald's began as a family business, founded in San Bernardino, California, in 1940 by two brothers, Richard and Maurice McDonald. More a roadside stand than a restaurant, the original McDonald's kept things clear, simple, and focused. It sold hot dogs, hamburgers, cheeseburgers, milkshakes, and French fries.

In 1953, the McDonald brothers began seeking franchisees and soon attracted the attention of a milk shake–machine salesman, Ray Kroc, who volunteered to help set up new McDonald's locations across the country. The chain grew slowly—34 restaurants in 1958, 102 locations by 1959— and then it quickly accelerated. Kroc eventually got so frustrated with the McDonald brothers' lack of long-term vision that he bought them out in 1961 for $2.7 million.

Kroc's goal was to make McDonald's the United States' leading fast-food chain, setting the stage for the enormous franchise known today as the McDonald's Corporation. It raised generations on Happy Meals and fed families with Big Macs, Quarter Pounders, Chicken McNuggets, and Baked Apple Pies.

McDONALD'S

- McDonald's sells more than seventy-five burgers every second.
- McDonald's has sold 3.6 billion Happy Meals.
- McDonald's has sold 550 million Big Macs in the United States alone.
- McDonald's has sold 9 million orders of French fries.
- Sixty-two million people visit McDonald's each day.

However, between 2004 and 2014, the most famous chain in the world was showing its age. To many it felt stale and unhealthy, a symbol of the harried, unrefined way the industrial world mass-produces, packages, markets, serves, and eats food.

Responding to quarter after quarter of nonexistent growth, in 2006 McDonald's found itself in a growth stall. It divested itself of Chipotle, Boston Market, and Donatos Pizza, and decided to focus on its core business of hamburgers and French fries and other flagship items—which is why the company's next decisions were so misaligned to its stated goals and the context of the market, almost bafflingly so. Instead of shrinking its menu—and eliminating non-core items such as chicken, fish, yogurt, cookies, coffee, salads, wraps, pancakes, desserts, and snacks—McDonald's decided to expand its menu and sell more items. Its goal? To sell more to existing customers while at the same time, hoping to attract new ones (**Customer and Product Diversification, Market Acceleration,** and **Customer Base Penetration**). To put that in context, between 2004 and 2014 McDonald's menu swelled by 75 percent. The result: between 2013 and 2015, McDonald's share price basically didn't move, and the company had lost more than 500 million visits since 2012.

Company executives spoke proudly of McDonald's "robust new-product pipeline," not realizing that employees who were once preparing 59 foods or combinations now had to juggle 121. McDonald's had cut Chipotle loose ostensibly in order to refocus on what it did best—but by expanding the menu, the company ended up doing the complete opposite. The chain didn't seem to understand that an option-heavy, visually chaotic menu overwhelmed customers, had led to slower customer service, quality control issues, and a muddled brand identity, all of which had a negative effect on top-line growth as well as bottom-line profit margins.

The company's slump didn't happen in a day, a month, or even a year. It was the culmination of dozens, even hundreds, of decisions McDonald's had made over the past decade that had a multiplier effect across the entire organization—and not in a positive way.

McDonald's (like Starbucks) had overrun its kitchens, its employees, and its customers with too many menu "choices" (products), resulting in a decline in customer satisfaction (**Customer Experience**), especially in the drive-through line. This lesson is about how McDonald's was pursuing organic growth while on the **Customer and Product Diversification** path, introducing new products not only to attract new customers but also to get existing customers to spend more by leaning into the **Customer Base Penetration** path. The combination of these two complementary efforts seemed feasible as a strong growth strategy "in theory"—and while there were pockets of success, overall the top-line revenue wasn't seeing as significant a lift as expected. Over the course of a few years McDonald's found itself in a pervasive growth stall. What could they do to course-correct?

Being on one of the ten paths and finding yourself in a growth stall doesn't mean you have to jump to another path altogether in order to recover—sometimes all that is required is to back away from one path, even slightly, to give the other initiatives a chance to take hold. In this case, McDonald's needed to retreat from **Customer and Product Diversification** in order to, once again, "refocus" on its core business of hamburgers and French fries and other highly desired menu items so that it could use **Customer Base Penetration** and **Customer Experience** as effective growth paths.

RECIPE FOR SUCCESS

In 1970, McDonald's franchisee Jim Delligatti began testing out some simple breakfast item ideas in his restaurants. Within a year, breakfast accounted for 5 percent of Delligatti's daily revenue. His idea caught the attention of Herb Peterson, who worked for Santa Barbara–based D'Arcy Advertising on the McDonald's account. "Borrowing" the idea of an eggs

Benedict sandwich being marketed on the West Coast by restaurant rival Jack in the Box, Peterson presented the idea to Kroc, who embraced it (and, as the story goes, ate two in a row). McDonald's executive Patty Turner later coined the name for what we all know and love as the legendary . . . Egg McMuffin.

McDonald's breakfast menu grew throughout the 1970s, a decade ahead of most competitors, and accounted for 15 percent of sales. Customers loved the breakfast menu. They loved it so much, they wanted it all day. And they asked for it. But for years and years, McDonald's didn't give the customers what they wanted. Why?

Speaking at the RBC Capital Markets Consumer & Retail Conference 2017, McDonald's chief financial officer, Kevin Ozan, said: "The reality was something like All-Day Breakfast. It was the number one most requested thing here in the United States. And our reason for not doing it always was it was going to be difficult operationally." He continued, "So, I don't know if we could really say we were customer centric when [what] we were really being driven by was 'is that going to be hurting . . . our ability to be efficient for operation?'"

TOO MANY OPTIONS, TOO LITTLE TIME

When McDonald's turned itself around, what decisions did it make to create a positive multiplier effect of successful growth? Getting itself out of a growth stall required McDonald's to "listen to its customers"; it had been ignoring the top request for a long time—thinking it knew what its customers wanted better than they did. But in the end, doubling down on a current product (breakfast), expanding its availability (all day), and improving customer experience (shrinking its menu) was the *combination* recipe for success.

Now comes the hard part. What had to change prior to rolling out the All Day Breakfast menu in 2015? It focused on the *sequence* of steps required prior to launch. McDonald's shrank the size of its menu to improve customer wait times and reduce the current complexity in the menu and the kitchen. The company convinced more than three thousand owner-operators to upgrade and reorganize their kitchens to accommodate breakfast alongside burgers and fries.

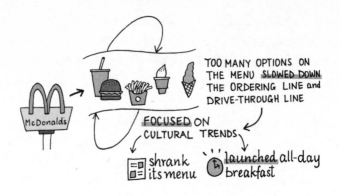

TOO MANY OPTIONS ON THE MENU SLOWED DOWN THE ORDERING LINE and DRIVE-THROUGH LINE

FOCUSED ON CULTURAL TRENDS

shrank its menu

launched all-day breakfast

What if McDonald's hadn't done those things? Chances are the twenty-four-hour breakfast option would have been a great idea that fell flat against high customer and market expectations. What if the company had launched its All Day Breakfast menu before reducing the size of its menu? Maybe the twenty-four-hour breakfast option would have still been successful, but consumers would continue to be overwhelmed and customer service would still be less than optimal.

McDonald's rolled out its new All Day Breakfast menu in October 2016, ten years after it had first found itself in a growth stall. Informing the *New York Times* that whatever progress McDonald's might make in the future was the result of "decisions being made today," McDonald's president and CEO Steve Easterbrook conceded that one or two quarters of growth didn't translate into a successful turnaround.

In fact, the smaller menu created the space for McDonald's to absorb All Day Breakfast. Expanding breakfast—a longtime request of customers—was a key part of the company's turnaround strategy, and it helped pull McDonald's out of a domestic (U.S.) sales slump. McDonald's shares rose 17 percent in 2015, and U.S. same-store sales were up 5.7 percent. In the first quarter of 2018, global same-store sales rose 5.5 percent, and U.S. stores grew 2.9 percent. Their success with breakfast created a "market share fight" between McDonald's, Taco Bell, and Burger King.

While the All Day Breakfast menu had shown positive returns, McDonald's continued to build upon the success of its All Day Breakfast menu with the launch of its value menu (2017), delivery (partnering with UberEats to test), and mobile kiosk ordering, all of which have proved to be a big hit among customers. Steve Easterbrook said, "We continued to build upon the broad-based momentum of our business, making eleven consecutive quarters of positive comparable sales and our fifth consecutive quarter of positive guest counts."

MCDONALD'S
KEY TAKEAWAYS

- The answer on how best to resolve a systemic issue of slow to no growth may have been staring McDonald's in the eye the entire time. Customers wanted breakfast all day—while it was mentioned in the **Customer Experience** path that you can't give your customers everything they may want, in this case, ignoring the consistent request was a mistake. Capturing, understanding, and responding to the voice of the customer (VOC) may in fact pull you toward the answers you are looking for.
- **Customer Base Penetration** is about selling more of your existing products to existing customers, but that *doesn't mean you have to continue to sell the same number of products.* You must be willing to put all options on the table when facing a growth stall. In this case, once McDonald's was willing to reduce the number of products they sold in order to focus on the most highly requested item—the Egg McMuffin—the All Day Breakfast campaign gave them the bump they had been looking for.
- The McDonald's story is a perfect example of how to use combination and sequence effectively. The growth strategy to launch the All Day Breakfast menu, which included products it already had (specifically, the Egg McMuffin), significantly reduced time to market; the growth paths were a combination of **Customer Base Penetration**, **Customer Experience**, and **Market Acceleration**; and the sequence was timed to ensure that each location would be able to update its kitchen to accommodate the new menu without negative impact to operational efficiency.

STORY

3

SEARS
UPROOTING RETAIL

We don't need more customers. We have all the
customers we could possibly want.

—EDDIE LAMPERT, CEO of Sears

BEFORE JEFF BEZOS (AMAZON), PIERRE Omidyar (eBay), and Sam Walton (Walmart), there was Richard Sears, a railroad station agent who in 1891 parlayed a surplus shipment of unwanted watches into the most famous and venerable retailer in history.

Even today, much of the marketing techniques used by Sears—he did it first—remain pretty much unchanged by online and off-line retailers around the world.

In the late 1800s, the American countryside was in a different world than the rest of the more urbanized country. All of that changed when Richard Sears and Alvah Roebuck hit upon *one of the greatest sales and marketing ideas of all time: the mail-order catalog*. The impact of Sears and his catalog on his time period was enormous. It allowed any person with access to the postal service to send in an order and payment and buy from Sears, which would then ship the merchandise via the post office or railroads, reaching customers wherever they are.

The company claimed the catalog "Tamed The West," and it was called "the farmer's friend" the "Wish Book," the "Book of Bargains," "The Great Price Maker," and "The Consumers' Bible." Country storekeepers were

SEARS INNOVATIONS

- Included customer testimonials in the catalog (brand advocacy)
- Mitigated the $0.25 shipping fee by applying it to orders over $10 (free shipping)
- Low price/best value was the mantra
- "Club order program" for neighborhoods to buy together (buying club)
- Specialty catalogs
- Seasonal catalogs
- "Your money back if you are not satisfied"
- Christmas catalog
- Emphasized customer satisfaction above all else
- State-of-the-art factories that helped to inspire Henry Ford's car manufacturing plants
- Offered credit cards
- Standardized size and quality

very opposed to the catalogs, so much so that Sears had to camouflage the cover (in some stores) so that store owners wouldn't throw them away. Its success was quite simple, yet profound for the time; people were delighted that a company could actually deliver all kinds of merchandise right to their homes. *It was the original disrupter in the early 1900s to mom-and-pop storefronts.*

The Sears catalog was the epitome of **Customer Base Penetration**—Sears knew its customers, and it knew what they wanted. Sears management decided, after early success with its current customers: Why not attract new customers and offer what it currently sells to more people? Then the catalog increased its products (**Product Expansion**) over its history, ballooning to hundreds of pages (like hundreds of items on McDonald's and Starbucks menus), selling anything and everything, including even prefabricated (Sears) homes. The early Sears playbook created a sizeable beachhead (the catalog)—which allowed it to further optimize sales when it expanded its reach by opening retail stores (**Market Acceleration**), keeping any competitors at bay, all while getting ever closer to its customers' purchasing habits (**Customer Experience**).

Customer Base Penetration served Sears well for many decades. During the 1950s–80s era of massive consumer market growth, Sears was often first on the list of virtually every home owner and child looking to purchase almost anything, with its convenient suburban and rural locations, selling toys, tools, clothing, and appliances. Does this sound familiar? It should. Replace the above scenario with what online retailers do today with the current technology and you have a modern-day e-commerce company that is a direct imitation of what Sears did more than a hundred years ago.

While pursuing a **Customer and Product Diversification** growth strategy, Sears was masterful in establishing product brands such as Kenmore, Craftsman, DieHard, Silverstone, and Toughskins, to name a few. It was a conglomerate during the mid-twentieth century, adding Dean Witter and Coldwell Banker Real Estate and introducing the Discover Card.

Ironically, given what came later, it might surprise you to know that Sears even started Prodigy as a joint venture with CBS and IBM in 1984. The company claimed to be the first consumer online service, offering its subscribers access to a broad range of networked services, including news, weather, shopping, bulletin boards, games, polls, expert columns, banking, stocks, travel, and a variety of other features. By 1990, Sears, via Prodigy, was the second-largest online service provider, trailing only CompuServe. And that wasn't their only venture into the Internet—Sears purchased the social search engine Delver in 2009.

ON LIFE SUPPORT

In a few decades, Sears has gone from being unstoppable to publicly admitting that it may not survive. Sears, at one time the nation's largest retailer, has lost money every single year in the decade leading up to 2018, bleeding more than $10 billion over that span. The once-iconic brand has been forced to pull the plug on countless stores (the company operated 1,002 stores in total at the end of fiscal 2017, compared with 1,430 in the year prior. In 2018 (January–April), Sears announced it would be closing one hundred additional stores, and will open more "smaller concept" stores later in 2018). Meanwhile, its stock price had fallen more than 72 percent since early 2017.

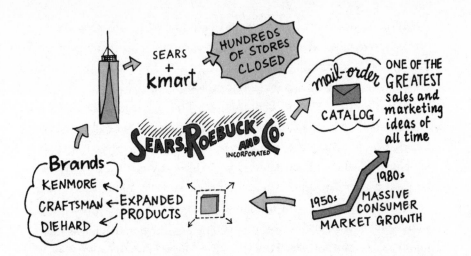

SEARS + kmart

HUNDREDS OF STORES CLOSED

mail-order CATALOG

ONE OF THE GREATEST sales and marketing ideas of all time

Sears, Roebuck and Co. INCORPORATED

Brands
KENMORE
CRAFTSMAN ← EXPANDED PRODUCTS
DIEHARD

1950s · 1980s MASSIVE CONSUMER MARKET GROWTH

Having played the role of upstart retail juggernaut in the 1890s, Sears now found itself in the same position as the rural general stores it used to drive out of business en masse. What happened? The customer changed, and Sears failed to change with it. In May 2017, Eddie Lampert, Sears CEO, blamed *shifting consumer behaviors that "changed the game."* In the past, it was the retailer who determined what a customer should want to buy and how they should shop. *Today, it's the customer who is defining the shopping experience*—and Sears has been unable to respond quickly enough to the changing market context.

In 1989, Sears was surpassed, after a century, by Walmart—a retailer that actually "adopted" the Sears model. They say imitation is the greatest form of flattery, but not when they do it and then supercharge it with technology and processes that streamlined its sup-ply chain channels and allowed for un-precedented price discounting. Other retailers, all using innovative technology solutions and more sophisti-cated marketing and sales techniques—Target, Best Buy, Home Depot, Costco—soon passed Sears, as well. Meanwhile, Sears decided to get rid of its "beachhead" and ended its mail-order business in 1993, just before e-commerce companies applied their very own "catalog" model to the Internet.

> *Skate to where the puck is going, not where it has been.*
>
> **—WAYNE GRETZKY, NHL hockey player and Hall of Famer**

PATH 2 CUSTOMER BASE PENETRATION

Unfortunately, Sears hung on to its **Customer Base Penetration** strategy for too long—and found it difficult to keep up with changing buyer preferences. So, instead, it chose to merge with Kmart, another struggling retailer, as a way to reinvigorate growth.

While Growth IQ is not about using mergers and acquisitions (M&A) to grow top-line revenue, the reason this deal happened highlights the fact that Sears missed the shift in market context altogether. It was not anticipating "where the puck was going to be"—it was solving for "where the puck had already been." The combined company wanted to make both brands more competitive by up-selling and cross-selling each other's flagship products, and gain access to each other's customers via new locations, in a classic **Customer Base Penetration + Market Acceleration** play.

Remember to consider the market context when planning for growth. Exposing Craftsman Tools, Lands' End, or Martha Stewart's home products at a Sears or Kmart brick-and-mortar storefront wasn't going to cut it against the rest of the industry and customer demands, which had already moved on. *The terrible irony of the Sears story is that many of the solutions to its problems have looked the company in the face now for nearly thirty years.*

"IF ONLY . . ."

The inventor of the mail-order catalog failed to see that the Internet was just a modern version of its original business model. It also failed to see the value in its still-healthy business of appliance installation, which gave the company unique access to American homes. It also failed to see the successful template for **Product Expansion** with its Kenmore, Craftsman, and DieHard brands and in its own Sears Canada store, one of the biggest e-commerce companies in that country, one that was more successful than competitors like Walmart. Sears had over one hundred years of customer data and buying preferences "in theory," and unfortunately . . . did nothing with it.

If only it had leveraged its access to America's kitchens and laundry rooms with its Kenmore and Whirlpool brands in 2012 to become the showroom for the *Smart House* of the future (and then buy the likes of Nest or Philips Hue Light Bulbs); had it used the Discover card to create a gigantic social network to move discounts and loyalty programs to its then millions of steady customers (or purchase start-up Square and integrate mobile payments and credit cards); or tied together its fitness equipment with its own FitStudio.com; or recast its Shop Your Way loyalty program to be less about discounts and create its own Gilt.com.

Instead, when Sears found itself in a significant growth stall, it made several significant decisions that validated the fact that it wasn't thinking about the twenty-first-century buyer, the customer base it already had, and how it could (1) penetrate them further and (2) keep them shopping at Sears—ultimately helping it get back to some level of growth. First, it began to sell off a few of its big-name brands. The most stunning was the sale of the Craftsman brand (after ninety years!) to Stanley Black & Decker in 2017 for $900 million (and a portion of future sales for fifteen years after the deal closed).

Sears lost more than a household brand—it sold an entry point to the next generation of smart homes, the Internet of Things (IoT)—which brings with it an entirely new customer base and category for growth. Furthermore, along with selling the brand, one of the most important and lucrative assets it got rid of was—its customers. *Sears didn't lose them, it just sold them*. Yet again, what a shame! Its loyal customer base had been unmatched in the industry for decades, so much so that other companies were willing to pay hundreds of millions of dollars to get their hands on them. A good question is: Was Black & Decker only interested in the products, or was it actually interested in the customer base? I'd argue the latter was a big part of its interest and valuation.

Let's put that into perspective: Why were those customers so valuable? Remember, acquiring a customer the first time is far more expensive than selling to them once they are in your brand's "orbit." Sears had them, by the tens of thousands, generations of them—and it completely ignored their intrinsic value to the business when it sold off these iconic brands. As many consumers continue to look elsewhere to shop, department stores have built robust and (customer) value-driven loyalty strategies. This is one area where some retailers, like Sephora, have used loyalty programs to reward their best customers and increase purchasing frequency. Will these decisions (negatively) impact the Sears Shop Your Way loyalty program membership? According to Sears, member sales penetration for the Sears Shop Your Way loyalty program has grown from 58 percent to 75 percent since 2011. Why are loyal customers important? Well . . . Nordstrom's ten million active loyalty program customers represent more than 50 percent of its total customer base.

The decision to sell off some of its major brands may have delivered a final blow to the once dominant seller of appliances that it may never be able to recover from. Shoppers will no longer be able to buy Whirlpool, KitchenAid, Jenn-Air, or Maytag appliances at Sears, following a pricing dispute that has ended a 101-year relationship between the department store chain and the country's largest appliance maker. The only part of their century-old partnership remaining intact is that Whirlpool will continue to manufacture appliances for Sears's private-label Kenmore brand. Sears characterized the decision as "an effort to support its customers." Seems a bit counterintuitive since the appliance business is one of Sears's last remaining strengths. _One of Sears's big selling points has been that it is the only retailer to carry all of the top ten major appliance brands._ Despite years of market share losses, the company is still #3 in the U.S. major appliance market. Sears may be a bit overconfident in its ability to continue to sell its historic volume of appliances with a much more limited brand selection. In July 2017, Sears struck a deal with Amazon (**Partnership**) to test-run selling Kenmore appliances on Amazon. This was followed in December 2017 with deals for Amazon to sell DieHard car batteries, tires, and other related items.

Let's reflect on the changing customer context. If you were to look backward (where the puck has been), then increasing the price of appliances may in fact disenfranchise even the most loyal of customers. But if you are looking forward (where the puck is going), to the twenty-first-century customer, and you are able to increase the value and the experience of a product, raising the prices doesn't seem as unrealistic.

Fast-forward to 2018:

- Whirlpool announced at CES (the official name of what had been called the Consumer Electronics Show) that Apple Watch wearers will soon be able to remotely control twenty connected home appliances. It would mean smart watch owners could change temperature settings on ovens, delay cycles on washers, or check how long is left to run on a dryer.

- Whirlpool has also announced that families will be able to control its 2018 range of appliances with voice commands to both Amazon's Alexa and Google's home assistant.

If only Sears had chosen to do these things prior to shedding all those well-known brands, the modern-day Sears story might look more different. Instead, the company chose to continue to milk its cash cow and leverage its massive real estate portfolio rather than fix what was wrong with its core business. Sears failed to see that the context of the retailing world was fundamentally changing with the Internet—and its customers were changing as well—so it stayed its course without deviating too far from what made it great for over one hundred years.

Sears wasn't on the wrong growth path by pursuing **Customer Base Penetration**—quite the opposite, Sears was right to try to sell more to its base, especially considering its sheer size. The mistake it made was not understanding that its customers wanted more, not less. They wanted cross-channel capabilities between brick-and-mortar stores and online commerce. They wanted a better (shopping) experience. They wanted more relevant and appealing products. They wanted a vast selection of products at the right price. *Unfortunately, what had made Sears so successful in the past was now holding it back.* It was, and continues to be, unwilling to make the necessary adjustments, especially when it came to **Customer and Product Diversification**, **Optimizing Sales**, and **Customer Experience**.

Sears had at its disposal all the right pieces for a strong showing against its competitors, but it lacked the willingness to look beyond the status quo. What Sears needed were more **Partnerships** (like Walmart and Uber or Kohl's and Amazon) not fewer, greater focus on **Customer Experience** (like Sephora, Ulta, Apple, and even Best Buy), and the key: keeping the customers it has by reducing customer defection (**Churn**). This isn't an either-or zero-sum decision. This is about how companies that are struggling to find growth can take the strengths they have, including large and loyal customer bases, and modernize them—with the right combination of technical advancements—and growth paths to further extend the life-

> *We can't afford to lose a customer.*
>
> **—RICHARD SEARS,**
> cofounder of Sears,
> Roebuck and Company

time value (LTV) of its customers—while at the same time allowing the company time to absorb the changes.

SEARS
KEY TAKEAWAYS

- Rather than leverage its assets that were tied to its customer base in order to strategically shift its business model, Sears sold off extremely valuable assets to double down on a deteriorating strategy.

- Sears wasn't on the wrong growth path by pursuing **Customer Base Penetration**—quite the opposite, Sears was right to try to penetrate its loyal and tenured base, especially considering its sheer size. The mistake it made was that its customers were beginning to leave (**Churn**) for retailers who were embracing the new economy—digital, social, and smart home technologies to name a few—and they weren't willing to make the necessary changes to keep them coming back . . . maybe until now.

- Just because it was "invented here" doesn't mean competitors won't use what made you great against you in the future. This is where market context becomes so important. If you get too internally focused, or believe that the only way out of a growth stall is to reduce expenses, or buy another company, then you have forgotten *the most important reason to do anything: the customers you serve*. Always keep them as your true north and allow them to guide you on when and why you would consider pulling back or accelerating on a particular growth path.

- As consumers are spending a larger percentage of their dollars online, retailers such as Sears will need to flip their value proposition to entice shoppers back into the store. Case in point: Target has been able to increase its digital growth by 25 percent in 2017 by arming in-store employees with mobile devices to help them facilitate orders placed online and picked up in the store, as well as facilitate online orders shipped to customers' homes from the store. Target claims as much as 70 percent of all purchases were shipped out of stores during the 2017 holiday shopping season.

- Even JCPenney has implemented a flexible fulfillment program with the rollout of "buy online, pick up in store"—same day to all stores. JCPenney has said that more than 40 percent of online orders are now picked up in the store, and more than 33 percent of those customers make an additional in-store purchase of $50. That is how you leverage **Customer Base Penetration** with a cross-channel sales and marketing effort.

PUTTING IT ALL TOGETHER

THE REASONS YOUR CUSTOMERS BECAME your customers in the first place will also impact the success of whichever growth path you choose. If customers joined you because you were offering the lowest price, it is highly likely that they will quickly move to another supplier who can offer an even lower price than you. But if customers joined you because of your amazing customer service (added value), then those customers are more likely to remain loyal and be positive recipients of cross- and up-sell propositions. Penetrating further into the existing base of customers means you must "find your niche"—and know what your most valuable customers look like, and why they buy from you. What trips up many companies that pursue a **Customer Base Penetration** path? They do not place as much emphasis on selling to the existing base as they do on acquiring new customers.

WHAT WORKS—AND POTENTIAL PITFALLS

The sequence in which you pursue this path is critical. Even if you have a large base of current customers who are disposed to buy more from you, it will backfire if you don't ensure that you **Optimized Sales**, plus allocate resources and dollars to make the marketing and sales efforts you pursue be more effective. The **Customer Base Penetration** growth path relies on detailed knowledge of the market and competitor activities. It relies on your having successful products in a market that you already know well. *Remember, this is about not only acquiring customers once but ensuring that you keep your brand top of mind when they "shop" again.*

You need to be talking regularly not just to your current customers but to your competitors' customers as well. Big data analytics can help you to bore down into the fine details of your customers' attitudes, behaviors, and interests—and, in the process, build a clear VOC profile. In the best of all scenarios, you know more about your customers and their relationship to your products than they do themselves. This will enable you not only to shift your pricing and marketing strategies at a moment's notice but to anticipate what your customers will want next and welcome them when they show up (i.e., "where the puck is going").

How can you apply the **Customer Base Penetration** growth path to your own company? This strategy will most likely succeed if the market you are targeting is still growing—or there are more "similar" customers to be found, or you have the ability to sell more to the existing base. A declining market, or one in which you have already scooped up 80 percent of potential users, is not likely to reward this path exclusively.

PATH 3

MARKET ACCELERATION

MARKET ACCELERATION

China is going to be the world's largest consumption place and that engine is going to drive the world economy.

—JACK MA, founder and executive chairman of Alibaba Group

WHY MARKET ACCELERATION MATTERS

- Global growth is projected to edge up to 3.1 percent in 2018 and ease slightly in 2019–20.
- Information-technology firms and construction-related companies dominate the fastest-growing industries in the United States.
- All twenty-three economies of "Emerging Europe" are set to record positive growth in 2018.
- China now accounts for 42 percent of global commerce as of 2018—more than France, Japan, the U.K., and the United States combined.
- Frost & Sullivan found 63 percent of respondents in a survey said they view customers in emerging markets as a future source of profits.
- By 2020, cross-border commerce is expected to account for approximately 22 percent of the global e-commerce market.
- In 2020, one out of five e-commerce dollars will be generated cross border.
- China will continue to see massive gains in retail e-commerce over the next few years, with sales topping $2.416 trillion in 2020. Spending via mobile phone is also booming and this year will account for 55.5 percent of all e-commerce sales and reach 68 percent by 2020.

CLOSER AND FURTHER

The greatest business successes in history—from General Electric to Facebook—have stemmed from a company's ability to grow by expanding into new markets. These markets can generate additional sources of top-line growth as well increase a company's customer base. The short-term appeal for most companies that choose to pursue this path is that they typically don't need to rethink their entire product strategy.

> *Competition should not be for a share of the market—but to expand the market.*
>
> **—W. EDWARDS DEMING, American statistician and author of *Out of the Crisis***

PERSPECTIVE
TIME TAKEN TO REACH FIFTY MILLION USERS

Air Travel	68 years
Automobile	62 years
Telephone	75 years
Lightbulb	46 years
Radio	38 years
Television	13 years
Personal Computer	14 years
Smartphone	12 years
AmEx	12 years
Uber	8 years
Internet	4 years
YouTube	4 years
Facebook	3.5 years
iPod	3 years
Google+	3 years
Pinterest	2.75 years
AOL	2.5 years
Twitter	2 years
Angry Birds	35 days
Pokémon Go	19 days

Market Acceleration closely follows the efforts of the previous **Customer Base Penetration** path. That said, it's still highly likely that product concessions will be needed to accommodate local, or retargeted, market needs. This carries a bit more risk than the prior path because it can be difficult to understand the context of a new market, its hidden complexities, its varying customer demands, and its geographic limitations when determining which combination and sequence is needed to support execution and implementation of this path.

However, the increased risk can be worth the reward this path can bring, especially with twenty-first-century technology. It used to be that accelerating the rate of adoption and number of users of a product would take decades, but with the changes in market context (Internet, social media, smartphones), decades has turned into days. It's mind-boggling that it took Air Travel sixty-eight years to capture fifty million "flyers" and today companies, like Angry Birds, are able to reach fifty million users in a mere thirty-five days! If you are looking to accelerate growth, expanding into new markets might just be the answer you've been looking for.

Market Acceleration *is the path of taking a brand's* **existing product** *into new markets, it is not selling entirely new products into new markets.* For this to work, a company will move laterally to take its existing products and find similar new customers. Those new customers may be in a new geographic area, in adjacent vertical segments that are not part of the current customer mix, or of different customer size (small business to midsize business). Or a company may even be selling to different people within a current customer base (such as switching from selling to IT [information technology] to selling to the marketing department) or geographic area. *The determining factor is that the market is in fact "new" for a company, outside of "to whom" or "where" it is currently selling.* If a company does decide to enter a new market, it is much easier to choose a target where customers already spend money buying more or less the same kind of product that a given company is selling. While it could be true that the product may be delivered or sold a different way, at the end of the day, getting a prospective customer to buy something familiar is much less risky than asking them to buy something that they don't understand.

An example might be Uber. Uber started out as an alternative to traditional taxi services with which people were already familiar—reimagined with their new business model. *If you do choose to pursue a market that is unfamiliar with the product or service you are selling, be prepared initially to spend more marketing dollars on product education and brand awareness than on driving leads.* That is why choosing a new market—with customers similar to those you currently have, with existing products—is an ideal way to test pursuing this particular growth path.

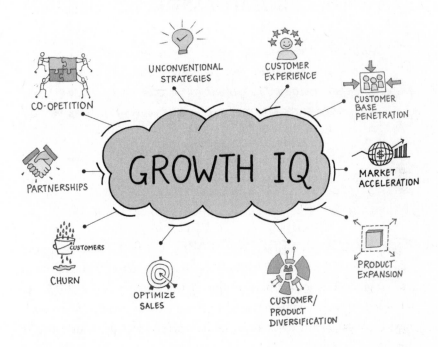

STORY

UNDER ARMOUR
SWEATY T-SHIRTS

Surround your disruptive core product, the thing that got you to the dance, with a whole product that solves for the target customer's problem end to end.

—GEOFFREY MOORE, author of *Crossing the Chasm*

THE GLOBAL SPORTS APPAREL MARKET is expected to garner $184.6 billion by 2020, with a compound annual growth rate (CAGR) of 4.3 percent during the forecast period 2015–20. The sports apparel market has seen strong growth over the past few years due to growing health awareness and increasing fitness activities such as yoga and spin classes. Three of the largest sports apparel companies in the world—Nike, Adidas, and Under Armour—have each taken advantage of these favorable trends in their industry, which should continue to support growth for many years and, probably, decades to come.

How each of these megabrands pursues growth is both similar and strikingly different—but one thing is for sure: there appears to be no slowdown in the heated competition among the three power brands. Each company is trying to outdo the others with large endorsement and sponsorship deals, innovative products such as 3-D printed custom shoes, and even basic T-shirts.

■　　■　　■

"I WILL"

In a row house in Georgetown in 1995, Kevin Plank started a company with about $15,000, some locally purchased fabric, and an ambitious plan to shake up the athletic apparel industry. Similar to Nike founder Phil Knight, who ran track, Plank was a special teams captain of the University of Maryland football team. Plank was looking for an edge against the faster, bigger guys he was competing against. That simple goal was what sparked a $1 billion business twenty years later. His idea was to make a better alternative for a short-sleeve cotton T-shirt in the summer and a long-sleeve cotton T-shirt in the winter to

> *Great entrepreneurs take one product and become great at one thing. I would say, the number one key to Under Armour marketing—to any company's success—plain and simple, is focus.*
>
> **—KEVIN PLANK,
> CEO of Under Armour**

help with sweat. After some of his University of Maryland teammates wore his shirts while playing lacrosse and baseball (not football), he realized he was onto something. As was the case with Red Bull, which was originally developed as a "non-carbonated" refreshment for factory workers and truck drivers to keep them awake through long shifts, Plank's idea saw a much broader appeal.

While Plank didn't invent "performance apparel," he was the first to see its potential, not just for athletes but also for the mass market. It was an entirely new concept to innovate a *T-shirt*, since it more than likely was never seen under a uniform and lacked the performance-enhancer label that other categories, such as shoes, enjoyed. Much of the innovation in sports was happening in equipment and shoes; apparel appeared to be an afterthought, which meant the category was ripe for the taking.

Why would anyone choose to compete in a category where brands such as Adidas and Nike were dominating? As with any successful "Blue Ocean" strategy, *don't go after the core business of the larger incumbents. Go after a smaller niche; win there. Learn the market. Develop a beachhead. Pull people into your product, your brand's orbit—and then, and only then, begin to expand your market and product offerings.* Like Red Bull, Under Armour was able to develop the right product with the right brand cachet

75

and endorsements, and market it in a unique way that captured the hearts and minds of aspiring athletes everywhere. Every one of its moves was carefully aimed at its "target market," a younger demographic, the millennials and Gen Z, who idolized professional and college athletes alike and wanted to dress and be just like them.

GO WHERE THE ENEMY ISN'T

For Under Armour, its early growth was the effect of a focused strategy around one product (T-shirts) to one market (football) to one target customer (athletes). Once it started to gain momentum, it took the former University of Maryland football player five years (to the year 2000) to turn it into a $5 million company. By 2004 it was over $200 million, and by 2017 it was over $5 billion in sales, all from a simple idea of a "tight, polyester-blend shirt that wicks away moisture while keeping muscles cool." How did Under Armour gain such incredible traction so quickly against much larger brands?

For the first five years we only had one product. Stretchy tee shirts.

—KEVIN PLANK, CEO of Under Armour

Under Armour made its first sale to Georgia Tech for about $17,000. Two dozen National Football League (NFL) teams soon followed suit. At the end of its second year, it had sold $100,000 in product. Like the Red Bull story, Under Armour caught the megabrands in the athletic apparel market off guard. It didn't start by attacking them head-on but rather at the edges of the category, with an innovative and new product proving you can think big, act big, start small, and still win big in the long run.

Once it knew it had a desired product (innovative T-shirt), knew who its ideal customers were (professional football players and aspiring athletes), and created customer buzz in the sportswear market, the next step was to accelerate that formula *laterally* into additional (new) markets with its existing product(s). The distinction here for Under Armour was the fact that taking its product into new markets didn't mean it had to reinvent what it was already doing; it just needed to determine the best way to sell more of its existing product to more customers like those it already had. In order to further pursue **Market Acceleration** beyond what it was doing on its own, it needed to combine its current efforts with third-party local retailers (**Partnerships**), which ultimately owned the (transaction) relationship with its ideal target customer base.

This decision was a perfect example of **Customer Base Penetration** and **Market Acceleration** in the right sequence. Had Under Armour decided to develop its T-shirt and immediately approach major retailers to create a partnership arrangement, more likely than not it would have been turned down for lack of brand awareness or consumer demand. It waited until it had enough buzz in the performance apparel market that large retailers would be very interested in striking a deal so that potential customers outside Under Armour's current sales channels could purchase its products easily.

Its first big-box coup came in 2000, when Galyan's Trading Company, a large retail chain eventually bought out by Dick's Sporting Goods, signed on, followed by thousands of others around the globe. Most recently it has begun to sell its shoes and apparel at Kohl's, the U.S. department store chain, as well as its shoes at DSW and Famous Footwear. It even opened its own "Brand House" stores (six so far in the United States, with international expansion expected next) to compete more effectively with Adidas and Nike, complement existing distribution channels, while at the same time upping its focus on the athlete and the (customer) experience.

When Under Armour went public in 2005, only 2 percent of its revenue came from outside North America. Since then, it has been investing heavily in (organic) **Market Acceleration** via international markets. In the fourth quarter of 2017, the international segment grew 47 percent, representing 23 percent of total sales, and it expects its international growth to be more than 25 percent, while its North American sales to be in mid-digit decline. It continues to grow its Brand House and Factory House stores internationally, and there is plenty of room to grow that footprint even further. Of course, the current efforts have a much broader product lineup than just a T-shirt, because of **Product Expansion** and **Customer and Product Diversification**—but Under Armour's desire to look for top-line growth via **Market Acceleration** continues today, twenty-two years after it was founded.

Retail partnerships were key to its growth early on, and even in light of the challenges retailers have been facing lately, it is still a major part of its growth strategy going forward, and the number of outlets carrying its products is about thirteen thousand. The only real difference now is that Under Armour is pursuing a much more refined retail strategy, one in which it takes a bit more control than in the past with its own branded storefronts. Don't be surprised if you start to see "pop-up" stores similar to Sephora in JCPenney and Apple in Best Buy with Under Armour taking over space in retailers such as Foot Locker.

"WHAT'S THAT ON THEIR SHIRTS?"

When hundreds of college football players descended on Lucas Oil Stadium in Indianapolis for the NFL Combine in 2011, quarterback Cam Newton and wide receiver Julio Jones were two of the hottest players to watch.

At some point during the week, people were asking the same question: What is that on their shirts? Newton and Jones were decked out in skintight red tank tops with a yellow . . . "thing" on it. It looked like a big round button you could push with an Under Armour logo in the middle and arrows flying out the sides.

It was actually the E39, a workout shirt with a removable biometric sensor measuring just about everything they did on the field. When Jones ran, his shirt tracked his heart rate, acceleration, and power. When Newton jumped, it measured the g-forces and power in his vertical.

Under Armour believed players could use the data to train better, and scouts could use it to make smarter decisions. This was the beginning of the next chapter for Under Armour and a full-circle moment for the company. This idea of a "smart shirt" started with a conversation a few years earlier, when Plank grabbed a 0039, the compression shirt he'd created in his grandmother's basement sixteen years earlier, the one that launched the Under Armour empire, handed it to his head product guy, Kip Fulks, and said, "Make it electric."

The **NFL Scouting Combine** is a weeklong showcase occurring every February where college football players perform physical and mental tests in front of NFL coaches, general managers, and scouts.

UNDER ARMOUR

STARTED WITH T-SHIRTS — HAS COME FULL CIRCLE BACK TO CONNECTED T-SHIRTS

FIRST SALE TO GEORGIA TECH FOR $17,000 → SOLD $100,000 IN PRODUCT AT THE END OF SECOND YEAR → then it was all about market acceleration

PARTNERSHIPS WITH LOCAL RETAILERS

While that project didn't work out—it didn't matter, it was the beginning of Under Armour's passion for combining technology + apparel + fitness. The T-shirt is just as much a part of its future growth strategy as it was back in 1995—the only difference now is that the T-shirt can tell you when it's time to replace itself.

UNDER ARMOUR
KEY TAKEAWAYS

- Over the years, Under Armour has remained true to its roots while simultaneously attacking a broader market with each new product category it enters. Early in its history Under Armour was right to stay very focused on what it did and did well. Instead of getting too far ahead of itself by pursuing an aggressive **Product Expansion** or **Customer and Product Diversification** strategy, it took what it learned from a single product—its T-shirt—and instead expanded the innovative fabric it had developed into other apparel categories adjacent to its core T-shirt. It wasn't until 2003 that it launched its first women's line of clothing, and it waited until 2006 to launch its "cleated footwear" line. In 2009, it went into a head-to-head fight with both Nike and Adidas with its first line of running shoes.

- Under Armour clearly understood early on the value of **Partnerships**, including high-profile endorsements. The decision not to open its own retail stores, especially in its first decade of hyper-growth, allowed it to reach more of its customers with less (financial) risk and a much larger sales footprint than it could have developed on its own. You must remember the market context when it first launched. In 1995 e-commerce wasn't even part of the equation. It was brick-and-mortar retail, mail-order catalogs, and other offline sales channels.

- _Build a beachhead, attack larger competitors from the edges, and build customer demand and loyalty without financially overextending yourself._ Under Armour first created buzz in the athletic apparel market with a single product, then they approached major retailers to create a partnership. This decision was a perfect example of **Partnerships** and **Market Acceleration** in the right sequence.

THE HONEST COMPANY
BETTER LIVING THROUGH CHEMISTRY

Forty-two percent of global respondents say they're willing to pay a premium for products made with organic or all-natural ingredients.
    —"DEEPER THAN DOLLARS" (2016 Nielsen report)

NOW, IN A FRESH TAKE on the pre–World War II slogan, "Better Living Through Chemistry," start-ups and large companies are embracing "green chemistry." Yale University chemistry professor Paul Anastas, known as the father of green chemistry, said the movement is "not simply choosing the next, less-bad thing off the shelf. It's about designing something that is genuinely good."

Once viewed as part of a fringe lifestyle, rooted in the hippie movement, natural and organic are going mainstream. Driven by regulations, consumer demand, and eco-friendly business philosophy, large corporations, retailers, and manufacturers are eliminating some chemicals, pulling products off shelves, and redesigning others, especially in the baby care market.

It wasn't until 2016 that the Toxic Substances Control Act of 1976 was updated, providing better transparency into the chemicals used in producing everyday items and protecting vulnerable populations such as pregnant women and children.

The global baby personal care market was valued at around $56 billion in 2017 and is expected to grow at an annual CAGR of approximately 7 percent from 2016 to 2024. It is experiencing significant growth in products that are "organic in nature and pose no threat to a baby's well-being."

Demand for organic personal care products is expected to provide a huge opportunity to baby personal care product manufacturers. Even though these products are more expensive, parents still prefer the best and branded products for their child, thereby disregarding the cost of certain products.

This growth, however, has gone disproportionately to (seemingly) small upstarts. In recent years, parents have been spurning Johnson & Johnson's infant staples for products containing fewer chemicals. In the first half of 2016, J&J's baby care sales fell below $200 million for the first time since 2007. Gerber (owned by Nestlé) has been losing market share to Earth's Best, Plum Organics, and Ella's Kitchen. Even baby diaper behemoths Procter & Gamble (Pampers) and Kimberly-Clark (Huggies and Luvs) are anticipating a dry spell.

NOT FOR MY DAUGHTER

First came the idea. In 2009, actress Jessica Alba gave birth to her first baby, a daughter. Like most new parents, the world felt toxic and perilous overnight. When her daughter developed hives after Alba used a store-bought clothes detergent, she decided to launch a consumer goods company committed to selling only nontoxic household products. Since then, The Honest Company has experienced amazing levels of growth. In 2012, its first year selling, it hit $10 million in revenue, and in 2016 it surpassed $300 million, and in 2017 it experienced a "flat year."

The Honest Company targeted the baby products market with a very specific buyer persona. *It was both responding to and creating consumer desire.* In particular, its message hit home with new parents who worried about the petrochemicals and synthetic fragrances in the baby goods they purchased. The context of the market was right for what The Honest Company was selling. Over the past two decades, "parenting" and "moth-

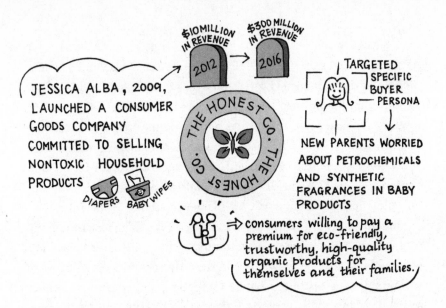

JESSICA ALBA, 2009, LAUNCHED A CONSUMER GOODS COMPANY COMMITTED TO SELLING NONTOXIC HOUSEHOLD PRODUCTS

DIAPERS BABY WIPES

$10 MILLION IN REVENUE 2012 → $300 MILLION IN REVENUE 2016

THE HONEST CO.

TARGETED SPECIFIC BUYER PERSONA

NEW PARENTS WORRIED ABOUT PETROCHEMICALS AND SYNTHETIC FRAGRANCES IN BABY PRODUCTS

⇒ consumers willing to pay a premium for eco-friendly, trustworthy, high-quality organic products for themselves and their families.

ering" have become branded concepts, and now as then, consumers are willing to pay a premium for eco-friendly, trustworthy, high-quality organic products for themselves and their families.

The Honest Company has used a number of growth paths in combination to achieve its $1 billion valuation. With its initial focus on diapers, infant formulas, and household cleaning products, The Honest Company was quick to maximize sales by offering more of its existing products to its existing customers via a subscription service (**Customer Base Penetration**).

The company launched (**Product Expansion**) the recurring $79.99-per-month subscription model for its diapers and wipes to improve both the customer experience and revenue predictability, based on its keen understanding of its customer base and what would appeal to them—it didn't want new parents to run out of diapers and need to make a midnight run to the store any longer.

The Honest Company also broke with industry tradition by eschewing traditional marketing such as advertising and brick-and-mortar retail. Instead, it focused upon direct-to-consumer (D2C) online sales and an image of purity and goodwill, not least in making major donations to charities right from the start (**Unconventional Strategies**). Hence why its e-commerce roots continue to run so deep even today.

WHAT GOT YOU HERE—MIGHT JUST GET YOU THERE

A cofounder and a former CEO, Brian Lee was a successful online entrepreneur, having cofounded LegalZoom with Robert Shapiro and ShoeDazzle with Kim Kardashian. He was instrumental in driving the company toward an industry-leading position, with its online prowess even outmaneuvering the industry stalwarts. The Honest Company's products were almost exclusively sold online, but as it pursued **Customer Base Penetration** and **Market Acceleration**, the off-line sales channel became not only more important to growth but a larger portion of overall sales.

Of course, it didn't hurt that Alba was a major movie star and one of the country's best-known new mothers. That star power helped her gain publicity that very few CEOs in the industry could ever achieve—including giving testimony before Congress about consumer product testing for dangerous chemicals. Because of Alba, The Honest Company enjoyed unequaled coverage in show business magazines and other non-traditional channels for reaching other new mothers. However, a celebrity name alone doesn't guarantee success or keep a company growing; if the products aren't good, there is no demand. You need both in order to capitalize on the effect of being a "celebrity."

For most companies discussed in *Growth IQ*, the decision to pursue a new growth path is made because the current one is either maturing or fading, or the company is encountering effective new competition. But for The Honest Company, the decision was made for the opposite reason—its runaway success. In particular, the company had found the ideal mix of the right market context, coupled with the right products, brand promise, and a clearly defined target market to deliver growth.

The interconnectedness of those individual attributes is extremely difficult to replicate, even by bigger brand names. If you think of a company trying new things to stimulate growth as moving at a "crawl-walk-run" pace, The Honest Company began by "crawling" in **Customer Base Penetration**. It focused on the company's foundation in the right sequence. It started "walking" and hired the right management teams, and putting in place the appropriate supply chain, built strategic **Partnerships**, and, as it grew, it began (running) to explore **Market Acceleration**, which included off-line partnerships.

Nick Vlahos, CEO of Honest, told *Fortune* in an interview that when he looked at the white space opportunities for the brand to pursue growth, Amazon was a clear target: a partnership with the e-commerce giant would make the brand more relevant online where more consumer spending is gravitating. The union, he explained, is part of an "omnichannel strategy that we are driving aggressively."

The Honest Company faced a dilemma. Should it continue to expand its business to its existing customers (that is, **Customer Base Penetration**) or pursue its planned growth (**Market Acceleration**) outside of its current North American market?

There was also a third option—one that was presenting itself with ever more clarity as the months passed: to begin to extend its product family to recognize that its first cohort of customers—babies and their parents—was now growing older, with changing needs and interests beyond simply baby products, now looking toward the entire home (**Product Expansion** and **Customer and Product Diversification**).

The diaper and wipes business proved it definitively. The Honest Company believed it could develop a single brand that carried its credibility across even more products in the nontoxic category.

It would also pursue these initiatives largely in parallel, through a combination that included massive funding (which was why the pursuit of an initial public offering was even on the table), the development of (geographic, chronological, and application) adjacent markets, and the addition of a brick-and-mortar component to its largely (80–90 percent) online ecommerce business.

In order to optimize sales, it chose to expand the places customers could buy its products and pursued **Partnerships** with various retailers in order to pursue the **Market Acceleration** growth path. The Honest Company was already selling through Whole Foods, Costco, and Target. Its products were also being sold in Nordstrom.

In mid-2017, it added CVS and Babies R Us. Then, in July 2017, it added the biggest player of all: Amazon—even though in 2015 at South by Southwest (SXSW), Alba publically stated she wasn't interested in pursuing Amazon (especially in light of the fact that it owned Diapers.com and

Soap.com). CNBC reported that "she wants to maintain the one-on-one relationship with the customer and does not want to give up control of the customer experience to Amazon." This decision to rethink her previous position highlights the brand's focus on **Customer Experience**. *Going where their customers are and responding to the ever-changing market context are what separates high-performing companies from the rest.*

The Honest Company could have done it on its own, but as you will see later in the **Partnership** growth path (and as you just read in the Under Armour story), this is a cost-effective and less risky way to accelerate sales in additional markets than going at it alone. This decision to open up its sales channels to more than its own online e-commerce store has proved a good one. The Honest Company now has a more balanced business, with about 50 percent of its current revenue ($300 million) coming from its more than eighteen thousand brick-and-mortar locations and online partnerships, such as Amazon.

The company that had, just two years before, sold primarily online to upper-middle-class parents was now marketing its products on two continents in mainstream stores, online and off-line, and pharmacies to families across the economic spectrum—and yet still managing to maintain its reputation for quality and exclusivity.

The zigzagging between growth strategies has been the very embodiment of *Growth IQ* and made The Honest Company one of the fastest-growing lifestyle companies in history, even when competing against some of the largest brands in the world. Similar to Under Armour and Red Bull, there was an opportunity, a "Blue Ocean," that was ripe for the taking—it was being ignored for the most part by other, much larger brands that were selling similar products, attacking the incumbents on the edges while improving its beachhead proved to be a good move.

From its beginnings as an online purveyor of diapers and wipes, the company grew quickly into an all-purpose lifestyle brand. Today The

For more than fifty million millennials over the age of twenty-seven, parenthood is becoming far more normal. Pew Research said earlier this year that sixteen million millennial women are moms, and 60 percent of all millennials say being a parent is important to their identity.

Honest Company sells more than 135 products, including cosmetics, toothpaste, sunscreen, multivitamins, kitchen detergents, and nursery furniture.

By looking at the combination and sequence of its decision making, we can better understand how the company grew as meteorically as it did, which is why understanding the market context can have such an incredible impact on decisions made.

Without those particular customer characteristics being in place, The Honest Company could have had a great idea, poorly timed for market demand. But instead, there continue to be rumors of an imminent IPO, the "Unicorn" status, and bringing in veteran CEO, Nick Vlahos (a consumer package goods [CPG] powerhouse previously from Clorox), signaling that it has no intention of backing away from a sizable market opportunity—regardless of who it is competing against.

Just as Under Armour put a modernized spin on T-shirts, The Honest Company, with new, artfully designed disposable diapers, keeps its beachhead product fresh, relevant, and fun—maybe even helping to capture entirely new customers along the way.

THE HONEST COMPANY
KEY TAKEAWAYS

- As with **Customer Base Penetration**, **Market Acceleration** requires you to have a deep understanding of the wants, needs, and purchase preferences of your target customer. This allows companies to meet customers where (online and off-line) and how (direct with a brand or via a third-party retailer) they want. Companies who choose to stick with what has worked in the past, without taking into consideration shifting buying patterns of its target customers, risk being left behind.

- Worth repeating: For most companies discussed in *Growth IQ*, the decision to pursue a new growth path is because the current one is either maturing or fading, or the company is encountering effective new competition. But for The Honest Company, the decision was made for the opposite reason—its runaway success.

- Just because your company does not have a "Blue Ocean" strategy doesn't mean you can't apply learnings from these companies. In the case of The Honest Company, Jessica Alba did not invent or instigate the "chemical free" movement. She took the shift in market context and applied it to an industry that had all but ignored this opportunity.

- Somewhat counterintuitively, *the quickest path to getting big in a new market is to aim small*. By creating a proposition that is good enough only for a particular type of buyer in a foothold market, companies can avoid the time and expense required to satisfy broad swathes of customers. The company then has a narrow target for its sales efforts. It also can attain scale within the niche, such as new and expecting mothers, that can serve as a powerful customer base, especially if those customers are vocal about their satisfaction with a brand or product.

STORY

3

MATTEL
TOYS WILL BE TOYS

Our vision is to inspire the wonder of childhood as the
global leader in learning and development through play.
As we shift our business aggressively in a new strategic
direction and transform how we operate, I believe we
have the assets to achieve this vision and shape the
future of the toy industry.

—MARGO GEORGIADIS, CEO of Mattel

As is the case with The Honest Company, as long as there are more than 130 million newborns each year across the globe, the need for toys isn't going away anytime soon. U.S. toy sales grew 5 percent in 2016, and 1 percent (United States and globally) in 2017, reaching $20.7 billion according to the NPD Group. From 2013 to 2016 the industry grew 16 percent larger across a number of key segments (games/puzzles, dolls, outdoor and sports, plush, and infant and toddler).

Founded in 1945, Mattel produces some of the most well-known brands in the world—American Girl, Fisher-Price, Hot Wheels, Matchbox, Thomas & Friends—and is the world's largest toy maker in terms of revenue ($5.45 billion in 2016).

In recent years, Mattel faced a problem. It had enjoyed almost continuous success and growth for more than a half century—most of it driven by one of the most iconic products of all time: Barbie. Now the company was in a growth stall. In a world where 85 percent of three- to five-year-olds have access to a home tablet where they watch shows and play games, toy companies are finding it harder to compete with this convenient and easy fix for a child's attention. This shift in market context contributed to the disappointing quarters and sinking margins Mattel was facing.

Throughout the course of 2016, company stock fell by 23 percent, which further increased when the company announced weak Christmas sales and a cut in its dividend to help fund a comprehensive turnaround plan. One of its turnaround efforts to boost sales was to focus on emerging markets where growth is still going strong as wages and quality of life steadily improve. The global market for toys and games is projected to reach $166 billion by 2024, with Europe representing the largest market and Latin America the fastest-growing market with a CAGR of 9.6 percent. *Just the kind of opportunity Mattel needed.*

However, in June 2017, at end of the quarter, investors anxiously awaited the results of that turnaround plan—and when it didn't materialize (sales were up only 2 percent over the previous year, to $974 million, while costs were up even more, to produce a net loss), they punished the company with a further stock drop of 7 percent. Mattel's stock was down 27 percent in 2017, trading at its lowest level since the summer of 2015.

Clearly, Mattel had made a terrible mistake. It had pursued a growth path (**Market Acceleration**) without fully understanding the implications of not having the other required growth paths (**Product Expansion, Customer and Product Diversification**, and **Partnerships**) shored up.

Remember, *it is never just one thing*. *The combination of products and sales channels wasn't right*. It had yet to give its flagship brands like Barbie and Ken a makeover for new markets—both domestic and international—considering both age and gender, it didn't have a comprehensive digital strategy, it was far too reliant on traditional (U.S.) retailers, and didn't have any lucrative licensing deal (**Partnership**) like Hasbro does with Disney—most notably, Star Wars, Marvel Superheroes, Disney Princesses, *Beauty and the Beast*, *Frozen*, and *Moana*.

Specifically, the toy maker's strategy to return to growth is fivefold:
1. **Create connected 360-degree play experiences.**
2. **Aggressively target emerging markets, especially China.**
3. **Fuel the innovation pipeline.**
4. **Improve internal operations.**
5. **Reignite the culture.**

The context of the toy business had shifted and Mattel had not responded in a timely way. As part of its turnaround strategy, Mattel acted, as one might expect, by following the money. The international sales projections were a strong proponent for Mattel to double down on **Market Acceleration** outside the United States. Even though Mattel had been selling its products globally for decades, what market could it specifically focus on to provide the greatest returns? It decided on China.

Targeting a large and relatively untapped market at first blush may seem like an easy decision to make when using **Market Acceleration** to reverse a growth stall. However, in the case of China's fragmented yet lucrative toy market, *the success for any brand interested in aggressively pursuing new or emerging markets hinges on its ability to navigate strict regulation and adapt to local consumer preferences.*

For that reason, Mattel quickly engaged in several **Partnerships** in China, in hopes of gaining greater market penetration. In particular, Mattel struck a deal with Chinese e-commerce giant Alibaba. With its (in-country) reach, it could give Mattel the momentum it needed. Along with Alibaba, Mattel teamed with two other companies specializing in child development: Fosun Group, to create play clubs and child-focused learning centers, and Babytree, to sell interactive learning products based on its Fisher-Price toys as well as to develop online parenting platforms to leverage China's preoccupation with education. The goal was to get Chinese consumers acquainted with, and excited about, the Fisher-Price brand.

All three of these partnerships marked a significant shift for Mattel. Remember, what got you here might not get you there. Its new strategy reflected an acknowledgment of the fact that *"one size does not fit all"*—especially in China, where one in every five customers prefers to shop for toys online rather than in "hypermarkets" and toy stores. Mattel was doing whatever it felt was going to provide it a better outcome than its first attempt into China back in 2002.

At that time, Mattel began selling Barbie dolls in regional stores and later introduced Ling, a Barbie with black hair and traditional Chinese attire (**Customer and Product Diversification**). Once in country, it then made an aggressive (**Market Acceleration**) push to expand further in 2009 by launching a thirty-six-thousand-square-foot "House of Barbie" store in Shanghai, the world's largest at the time. The decision to open a store with existing toys was a mismatch against the existing market context (what customers wanted and expected). Unfortunately, it failed to gain traction and was closed two years later due to high costs and low sales. The setback proved that Chinese customers preferred tailor-made products and that their buying decisions were not always price driven.

A NEW LOOK

What makes this growth stall worse was that the decline Mattel was experiencing wasn't just in its bedrock Barbie line but across its other product lines, including American Girl dolls, Fisher-Price, and Power Wheels. That meant that it couldn't use one product family to hold the fort while the others turned around—it had to come up with a new strategy, and *now*.

The Chinese market was only part of Mattel's turnaround strategy and the company also planned to put into play its flagship product, Barbie, with a change of look. In the age of social media and an increasing interest in diversity and inclusion, the blond bombshell look of traditional Barbie looked increasingly anachronistic.

Mattel had recognized this change in market context as early as 2000, even as it was expanding into China and introducing Ling, but it had been very conservative beyond that in its response. Now the company was prepared to go all in: new bodies for its dolls—petite, tall, and curvy—and a wide range of races and clothing styles. Mattel has even pushed the envelope on Barbie career dolls with a president, a doctor, a teacher, and

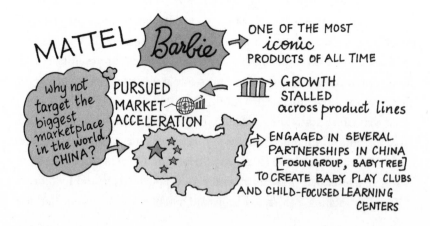

a game developer to raise awareness of STEM (science, technology, engineering, and math) for girls.

It was a massive risk for Mattel, because to many people, Barbie is more than just a doll, she is part of the American culture. The brand does $1 billion in sales across more than 150 countries annually, and 92 percent of American girls ages three to twelve have owned a Barbie, thanks in part to her affordable $10 price tag.

"LET IT GO"

What is important to keep in mind as you read this lesson is the fact that if you are going to pursue the **Market Acceleration** growth path, you *must consider not only the products you plan on selling but the broad set of partners needed to support and fuel your growth.* So, while all of these product changes were good for Mattel, and necessary, it will all be for naught if it doesn't maintain and nurture its highly coveted, industry-leading partnerships such as the one with Disney.

Mattel had worked with Disney since 1955 when it was its first sponsor of *The Mickey Mouse Club*. In 1996, Mattel had become Disney's chosen doll maker for their Princess Dolls, including Jasmine, Cinderella, and Sleeping Beauty. The contract was said to be worth some $500 mil-

- Mattel, which makes Barbie dolls, has worked with Disney since 1955.
- Since 1996, the company has been making the Disney Princess dolls.
- But now the lucrative contract belongs to their biggest rival, Hasbro.
- Despite being the biggest doll maker on the market, Mattel lost the contract to a company known primarily for making boys' toys.
- One of Disney's biggest success stories of late, the 2013 movie *Frozen*, is counted as a separate franchise, and another half billion dollars' worth of dolls and dresses based on Princesses Elsa and Anna were sold in the United States last year, according to NPD Group.

lion, not even including the new most popular doll among girls, Elsa from Disney's *Frozen*. However, when Barbie sales began to slow, Disney felt "overlooked" as Mattel appeared to focus more attention on their flagship product than in partnership and opportunities it had with Disney. As it continued to look for new revenue streams, in 2013 it introduced "Ever After High" (**Product Expansion**), a line of dolls based on characters from fairy tales, which spawned a Web series, a movie, and two book series that in many ways directly competed against the Disney Princess brand.

Unfortunately, after a series of internal decisions Mattel made, in September 2014, Disney officially took its doll business to Hasbro, which already had their Marvel and Star Wars licenses. Although Mattel still makes toys for the company, including Mickey Mouse, the loss of that contract cost Mattel 7 percent of its annual sales, or roughly $450 million. "*We took Disney for granted, we weren't focusing on them. Shame on us,*" admitted Chris Sinclair, a Mattel board member who became CEO at the start of 2015. It is a reminder that choosing a new growth path or doubling down on an existing growth path cannot happen in isolation.

This is an example of where things can go woefully wrong if you aren't careful about the implications of certain decisions made across groups or divisions. If product development isn't aligned with the partnership and alliance team, one can actually end up competing against the other or, worse yet, become the catalyst to destroy long-standing revenue streams. The implications can be catastrophic, as in the case of Mattel and Disney.

MATTEL
KEY TAKEAWAYS

- Consumers are demanding greater flexibility in sales channels, and companies that are considering **Market Acceleration** to recover from a growth stall can't just use the same tactics (i.e., selling via retailers with some products) to spark a turnaround.

- At the same time as it was attempting to grow into new markets, Mattel was playing catch-up to the current market context with its product lineup, which meant that the sequence of efforts really mattered. Pushing into new markets without the appropriate products can hurt a company's chances to succeed. You may have the right growth path in play (i.e., **Market Acceleration**), but you may be selling the wrong products (not regionally adjusted or outdated) or the market you are expanding into may itself be in decline and not worth pursuing.

- Global brands, or brands that aspire to be global, must take into consideration the regional adjustments required and make those adjustments (minor or major) prior to launching an existing product.

PUTTING IT ALL TOGETHER

REMEMBER, IN THE **Customer Base Penetration** path, the benefit of doing the work to research and better understand your current customer will guide you if you decide to pursue growth by targeting similar customer types in new markets. Rarely does this path sit alone: if a company wants to expand into new markets, it better ensure it has established the necessary sales and marketing capabilities prior to officially entering a market (**Optimize Sales**). It may be appealing to explore **Partnerships** to mitigate some of the risk and realize a faster time to market. The amount of planning you do to prepare for a new market largely will depend on how similar it is to your current efforts and your understanding of the context of the new market— whatever that might be.

First and foremost, you must be able to identify the best markets to pursue, based on future growth projections of your category/product/ customer segment, as well as those to avoid. The trick is to understand market context in such a way that you can adjust product, marketing, and sales capabilities quickly enough to realize a return on your investments. This will ultimately put far more pressure on your sales and marketing organizations or your partnerships (rather than products), as they are more likely to limit the speed at which this particular path can be executed.

WHAT WORKS—AND POTENTIAL PITFALLS

THE LONG-TERM IMPACT OF A MARKET ACCELERATION PATH CAN BE SIGNIFICANT, IF YOU GET IT RIGHT:

- Opens up previously excluded market and customer segments for growth, further extending market share.
- Offsets a current growth stall, which may be occurring in home market(s) and the customer base, with new revenue sources.
- Allows for more aggressive pricing, marketing, and sales efforts to be isolated to certain markets, avoiding channel "conflict."
- Taps into developing markets that are experiencing high growth in your product category, which provides your company with the ability to fund other growth paths in your home market.

THE LONG-TERM IMPACT OF A MARKET ACCELERATION PATH CAN BE SIGNIFICANT, IF YOU GET IT WRONG:

- You overextend yourself so much that product quality and customer experience are negatively impacted.
- You pursue a market aggressively, only to pull out when things start going wrong. This will leave you exposed if you ever try to enter the same market again. Customers may remember your previous entry and exit and worry that you will do the same thing again.
- Going global means that you must be sensitive to local customs and laws. If you aren't, you risk offending potential customers with your lack of consideration, and that is extremely difficult to recover from.

- Using partnerships to extend reach and gain access to new markets is a viable way to improve the likelihood of success. However, if you make it too one-sided (i.e., it's all about you), you will discourage additional investments.

COMBINATION: PATH 3—
Market Acceleration + Path 8—Partnerships

This one stands to reason: you've successfully entered into a new market with a variant of an existing product. Now that you are established, the next challenge is to spin out and exploit all of the new opportunities this move has created.

If you've done your homework and already identified the key players in your new market, then it should be a simple step to prioritize potential strategic partnership, relationships, and channels that will make you even more efficient and competitive.

Ultimately, your place in the ecosystem of this new market should be at least as complex, influential, and sophisticated as it is in your original market. As was seen with Under Armour, its retail partnerships were invaluable when it wanted to expand even further, both domestically and internationally, emphasizing the importance of establishing local partnerships with recognizable and reputable brands that have customer bases it could leverage.

COMBINATION: PATH 3—
Market Acceleration + Path 6—Optimize Sales

You've charged into your new market and established momentum. But your relationship to that market and its participants is still rough and unproven. What may look like a long-term success may in fact still be just novelty.

You need to consolidate your position in this new market. One of the best ways is to make your sales operation efficient, responsive, and adaptive. It needs to get you to that repeat sale and, in the process, a steady, then loyal, then generational customer base. These two growth paths—

Market Acceleration and Optimize Sales—are inextricably connected. If you are going to expand into new markets, your sales efforts must be aligned.

COMBINATION: PATH 3—
Market Acceleration + Path 10—Unconventional Strategies

This is the riskiest of the three combination growth paths—so why take it? The start of a new market, when the situation is less defined and more fluid, may be the best time to try something new. If you swing for the fences and fail, the loss could be small and the market will barely notice.

If you are ever going to sweep the table on a new market, there is no better time than when you first enter it, when consumers are curious, competitors are unprepared, and you enjoy a novelty and freedom to maneuver. While the risks are there, they are small: succeed, and you spare yourself a fortune and years of hard-slogging competition.

PATH 4

PRODUCT EXPANSION

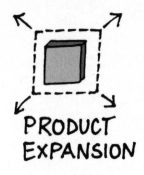

PRODUCT EXPANSION

When we buy a product, we essentially "hire" it to help us do a job. If it does the job well, the next time we're confronted with the same job, we tend to hire that product again. And if it does a crummy job, we "fire" it and look for an alternative.

—CLAYTON CHRISTENSEN,
author of *The Innovator's Dilemma*

WHY PRODUCT EXPANSION MATTERS

- Existing customers are 50 percent more likely to try new products and spend 31 percent more, when compared to new customers.
- Sixty percent of global consumers with Internet access prefer to buy new products from a familiar brand rather than switch to a new brand.
- In the consumer products business, forty-two of the fifty-four major categories have lost market share to younger, previously unknown companies.
- By 2025, Thomson Reuters data shows that 72 percent of the world's consuming class will live in the developing world.
- One in three hundred products makes a significant difference to customer purchase behavior, the product category, or the company's growth trajectory.

WHAT IS A PRODUCT?

In today's fast-paced, fiercely competitive business world, it's no longer possible, or necessary, for companies to rely solely on high research and development (R&D) budgets and long, sequential production schedules when contemplating developing and launching new products to drive growth.

> *Don't find customers for your products, find products for your customers.*
>
> **—SETH GODIN, author of *Linchpin***

For example, I met with a very large technology company several years ago to discuss a new product they were planning to launch targeted at the small and midsize business (SMB) segment. The product itself was not "new" per se, but it was an extension of an existing product built with a very specific customer segment and buyer in mind. This provided huge economies of scale, faster time to market, and institutional knowledge they could tap into of what had worked (and not worked) in the past. The company was already a market share leader in the SMB space for many other products and services in its portfolio, making it an existing market, which made this launch a perfect **Product Expansion** adjacency play because it was looking for additional top-line growth. This effort became the most successful in the history of this product line for a company that sold millions of units in this (product) category each year.

What this shows is that if the **Product Expansion** path is something you are considering, you don't always need to go back to the drawing board and start from scratch in order to design a "new" product. *The first and most important reason for any new development should be to provide "value" to a customer by solving a personal, business, or societal need.* Without this, there is no reason for them to pay for what it is you are offering. *The new and increasing value is what keeps customers coming back and companies growing.* If the value offered is not increasing, or a product stagnates, the company risks losing ground in the market as competitors, or even newcomers, increase their value and leave it behind. In this case, this company's product hit on all the customers' value-based needs.

But in the twenty-first-century climate, the definition of what a product is and what value it can bring might not be as cut-and-dried as my example above.

FORBES'S TOP TEN OF THE WORLD'S MOST INNOVATIVE COMPANIES

All you have to do is look at the 2017 *Forbes* Annual List of the World's Most Innovative Companies to understand that the "products" these companies sell are far from monolithic. Some of these companies are twentieth-century companies still innovating in the new century, while others have had the benefit of twenty-first-century technologies to build extremely innovative and disruptive products. In the service realm, the sharing economy has turned the idea of product "ownership" on its head. Uber owns no cars. Airbnb doesn't own any hotels. Yet, they sell a lot of rides and rooms to rent. They are merely a conduit, a digital market of sorts, for customers to gain access to a network of available products (cars and rooms). So, what exactly is the product?

The truth is: it may be all of those things, which makes this particular growth path as full of challenges as it is full of opportunities.

It isn't sufficient enough to have a great product and expect to succeed. *Only having a great product—even if it's the best of breed—is no longer enough.* You obviously need to invest in developing your product, and

Forbes's Top Ten of the World's Most Innovative Companies (2017):

Rank	Name	Country	Industry
1	SALESFORCE.COM INC	USA	Application Software
2	TESLA INC	USA	Automobile Manufacturers
3	AMAZON.COM INC	USA	Internet and Direct Market Retail
4	SHANGHAI RAAS BLOOD PRODUCTS CO LTD	CHN	Biotechnology
5	NETFLIX INC	USA	Internet and Direct Market Retail
6	INCYTE CORP	USA	Biotechnology
7	HINDUSTAN UNILEVER LIMITED	IND	Household Products
8	ASIAN PAINTS LIMITED	IND	Speciality Chemicals
9	NAVER	KOR	Internet Software and Services
10	REGENERON PHARMACEUTICALS	USA	Biotechnology

there is nothing wrong with being "product-led." Regardless of whether you make apparel, cupcakes, camping equipment, or luggage—it doesn't matter.

It's when you are too product-focused that you get into trouble. What the market demands today is much greater flexibility and focus on the customer, otherwise known as being "market-led" or "customer-led." This is where a company seeks to determine what products a customer *might* want in the future and then moves to develop those products. Large or small, it doesn't matter. There are so many ways to execute this path—more than this chapter could ever do justice. But what this chapter will cover are some great examples of how companies used a combination of decisions, together with their current market context, in the right sequence, to give them the competitive advantage.

STORY

1

KYLIE COSMETICS
KEEPING UP WITH KYLIE JENNER (#KUWKJ)

[Millennials] create a community and their own language and their own world and communicate and consume in a different way.

—JO MALONE,
founder of Jo Malone and Jo Loves

THE TRADITIONAL MAKEUP MARKET WAS down 1.3 percent in 2016. But independent brands were up 42.7 percent. The growth of these smaller independent brands is a direct reflection of a change in market context, consumer tastes, and buyer demographics. Case in point . . .

One of the most successful recent examples of a company executing a highly targeted and effective **Product Expansion** growth strategy is Kylie Jenner, best known as being the youngest of the Kardashian-Jenner empire.

Regardless of what you may think of reality TV or the Kardashian family, this is an impressive story that takes advantage of many of the bene-

In the United States, "women are spending more [on beauty products], 13% more on foundation, 18% more on concealer, 35% of women use more than five makeup products every day and 80% use three skin care products every day . . . and six mascaras are sold per minute in the U.S. . . . Sixty-five percent of teens rely on social media to discover and select beauty products."

fits that technology and changing consumer behavior provide companies today, which is at the heart of *Growth IQ*.

Taking full advantage of her exposure on the *Keeping Up with the Kardashians* television show, Kylie became an influential voice on makeup and fashion. In 2012, when she was only fifteen years old, she collaborated with the clothing brand PacSun, along with her sister Kendall, and created a line of clothing, "Kendall and Kylie," targeted at teenage girls, which was their natural fan and target customer base. In 2014 and 2015, *Time* magazine listed the Jenner sisters as one of their "Most Influential Teens in 2014." If that wasn't enough, in 2015 Kylie launched her own cosmetics line, Kylie Cosmetics. What made her believe she could successfully enter the cosmetics industry occupied by some of the most famous brands in the world?

> *Ever since I was probably fifteen I've been obsessed with lipstick. I could never find a lip liner and lipstick that were a perfect match. So that's where I thought of the idea that I wanted to create my own product.*
>
> **—KYLIE JENNER**

First, she had a passion for makeup and fashion. Second, she had the ability to leverage a huge platform from both the show and her growing fan base, which allowed her to form (required) manufacturing and distribution **Partnerships**. Third, she saw an unmet need in the market. Fourth, she wanted to focus on customers who were just like her—teenagers.

Let's focus in on the second one for a moment, because it is an important piece of this lesson. In December 2017, at twenty years of age, she reached 100 million followers on Instagram alone. She also has more than 24 million Twitter followers and 20 million Facebook followers, bringing her social media reach to more than 150 million people. In short, she had one of the largest social media followings on the planet (maybe only rivaled by her big sister Kim).

As part of a **Product Expansion** strategy, its initial collection of discrete cosmetic products was expanded over subsequent months (yes . . . months) in two different directions. One direction was related cosmetic categories: Kyshadows (eye-shadow palettes), Kyliners (eyeliner), Snap-Chat tutorials (which average ten million views), a mobile app, and other

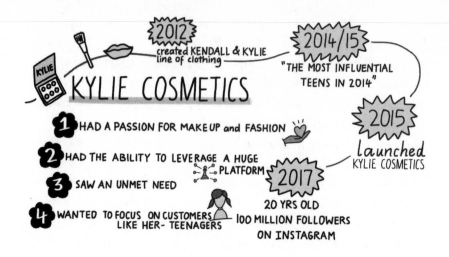

2012
created KENDALL & KYLIE
line of clothing

2014/15
"THE MOST INFLUENTIAL
TEENS IN 2014"

KYLIE COSMETICS

KYLIE

1. HAD A PASSION FOR MAKEUP and FASHION

2. HAD THE ABILITY TO LEVERAGE A HUGE PLATFORM

2015
launched
KYLIE COSMETICS

3. SAW AN UNMET NEED

2017
20 YRS OLD
100 MILLION FOLLOWERS
ON INSTAGRAM

4. WANTED TO FOCUS ON CUSTOMERS LIKE HER- TEENAGERS

fashion products. The other direction was the bundling of products thematically (Kylie's Vacation Edition, Kylie's Valentine Collection).

Now firmly established in her target market, Jenner leveraged a personal milestone to stretch the edges of that market with these new products—to continue to be relevant to her aging, yet still teenage, customer base—with the #KylieTurns20 product campaign.

The success of this strategy depended heavily on both combination and sequence. Yes, there is no question that part of her success is based on making the most of her massive platform, but that will only get you so far. Similar to what we saw with Jessica Alba and The Honest Company, being a celebrity might get your foot in the door, but without great products, a loyal customer base, and a strong customer experience, it won't matter.

Many other (much older and more established) celebrities have attempted to extend their brand by venturing into the business world, only to fail. Jenner—along with her business manager and mother, Kris Jenner, and her extended business team, including Laura Nelson and John Nelson of Seed Beauty—had to first capture a sizable share of her target market by playing off the context of Kylie's teen stardom and massively loyal fan base.

The sequence of this massive growth was critical. Kylie started by establishing her personal brand first, before she endorsed or released any products on her own. Next, she created her own niche within the family empire, different from her siblings, and stayed focused there, with vari

> Karin Tracy, Facebook's head of Industry–Beauty/Fashion/Luxury/Retail, noted: "Facebook has 1.9 billion users, WhatsApp has 1.2 billion, Instagram has 700 million and Facebook messenger has 1.2 billion. On those combined platforms there are 60 million businesses and every day there are 526 million posts that relate to the beauty industry."

ous endorsements and partnerships. Then, once those efforts had shown promising results, she launched her own line of "Lip Kits"—in a limited run, at a premium price—which sold out in minutes.

Some might argue that this is the classic "scarcity" marketing tactic, and they may be right. Was it intentional or not? Who knows, but she has become a master at knowing her customer base (or, rather, fan base), catering to their needs and continuously pursuing **Product Expansion** to extend her product line as her customer base ages into adulthood.

The combination of her marketing and social media moves was a critical component of its success. As social media replaces traditional media, it's possible you won't see an ad in *Teen Vogue* anytime soon from Kylie Cosmetics. Kylie is leveraging all aspects of social media marketing (video, Instagram, Twitter, Facebook) to stretch the boundaries of customer engagement.

Fabrizio Freda of Estée Lauder observed: "Younger generations are defining the culture with images of self-expression. They take more pictures in a day on average than their parents took in a year. Sixty-five percent of teens rely on social media to discover and select beauty products. . . . Volatility and the pace of change are not diminishing. What we're living through is not a moment in time, it's the new reality. . . . The art of leading through change is understanding what has not changed and how to leverage our historical strengths."

In less than two years, and with no paid advertising campaigns, Kylie Cosmetics is now a full-service, direct-to-consumer (D2C) beauty brand and social media powerhouse, with an estimated $600 million in revenue. Jenner was recently named #57 on the *Fast Company* list of the hundred most creative people in business in 2017.

Let's put this all in perspective. How does Kylie Cosmetics revenue performance measure up against other beauty titans? Well, it took fash-

Spending zero dollars is effective when it's authentic. Digital isn't a strategy or a channel; it's where we live. Our products are promoted by people who don't work for the company. The team is endless. . . . Direct interaction [with consumers through social media] allows four-day product creation and no focus groups. When product development lead times are days, you don't have to commit to inventory on a best guess basis.

**—LAURA NELSON,
cofounder and president,
and JOHN NELSON,
cofounder and CEO,
of Seed Beauty**

ion genius Tom Ford ten years to reach half a billion dollars in sales after he launched his beauty line in 2006. It took L'Oréal's Lancôme cosmetics line eighty years to hit $1 billion. It took MAC thirteen years to achieve $250 million and another ten years to reach $500 million, even with Estée Lauder owning a majority and then all of it during that time frame.

As for Kylie Jenner, the current rate of growth of her company suggests that she will rocket past the $1 billion mark by 2022 while still picking up speed. And there appears to be no end in sight.

KYLIE COSMETICS
KEY TAKEAWAYS

- The sequence of this massive growth was critical. Kylie started by establishing her personal brand, before she endorsed or released any products on her own. Next, she created her own niche within the family empire and stayed focused there, with various endorsements and partnerships. Then, once those efforts had shown promising results, she decided to launch her own line of "Lip Kits." Had she launched Lip Kits prior to realizing that her personal brand was growing and her target demographic wanted more from her, it may have been a fad that fizzled out as quickly as it had started.

- Kylie Cosmetics has a deep and personal understanding and connection to its massive customer (fan) base. Kylie identified an unmet need for herself and decided to fill it for others like her (teenagers who enjoy makeup). She didn't open an R&D lab and test products over the course of years before she launched. She took advantage of the capabilities of a strategic partner (**Partnership**), Seed Beauty, which had seventeen years of beauty experience to help her company fast-track production and time to market.

- Kylie Cosmetics was able to grow using multiple paths in combination. It wanted to sell more existing products (Lip Kits) to its existing customers (**Customer Base Penetration**). In addition, it launched new products (**Product Expansion**) to sell to its ever-growing customer base and attracted new customers (**Customer and Product Diversification**) with all of the new products it was putting out. It also **Optimized Sales** as it struggled to keep up with demand from sales channels, so it had to find a cost-effective way to get its products into the hands of more people.

STORY
2

JOHN DEERE
AND THE "BEET" GOES ON

Necessity is the mother of invention.

— PROVERB

T THE TURN OF THE twentieth century, most Americans were farmers or came from farm families, and almost half of the U.S. population still lived on farms. There were almost six million farms, and that number was still growing, as was the amount of land used for agriculture. Several factors accounted for this extraordinary achievement. One was the expansion to the West. Another was the application of machinery to farming.

These increases continued well into the 1900s, but by mid-century both trends had been reversed. The 1920s saw the beginnings of large progressive changes from horse to tractor and advancements in "horsepower," and by the start of the twenty-first century, the market context had dramatically changed.

The total number of farms had shrunk to fewer than two million. Less than 2 percent of the total population now lived on farms or worked in agriculture, and agriculture contributed a much smaller share to the total economy than in 1900.

Yet, with only one-third as much total labor as in 1900, by the end of the twentieth century, U.S. agriculture was producing seven times as much output, and average farm family incomes had risen to equal or surpass nonfarm family incomes. Farmers—and those who provided products and services to farmers, such as John Deere and Sears Roebuck (yes, that Sears)—were growing.

PLOWING AHEAD

When you think of the world's most innovative industries, farm machinery probably doesn't come to mind. Yet, 180-year-old John Deere, with its iconic green tractors and other farm equipment and its yellow leaping buck logo, is not only one of the world's largest companies; it also puts most other product innovators to shame. And when it comes to selling new products to its existing customer base, at the right time, the right combination of direct sales, and with partners, it's nearly unmatched.

Product Expansion has always been the story of John Deere. In fact, the company was founded by the eponymous Mr. Deere in Grand Detour, Illinois, in 1837 to exploit a new invention. A blacksmith by trade, Deere noticed that the rich local soil tended to stick to the face of traditional iron plows. So he took a Scottish saw blade and worked it into a plow blade. It worked brilliantly; the dirt slid right off the smooth surface, without the need to be regularly "scoured" off.

The John Deere scour-less plow blade took the market by storm—it was a great product, filling a specific customer's (farmers) need, sold via the right sales channels (storefront), with effective payment terms. The combination of these things from John Deere is given considerable credit with helping to open the Great Plains to agriculture. The rest is history.

The new century brought new challenges, especially for heavy equipment manufacturers. The first came at the very beginning: gasoline-powered tractors, pioneered by a new company, International Harvester, quickly made John Deere's current equipment line all but obsolete. John Deere needed to get into the tractor business, and after an internal effort to build its own engines proved unsuccessful, it decided to purchase the Waterloo Gasoline Engine Company, a maker of small, two-cylinder motors, in 1918.

John Deere could have resisted the change in market context—it could have ignored what its customers in the farming community wanted. The business world is littered with companies that didn't want to change—even when the market was changing around them. Instead, for the rest of the century, John Deere regularly introduced a new generation of tractors, self-propelled combines, harvesters, seed drills, cotton pickers . . . and, increasingly, construction equipment, as well, once every twenty years or so, following the traditional twentieth-century-long product expansion process.

> It's very important that we take the voice of the customer into our design process. That's our job, and we have people all over the world who are talking every day to customers. It's important to John Deere that we design our product—no matter what type—to meet the needs of our customers.
>
> **—GREG DOHERTY,**
> **group director, product and technology marketing, for John Deere's worldwide commercial and consumer equipment division**

At their introduction, each of these generations of machinery represented the pinnacle of new innovation in agricultural equipment. You may think that, due to their product expansion prowess, Deere was a product-led company. This was only partially true.

John Deere developed new products based on years of studying and querying farmers about their needs, and while its competition struggled to build a network of salesmen, John Deere's equipment dealers were an open secret of its success. Dealers worked closely with farmers to customize a machine's weight, traction, and accessories. A strong dealer network combined with the right products allowed John Deere to dominate the market.

A SOUND IDEA

A telling moment, for the purposes of our story, occurred in 1972, one hundred thirty-five years after John Deere was founded, with the introduction of the company's "Sound Idea" generation of tractors. Mechanically, the Sound Idea line was almost identical to the prior New Generation models but with a modernized approach. The crucial difference was what could be called a shift to a "software" orientation. This was not to say that John Deere was going to abandon its "hardware" by any stretch of the imagination. Rather, it knew that the proven John Deere hardware with new software capabilities would be a game changer for the future of the business.

In particular, the driver's experience for the first time took priority. *The shift was not to a **Product Expansion** growth path, but within the Product Expansion path: a shift from a product-centric to a customer/user experience-centric approach.*

Or: they had already deployed the **Product Expansion** path, but they decided to combine it with the **Customer Experience** path. It moved from a product-led to a customer-led design paradigm, which was a radical shift, not only for John Deere but for an entire industry. Now there was no going back.

The new tractors featured enclosed cabs, heaters, radios, and adjustable seats. To our eyes, these may seem like minor changes, but at the time they were significant product enhancements—and ones that set the company on a brand-new, very lucrative growth path.

Customer Experience (the farmer) was actually becoming the product—not the tractors. Most important, these decisions had set the company on a trajectory toward the digital age.

JOHN DEERE
KEY TAKEAWAYS

- John Deere could have resisted the change in market context, believing that its long-standing history in the farming community would continue to engender customer loyalty. Instead, it realized that the proven John Deere hardware with new software capabilities would be a game changer for the future of the business and would help it keep pace with what twenty-first-century farmers wanted.

- Maybe the biggest shift for John Deere was to put the farmer, the customer, first when developing its products in a much more holistic way. The shift was not to a **Product Expansion** growth path, but within the **Product Expansion** path: a shift from a product-centric to a customer/user experience–centric approach.

- Any company must be willing to disrupt itself before it can ever hope to respond to a market being disrupted around it. John Deere put everything on the line. The definition of a "product" has forever changed. With its push into digital, it is now both a product and a platform company. It has opened the door to compete not only with other farm equipment manufacturers but with AgTech companies as well.

- Selling new products into existing markets requires a deep understanding of the market itself, including the customers. Capturing data about its equipment can help identify ways in which it can improve performance. Capturing customers' usage patterns, on the other hand, will help it to further extend its customer-driven **Product Expansion** efforts.

BLOCKBUSTER
"BE KIND, PLEASE DON'T UNWIND OUR BUSINESS"

OK, Houston, we've had a problem here.

—JACK SWIGERT, NASA
command module pilot of *Apollo 13*

THERE SHOULD BE NO QUESTION that Blockbuster owned the video rental category—until it didn't. The company opened its doors in Dallas in 1985. Nine years later, Blockbuster was acquired by Viacom for $8.4 billion. It is almost difficult to remember now, but a decade ago Blockbuster, with its ubiquitous, brightly lit stores, was a centerpiece of American weekend life. Every Friday, tens of millions of people jammed into the company's stores to rent videos and DVDs—and fight over the latest releases. It had a stronghold on this industry, with the full support of all of the major movie studios, and a formula that worked—it was a license to print money.

Unfortunately, over a ten-year period (1987–97), its rapid hyper-growth and aggressive expansion, as well as M&A activity, began to take its toll. Blockbuster found itself in a growth stall. In an attempt to course correct, it began conducting joint promotions (**Partnerships**) with Domino's Pizza and McDonald's. It began ad campaigns. It pushed into international markets (**Market Acceleration**). It began to offer video game equipment and Sega Genesis video games at some of its stores. The company considered selling audiocassettes and CDs. It even acquired the right to market tapes of the 1992 Olympic Games (**Customer and Product Diversification**). It was an all-out blitz. In the United States, it had opened its twelve hundredth store by June 1990; new locations were opening at a rate of one a day.

At the same time as it was fully committed to all of these various initiatives, a slowdown in the video rental industry was becoming evident. Even though the company's earnings grew an astronomical 114 percent in 1988, it contracted to a still-impressive 93 percent rate of growth in 1989, followed by a rate of 48 percent in 1990. In keeping with this trend, first-quarter financial results for 1991 were disappointing.

There was no question that all of this growth had made Blockbuster the market leader, the de facto video rental choice for families around the United States. With a strong brand, it was able to acquire customers easily and was able to keep them coming back due to its large inventory, but much of that may have been due to the fact that there was no alternative. *Launching loyalty cards is one thing. Engendering loyalty among one's customers is another.* Serving approximately three million customers per day in its ninety-one hundred stores in the United States, its territories, and twenty-four other nations isn't easy. Just ask Starbucks. It's hard to tell for sure if it ever pivoted to **Customer Experience** as a way to increase rental frequency or the number of movies rented with each visit, but from the outside looking in (and as a former customer), that didn't appear to be the case.

The experience of renting a movie could be somewhat frustrating due to the lack of inventory (hot new releases), and it could be time-consuming for the customer walking up and down the aisles as if on a scavenger hunt, hoping the movie was in stock. When the movie was found, the customer had to check that the box matched the movie inside and that the movie was actually rewound. If it was the right movie, the customer would take it home for a two- or three-day rental and then have to go out of the way to return it, often returning it late. Customers began to push back on excessive late fees, which in some cases were actually more than the movie rental itself. It may have been those very late fees that were the catalyst to customers turning away from Blockbuster in the first place and looking for an alternative.

YOUR LATE FEES ARE WAIVED

While Blockbuster had standardized the video rental market, and entertained families for a decade, the company was about to face a challenge that would forever change the company's history and legacy. First and foremost, *Blockbuster wasn't prepared for the speed with which the context of the market would change around them*. The Internet was making its way into homes across the country and consumer preferences were changing right along with it. These circumstances opened the door for alternative, competitive threats.

The company leading that change was a Silicon Valley start-up. In 1997, a man named Reed Hastings returned a late copy of *Apollo 13* to his local Blockbuster Video store. He was assessed a $40 late fee. A year later, inspired to eliminate late fees once and for all, he founded Netflix. Netflix's beginnings were humble: it was one of the first during the dot-com boom to disrupt an incumbent by targeting the same customer base with an innovative business model and product offering leveraging newly developed Internet technology.

> *Neither RedBox nor Netflix are even on the radar screen in terms of competition.*
>
> **—JIM KEYES,
> former CEO of
> Blockbuster**

Netflix began by attacking Blockbuster where the latter company was already feeling the pain. Netflix provided an easier way to rent and return movies, which removed many, if not all, of the friction Blockbuster was causing its customers—especially with its highly profitable late fees.

Netflix was very early in analyzing user preferences, past rentals, and wish list data (similar to what Amazon does today) to recommend movies to its customers. This move was actually a masterful usage of the sec-

IN 1997, **BLOCKBUSTER** → a late fee that changed it all — FOUNDED **NETFLIX** to eliminate late fees — INNOVATIVE BUSINESS MODEL and PRODUCT OFFERING provided an easier way to rent and return movies

CHARGED $40 LATE FEE TO REED HASTINGS

ond growth path—**Customer Base Penetration**. The company stayed committed to its core, movie rentals via mail, and found ways to entice customers to spend more with it, more frequently, all of which produced their early success.

We don't have any concern there. Netflix is a great service, it's a great in-home service. They've had other movies. Netflix is very much a television network and not unlike what HBO and Showtime have done for years, they have some original product that goes out there. So it's not playing in theaters, it's playing on Netflix and we hope they have great success with it but I don't see it as an issue relative to the theatrical business. It's not one really that we talk about.

**—MARK ZORADI,
CEO of Cinemark**

As Netflix was gaining ground, Blockbuster remained in denial about sweeping changes in technology and consumer preferences. In 2004, five years after Netflix's founding, Blockbuster at last entered the online DVD rental market. In November 2006, Blockbuster began its **Product Expansion**, right in Netflix's sweet spot—launching Total Access DVD, where customers could rent movies online, receive DVDs by mail, then return the DVDs to a Blockbuster Store in exchange for a "free rental coupon." But it was too little, too late. By 2007, Blockbuster counted 2 million online subscribers, while upstart Netflix raced ahead to 6.3 million.

But Blockbuster didn't have to die—especially for the reason it did. Previous acquisitions and partnerships showed that Blockbuster had the appetite and willingness to expand its product offerings. In 2000, it partnered with Enron in an attempt to create a video-on-demand service. Initially, the partnership was supposed to last for twenty years. However, Enron chose to terminate the deal only a few months later over fears that Blockbuster could not provide sufficient films for the service.

The unfortunate coda to this story is that Blockbuster had all that same information that Netflix did, if not more, yet did little with it—even with its history of **Product Expansion** (Blockbuster Music, Blockbuster Block Party, Total Access DVD rental service, and Entertainment with Republic Pictures and Spelling Entertainment Group), Blockbuster was unable to see the need to make one more crucial decision—it turned down a chance to purchase the still-fledgling Netflix for $50 million in 2000.

Blockbuster feared change and hung on too long—the context and the customer got too far away from it to recover, and Netflix continued to gain new customers, many at the expense of Blockbuster. This is where Netflix began to make strides and gain market traction, putting huge pressure on Blockbuster. The sequence in which Netflix made these decisions is critical. Had it bypassed mailing DVDs and jumped right to streaming video rentals, it may have found the same fate as many others during the dot-com bust. Netflix captured customers in a proven market—DVD rentals (which still has four million–plus subscribers)—and became highly operationally efficient in that business producing significant profits.

Having beat Blockbuster at its own game, Netflix today faces even more formidable competitors in the business of content creation and delivery—notably from the likes of Disney, following their $52.4 billion acquisition of Fox in 2017: "Disney's chief executive, Robert A. Iger, is steering the company into streaming services to compete with Netflix, Apple, Amazon and Facebook."

BLOCKBUSTER VS. NETFLIX
KEY TAKEAWAYS

- From the beginning, Blockbuster seemed not fully to understand what its "product" actually was and what value it had for its customers. It assumed the product was the movie customers came to the store to get, so it built a large selection of movies to choose from and set up a massive distribution network for the movie studios' product. *What it missed was that its customers were buying the experience of watching a movie with family and friends.* This meant it was completely exposed if customers started wanting to get/consume/use the product in different (distribution channels) ways.
- Blockbuster's success resulted in its complacency. Being the longtime front-runner in video rentals impaired its ability to see the looming shifts in market context, and thus the potential

threat that Netflix posed for the future of its business. At the turn of the new millennium, customers had started looking for easier, more effective ways to get things done through technology. As a result, companies from every industry were having to rethink their entire value proposition and go-to-market approach, giving serious consideration to the possibility that their biggest rival might not be the competitor down the street but rather a faceless, virtual store with lower overhead and a clear understanding of how the Internet and its users work.

- Blockbuster wasn't just slow to enter the world of online video rental; it also failed to capitalize on its unique selling proposition once it arrived. With a large customer base, Blockbuster should have entered the online arena like a gangbuster, touting the obvious advantage it had over Netflix—rent online, return at the store. Instead, Blockbuster made its grand entrance by copying what Netflix had already done . . . except that Netflix was doing it better and more cheaply and had already begun to chip away at Blockbuster's customer base.

- Pursuing multiple growth paths simultaneously requires thoughtful attention to sequence. When Blockbuster found itself in a growth stall, it was trying multiple paths trying to course correct. The combination of too many growth paths meant it wasn't really committed to any one of them but beholden to all of them.

PUTTING IT ALL TOGETHER

Great companies are built on great products.

—ELON MUSK

IF YOU ARE GOING TO pursue this growth strategy, it would be valuable for your product marketing and market intelligence departments to constantly look for opportunities that can be filled by new products, enhance existing offerings, or even form new partnerships to gain access to new customers.

It is true that new product introductions are always risky endeavors, but less so now with the new twenty-first-century definition of a "product." In a **Product Expansion** growth strategy, the particular challenge is to not confuse your current customers with a fundamentally new product that, cognitively, doesn't quite fit with the core products they associate with your company. Rather, *think about staying close to your core and choose adjacencies to your existing base.*

The **Product Expansion** growth path, when successful, opens the door to two of the most exciting combination paths, both of them relating to working with other companies—even competitors—and they are **Partnerships** and **Co-opetition**. This may not seem intuitive, but keep in mind: *bringing a new product to market is often a very cost- and labor-intensive activity.* Expenses may include research and development, prototyping, laboratory testing, field testing, establishing manufacturing lines, intellectual property (IP) filing, training a dedicated sales force, new service programs, manuals, marketing, and advertising.

Thus, *even when the potential for reward is great, so, too, is the risk.* The best way to minimize that risk—even if it means losing some of the potential revenues—is to share it with others through **Partnerships**, especially those with unique or established skills that your own company may not (yet) have. Some of those new competitors have more complete distribution channels and retailer relationships, and deeper understandings of customers than you do. There is no time to go slow—and doing so will not reduce risk but likely increase it. The profit advantage you gain by being first in the market will soon be gone. Move quickly—the best way to do that is to work with others. In such a scenario, even your worst competitor can be your best friend—at least for a while.

WHAT WORKS—AND POTENTIAL PITFALLS

It is a bad idea to expand your product offering when you haven't thought through the implications of doing so. But when you do think it through, it can lead to growth. For example, initially McDonald's did not launch All Day Breakfast—a **Product Expansion**—despite huge demand in the marketplace, until it was first able to operationally implement the expansion across its massive network and supply chain. Otherwise, McDonald's would risk getting in over their head and failing to keep up with customer demand, which could have resulted in serious reputational brand damage.

COMBINATION: PATH 4—
Product Expansion + Path 8—Partnerships

In **Product Expansion**, you are just as likely to adopt this or the other combination path almost immediately. The reason is that, as just noted, a new product cannot achieve its true potential until it is surrounded by an entire supporting ecosystem (i.e., service, sales, and marketing).

This combination path is the template for creating that ecosystem by locating, and associating with, companies that can fill in the "holes" of your company's go-to-market program for a new product or portfolio of products. That can include expanding your company's sales footprint by establishing original equipment manufacturer (OEM) relationships with other firms or licensing sales in particular vertical markets you are unlikely to exploit for a long time to come.

If your proposed product is going to require an expensive development effort, you may want to enter into a codevelopment contract with an aging company that has more capital but less innovation. You might also partner with a company that already has established and robust distribution channels but lacks products to fill it. Or you might partner up to get access to another company's already extensive user base in your newly targeted market.

If you are pursuing a path based on **Product Expansion**, you don't have to go it alone. Hitting the market quickly with your new product, backed by established supply and distribution channels, scalable manufacturing, and a tested marketing and sales program aimed at established customers—all or part of which is delivered by partners—is almost always better than trying to go it alone and learn as you go.

COMBINATION: PATH 4—
Product Expansion + Path 9—Co-Opetition

In this case, your new partner may also be a perceived or real competitor. Why would you choose to team up with a company whose goal, at best, is to take your business away—and, at worst, is to crush you into oblivion? Pragmatism.

The reality of the business world is that there is almost no company that is your perfect, pure competitor. There are always points of contact where you both share the same interests or suffer the same weaknesses—situations that can only be improved by working together. These arrangements are given various titles—including joint ventures, outsourcing agreements, coalitions, associations, cooperative research, and product licensing—but all have the common theme of companies that are otherwise competitors finding ways to work together for common interests—even as they are locked in ferocious competition the rest of the time.

125

Unfortunately, competitive collaboration between companies often is the result of desperation, when both companies are under serious, existential threats, or the entire industry is. A far wiser growth strategy is to enter into these agreements when times are good and the opportunity is at its peak—that is, when you first enter a new market with a new product or line. Only then can **Co-opetition** be a true growth path, not just a last-ditch attempt at survival.

PATH 5

CUSTOMER AND PRODUCT DIVERSIFICATION

CUSTOMER/ PRODUCT DIVERSIFICATION

Taking an established American brand into an emerging market requires a careful assessment of the local landscape and tastes and a flexible approach to your product's place in it. There's got to be a balance. We call it "glocal." It's the global together with the local that's the winning brand.

—IRENE ROSENFELD,
CEO and chairman of Mondelēz International

WHY CUSTOMER AND PRODUCT DIVERSIFICATION MATTERS

- Almost two-thirds (63 percent) say they like it when manufacturers introduce new products, and more than half (57 percent) say they purchased a new product during their last shopping trip.
- Consumers want more new products on the market that are affordable, healthy, convenient, and environmentally friendly.
- Trade growth in 2018 should pick up slightly to between 2.1 percent and 4.0 percent.
- The value of global goods trade is expected to grow in real terms to around $18 trillion in 2030 or implied real trade growth of 3.3 percent per annum.
- By 2030, the trade links between China and India, as well as other Southeast Asian economies like Malaysia, Indonesia, and Singapore, will become ever more important to global trade.

TO DIVERSIFY OR NOT

The **Customer and Product Diversification** growth path happens to be the last modernized take on the Ansoff Matrix within Growth IQ. The key differences between this and the previous (three) paths (not including **Customer Experience**) is that the others have centered on varying levels of risk, reward, and investments as they relate to customers, products, and markets respectively.

> *I believe the auto industry will change more in the next five to 10 years than it has in the last 50.*
>
> **—MARY BARRA, CEO and chairman of General Motors**

It's rare to find a single market or a single product that continues to perform in its original state over the long term. *When the need for something becomes imperative, you are forced to find ways of getting or achieving it.* It is a common misperception that companies facing a growth stall need to completely rethink their current products or services and customers. Poor performance alone should not be the catalyst for a company to pursue the **Customer and Product Diversification** path. I have observed far too many companies on this growth path that bite off more than they can chew with little consideration for the impact this kind of effort can have on the entire organization.

First of all, *culture matters a lot in this case*. If you decide on this path, you'd better make sure you have employees who are open to this much change: in other words, *a culture of innovation. Before you even consider this growth path, make sure you fully understand your company's market context*. Furthermore, you must be keenly aware of the sequence with which you pursue this path and what combination makes the most sense for you. If you aren't sure about the company's ability to launch new products—and everything that goes along with that, while at the same time acquiring an entirely new customer type—then it might make more sense to start with **Product Expansion** and **Market Acceleration** to test capabilities. *Then, and only then, double down by pushing further into new products, markets, and customers.*

The nature of this path is that it allows companies to pursue top-line growth by developing new products for completely new markets and customers. As such, it is inherently riskier than **Customer Base Penetration**,

Product Expansion, or **Market Acceleration** because, by definition, the organization has little or no experience of the new product, customer, or market segment. In addition, there will be new skills needed, especially if a company has never attempted to expand beyond its core product lineup. It absolutely will require new capabilities in terms of marketing and sales to effectively execute this path. Taking an existing sales strategy—in an existing market with an existing product—does not just "lift and shift" without careful consideration to the new market context a company will encounter when pursuing **Customer and Product Diversification**. Partnering with other companies (via either **Partnerships** or **Co-opetition**) can help to offset some internal capability gaps. However, those efforts may only be a portion of the overall go-to-market efforts. It may still be necessary to have in-house dedicated resources building out direct sales capabilities.

So while this path may seem familiar or even something you have successfully, or unsuccessfully, done in the past, this still remains one of the most challenging decisions a company can make. *The risks can be extraordinary—but so can the rewards.* You should ensure that you clearly understand whether you have captured all of the options available to you with the existing products and services you offer prior to considering this path. It might make more sense to start with **Customer Base Penetration** to see if you can stimulate additional growth within the existing customer base. Or would choosing the **Optimize Sales** path involve less risk and allow you to improve sales performance of the existing set of products you have? Or could you take existing products into new markets through a local partnership (**Partnerships**) instead? Meaning: Could you improve performance without taking such a potentially capital- and people-intensive path? Then and only then can you analyze:

1. Whether you should be pursuing this path at this time;
2. If you have the resources (people and capital) and capabilities to develop entirely new products or even modify existing ones;
3. If you have the proper sales, distribution, and partnership capabilities in place to enter new markets or new customer segments without overwhelming the existing business.

Success stories abound—think how the Walt Disney Company has diversified its customers and products over the decades with tremendous success. It expanded from its core animation business into theme parks, live entertainment, cruise lines, resorts, planned residential communities, TV broadcasting, and retailing by buying or developing the strategic assets it needed along the way, all in pursuit of new customers.

But with the good also come stories of infamous and costly failures even with companies who seem unstoppable in their constant pursuit of diversification. Let's take Amazon and its Fire Phone, which debuted in 2014. It was initially priced at $199 with a two-year contract. Sales plummeted in the weeks and months following the phone's release. Executives on the Fire Phone team later acknowledged that they didn't get the price right when they launched. Eventually, Amazon had to write down $170 million in costs associated with Fire Phone inventory. Don't forget, *even in failures there are lessons, which, if you're paying attention, can be applied in other situations.*

By definition, *a new product is an untested product, one whose market reception you do not yet know.* You may have a superstar on your hands, or you may have a complete profit-sucking dud. By the same token, a new market is one that you may have learned something about but you haven't yet experienced. You likely know no one in that market, you don't yet understand the nuances of customer desire, and you face well-established competitors—it's like you're laying siege to a castle.

The best time to pursue a **Customer and Product Diversification** strategy is when your company isn't coming from a place of desperation but rather when the company is prospering. Why? That's when you are most impervious to failure, and you have both momentum and capital reserves. It is also when shareholders and employees are most likely to support your strategy. *Unfortunately, many companies only resort to diversification when they are in trouble*: their current market is shrinking or their current products increasingly are becoming uncompetitive. In this weakened state, unless you have considerable cash reserves, or another growth path is available to combine with **Customer and Product Diversification** while this longer-term investment takes hold, this path can potentially be a mistake (sometimes fatal).

STORY

1

MARVEL
SUPERHERO SAVES THE DAY

Companies are successful or not because they get market transitions right.

—JOHN CHAMBERS, former chairman and CEO of Cisco

IMELY PUBLICATIONS (MARVEL'S ORIGINAL NAME until 1961), founded in 1939, during the first "Golden Age" of comics, had always been a second-tier but financially healthy player operating in the shadow of mighty DC Comics, home of Superman and Batman. But, thanks to several popular creations—notably Captain America—Marvel was able to carve out a sustainable niche.

While the government investigations of the morality of comic books in the 1950s and the aging of baby boomers in the 1960s wiped out much of the competition, Marvel managed to hang on. In fact, thanks to a new group of creators, most famously Jack Kirby and Stan Lee, Marvel not only gained ground against an aging DC Comics but developed a cultlike following among a new generation of comic book fans that admired the maverick and iconoclastic nature of its characters and plots.

Beginning in 1993, the business began to show signs of a growth stall. Unfortunately, Marvel's management for its part made a number of short-sighted and costly decisions, which put the company heavily in debt. How is it that a brand steeped in fifty-plus years of history, revered by loyal customers and a stable of five thousand beloved comic book characters including the Hulk, X-Men, the Fantastic Four, and Spider-Man, found itself facing an uncertain future? In fact, the crisis erupted quickly.

Looking back, you can clearly see that the leadership team misjudged the market context at a crucial time in the company's history and then exacerbated the problem by raising prices in a declining industry of comic books and trading cards, not understanding the impact of the collapsing newsstand market, misjudging the most active customer cohort (collector/speculators) who were exiting the market, and, finally, according to some industry insiders, producing poor-quality product. Together, these bad decisions, coupled with management infighting, caused a perfect storm of internal and external threats facing this iconic brand.

A cult following and critical acclaim simply weren't enough to fend off disaster. On December 27, 1996, Marvel filed for bankruptcy. A third of its employees were laid off, and, worse, it owed a lot of money. In 2000, the company declared a loss of $105 million. The new century began with Marvel facing an uncertain future.

IRON MAN: B-LIST CHARACTER

By 2008 when *Iron Man* hit movie theaters around the globe, Marvel had not only turned around its fortunes, but it was about to capture global preeminence in the field of character-based entertainment.

How the company performed this apparent miracle is a story of a brilliant application of the right growth path in the appropriate combination and sequence applied with precision in a changing market context. Indeed, so successful was this initiative that Marvel has in recent years bent the context to its own advantage.

How did Marvel do it? It realized that the *value of its brand wasn't actually comic books but the comic book characters themselves*. In 1997, Toy Biz and Marvel Entertainment Group merged to end the bankruptcy, forming Marvel Enterprises Inc. Though the newly named company was destined to continue bleeding cash for several more years, Marvel had a vision—more precisely, **Customer and Product Diversification** and **Product Expansion** strategies—to get back to growth.

Remember, these growth paths are about producing new products—to both existing and new markets and customers. *It was a "bet the com-*

pany" risk meant to leap into hot new markets or make investments in new, uncharted territories.

While it sounds complicated, it really was quite simple. In this case, **Customer and Product Diversification** could have only focused on creating new comic book characters for new kinds of readers (customers). But instead, Marvel chose to bet big. It was able to stay close to its core and innovate by taking advantage of its already developed assets (products), which nobody else could replicate—*Marvel's indisputable stable of iconic comic book characters.* Because those characters had engendered a loyal customer base, it was able to diversify the "product" by thinking of other "mediums" in which it could use those assets to its advantage, and it chose . . . *movies.*

However, just because Marvel was a large company with a globally recognized brand didn't mean it could diversify both products and target customer without any issues. Marvel actually had been burned before when it pursued **Customer and Product Diversification** with its launch of "Marvel Mania" theme restaurants, Marvel interactive CD-ROMs, and a new trading card initiative with SkyBox. After opening one location of Marvel Mania in 1998, it was closed a year later. Also, the CD-ROM and trading card plans never happened. They may have been the right ideas when the concepts were first discussed, but by the time they had launched or planned to launch *the context of the market had already shifted.*

When Marvel realized that the context of the market had shifted but still wanted to diversify its portfolio, it had to come up with another option. Marvel chose to work with various movie studios by pursuing the **Partnership** and **Customer and Product Diversification** paths in combination. Unfortunately, like its previous attempts, this effort proved to be misguided as well.

PATH 5 CUSTOMER AND PRODUCT DIVERSIFICATION

> For many consumer entertainment and media businesses, avid or loyal fans—who typically represent 10 to 20 percent of a franchise's user base—can drive 80 percent or more of that franchise's overall business value. Content efforts therefore must prioritize initiatives aimed at super-serving them—deepening engagement with avid fans and simultaneously extending the brands and franchises associated with these passionate fans into new areas.

Why? Among *Spider-Man*, *X-Men*, and *Blade*, the licensing deals they made with 20th Century Fox and Sony proved to be highly lucrative . . . for the studios, but not for Marvel. *Blade* was a modest success, *X-Men* helped relaunch the era of superhero movies, and *Spider-Man* grossed $400 million. Yet while *Blade* made $70 million at the U.S. box office, Marvel took home only a flat fee of . . . $25,000. It had the same flat-fee scenario with *X-Men*. Maybe it seemed like a great idea on paper, but without a new strategy they were "giving away the farm" . . . literally. The partnership arrangement was a tremendous top-line revenue generator for its partners, and dismal for Marvel.

Now, even at its darkest hour, Marvel had to find a solution to its critical situation. In 2003, Endeavor talent agent David Maisel pitched Marvel on a simple but radical idea: Why, he asked, should Marvel continue to give away its best assets to other companies for pennies on the dollar? If Marvel wanted to take advantage of its existing core assets (thousands of characters and story lines) and introduce them into another medium (movies, video games) and satisfy the loyal customer base, why not create a production studio of its own? Such a studio could develop and produce the titles that had been at the mercy of less-than-interested movie studios for decades, and Marvel could retain 100 percent of the profits. Now Marvel had to make a full pivot to **Customer and Product Diversification**, which required significant change in talent (people, including executives), products, and asset investment.

While it wasn't a quick decision, Marvel eventually agreed to a seven-year, $525 million deal through Merrill Lynch that put up ten of its most prized characters, including *The Avengers*, as collateral . . . and Marvel Studios was born.

To say Marvel was faced with an "all or nothing" proposition would be an understatement—it was literally an existential bet. If the movies had failed, Marvel would have disappeared forever. If they had done nothing, they would have surely suffered a similar fate. At least with the infusion of cash, they had a chance to save themselves.

As luck would have it, New Line Cinema let its option on Marvel's Iron Man character run out two months after this deal was done, which gave Marvel the rights back to the character. But there was a catch. Because Iron Man was not one of the ten properties included in the Merrill Lynch deal, if Marvel wanted to make this movie, the company would have to use its own cash. Regardless, Marvel was determined. It wanted to launch its first film with a character that had never been in a live-action production—and Iron Man fit the bill. The rest is history.

Since its release in 2008, *Iron Man* has grossed over $585 million, making it one of the highest-grossing films of all time, and since then the Iron Man franchise has grossed close to $2.5 billion in worldwide box-office receipts. Its success set the stage not just for Marvel's turnaround but its dominance in film over its biggest competitor, DC Comics.

MARVEL UNIVERSE

This could have gone very differently had Marvel not taken such risks and had it not done it in the right combination and sequence—and a bit of good luck, too. The result, adopted from the comic's print history, was the Marvel Universe. Moviegoers would now see, at the beginning of each film, the Marvel studio logo—an animation showing these historic comic book characters rising from the turning pages into the real world. Then, for the keen-eyed, those films also contained Hitchcock-like cameos by the octogenarian Stan Lee. The same moviegoers could also delight in seeing their favorite Marvel characters appear in other company films.

It wasn't long before Marvel had developed the practice—first used decades before in the comic books—of introducing new characters in minor roles in one series, then moving them to their own series of films and (if successful) eventually adding them to group productions. This mixing and matching enabled Marvel to create an almost infinite combination of stories and characters . . . and if one failed, that character could just be dropped back into the pack to be replaced by another candidate.

Marvel accomplished all of this not by hanging on to its limited product of "comic books" but by pursuing **Customer and Product Diversification**. It went all in on creating movies and significantly changing its products based on the changing market opportunity (context), rethinking and revamping the combination of its products (less print/more film-famous characters/lesser characters/group films), and then sequencing their appearance and interaction over the course of a decade.

Marvel was back. In August 2009, it was announced that the Walt Disney Company was acquiring Marvel Entertainment for more than $4 billion. In other words, eleven years after declaring bankruptcy, and just nine years after it was at death's door, Marvel had turned itself into one of the world's best-known companies—and had more than paid back its investors and entertained its loyal customers as well as captured new ones along the way. Disney's acquisition of Fox in December 2017 is a portent of things to come for the expanding Marvel Universe—"the once unthinkable acquisition promises to reshape Hollywood and Silicon Valley."

MARVEL
KEY TAKEAWAYS

- Had Marvel shied away from **Customer and Product Diversification**—after its failed attempts with its push into "Marvel Mania" theme restaurants, Marvel interactive CD-ROMs, and a new trading initiative with SkyBox—the Marvel we know today would not exist. More likely than not, failure will be part of the learning curve you will experience on this path, which is why culture really matters. If you don't possess the internal fortitude to weather the tough times as you search for new ways to stimulate and drive growth, you are guaranteed to find yourself on a tough road. *If you're not careful, the fear of failure can keep you away from your greatest innovations.*

- The **Partnership** path may have been the right choice at the time between Marvel and 20th Century Fox and Sony, but the financial model made it an ill-advised route for Marvel to continue to pursue. You will learn in the **Partnership** path what to look out for when striking up deals like this.

- In the case of Marvel, pursuing the **Customer and Product Diversification** path was focused on taking an existing "asset" (comic book characters) to a new medium (film), which allowed it to stay close to storytelling and its loyal customer base. The lesson here is, *know why customers like your brand, like your products, and are willing to spend money with you.* If you ignore those things when deciding where to invest, you will do so at your own risk.

STORY

2

PAYPAL
BANKING ON THE FUTURE

The price of inaction is far greater than the cost of a mistake.

—MEG WHITMAN, CEO of eBay

FOUNDED IN 1998, AROUND THE same time as Netflix—capitalizing on the changing customer and market context—PayPal was one of the more memorable creations of the first era of e-commerce. Founded as the online alternative to traditional money transfers via checks and money orders, the company was perfectly timed for the boom in online retailing and auction sites.

In the years to come, PayPal would also become famous for giving a start to some of the most famous figures of the digital world in the twenty-first century, including financier Peter Thiel, entrepreneur Elon Musk, and venture capitalist Reid Hoffman.

The company took off fast: riding the dot-com bubble, it managed to go public with its first IPO just four years later, in 2002. Later that year, an even bigger e-commerce success story, eBay, and its CEO, Meg Whitman, spotted a chance to supercharge the financial side of its auction service and acquired PayPal for $1.5 billion, taking the company from online auction house to e-commerce powerhouse.

By 2010, PayPal was the acknowledged industry standard for online payments. Revenues approached $3 billion. Total users reached one hundred million in nearly two hundred countries. By 2012, PayPal represented 40 percent of eBay's revenue (up from 15–20 percent at the time of the deal) and 31 percent of operating profits. Revenue grew at 25 percent annually, operating profits were near 40 percent growth, and free cash flow growth was above 10 percent. The company's total financial volume was nearly $150 billion.

Yes, these are impressive numbers, of course. But what these numbers don't tell you is that the context of the market had changed dramatically in the decade since the acquisition in 2002. *By 2012, billions of people had access to smartphones, the Internet, and ubiquitous e-commerce and local businesses that had global reach.* Buying and selling with "1-Click" (from Amazon) changed the entire dynamic of PayPal's business. How was it going to capitalize on the *next* billion people coming online and setting up storefronts, needing to bank and have access to more financial tools?

PayPal might have stayed on their upward trajectory—likely with diminishing returns—had an outside force not intervened and changed everything. In 2013, legendary hedge fund investor Carl Icahn flexed his equity holdings in eBay to demand that the company spin off PayPal. eBay did just that, in July 2015—PayPal was once again independent, although still the preferred payment platform for eBay until that deal ends in 2020 (at which time Dutch fintech company Adyen will become eBay's primary payments processor). Former eBay CEO John Donahoe became company chairman and Dan Schulman, a veteran of AT&T, Priceline, and American Express, became CEO. Rather than return to the status quo, Schulman saw this moment as a unique opportunity.

The vision of a "new PayPal," as he formulated it, Schulman admitted, was a "very interesting—and perhaps even a paradoxical—path." In particular, Schulman had decided that it was time to take PayPal on a new growth path, one that would require PayPal to find relevant gaps—white space—in the market and fill them with new products—**Customer and Product Diversification**—that added value: ones they developed in-house, or acquired, or partnered to deliver, especially if they wanted to go after an entirely new market and customer set.

But after all of these years, Schulman believed "the ship had sailed" on the traditional e-commerce transaction business. The U.S. market was saturated, and they needed to look for growth elsewhere.

> By 2020, the global payments industry will generate an estimated $2.2 trillion in revenue.

What was it about this **Customer and Product Diversification** path that was so valuable that PayPal was willing to risk all of its advantages? It wanted to be more than a button on a website, and there was a massive opportunity becoming more apparent with the adoption of smartphones and mobile apps.

My goal is to get us laser-focused on who we are going to serve and who we are going to hyper-serve—and how.

—**DAN SCHULMAN,
CEO of PayPal**

PayPal aspired to be at the center of as many payment transactions as possible, via mobile devices or in a physical retail store. It wanted to develop the right products so consumers and businesses would opt for it no matter the scenario. Schulman knew he needed to be "more than a button on a website"—he needed to evolve its technology to a platform to enable developers (**Partnerships**) to extend its products and enable its customers (sellers) to have tighter relationships with their customers.

But how was he going to do that? In order to pursue the **Customer and Product Diversification** path, it first needed to fix some internal organizational issues. *The sequence in which these adjustments were made would have material impact on future results.* It began when Schulman realized he had to reorganize the company into two groups—merchants and consumers—in order to better align with its target customers. Next, he had to develop a suite of targeted products for both. A new product, Venmo, was developed to serve the millennials market using smartphones

and social networks to transfer money, [in 2017 it processed nearly $35 billion]. Next, it acquired Xoom, which gives people the ability to move money internationally via mobile phones [since the acquisition, Xoom's customer base grew 30 percent and transactions have grown by 50 percent a month]. By diversifying and launching these two new products, it was able to diversify its customer base by attracting millennials. In Q1 2018, PayPal processed approximately $49 billion in mobile payments—a 52 percent growth year over year (YoY). For merchants, it developed Working Capital, which lends money to small businesses that use its service—so far it has lent more than $2 billion.

How did PayPal do with the radically new **Customer and Product Diversification** strategy? Well, at first, investors were curious but skeptical. While Schulman saw a slowing of PayPal's revenue streams, the shareholders seemed happier with the status quo. Schulman had to show that PayPal could maintain its current business success—in particular, hang on to all of those point-of-sale customers—even as it transformed itself. Not an easy proposition, especially for a publicly traded company with demanding shareholders.

That's a big reason why PayPal stock price dropped more than 10 percent in the months following Schulman's announcement. However, it is good to note that as this is being written, PayPal's stock is up 50 percent from before it became "The New PayPal." PayPal added a record 29 million new active users in 2017, to reach 227 million active accounts, including 18 million merchants, and grew its total payment volume by 25 percent, to $99 billion. In the first quarter of 2018, PayPal operates in 202 markets and has added 8.1 million active accounts with net new actives up 35 percent, and $2.2 billion in payment transactions—up 25 percent—with total payment volume of $132 billion. Partners are encouraging their customers to create PayPal digital wallets because it helps them increase

Successful product launches are the culmination of organizational focus and commitment to product development, creative marketing, smart leadership and, above all else, an in-depth understanding of what drives consumer preferences.

**—JOHAN SJÖSTRAND,
senior vice president
and managing director
of Nielsen Innovation
in Europe**

their own transactions and increase the quality of the customer experience. Dan Schulman noted: "Our partner relationships in the U.S. and across the globe continue to grow and flourish."

It won't be enough for PayPal to rewrite its deeply embedded role as a leader in the finance industry's larger Web-based information ecosystem as the explosion of mobile commerce makes its way into every corner of the globe. So far, its **Customer and Product Diversification** strategy move appears to be working.

PAYPAL
KEY TAKEAWAYS

- In order to pursue the **Customer and Product Diversification** path, PayPal was aware of the sequence of decisions and internal changes it needed to make first. Had PayPal not reorganized prior to launching Venmo and Xoom, it may have failed under the weight of internal inertia.

- *It isn't possible to put everything else on hold when you decide to make significant adjustments to an organization, products, and customers.* Unfortunately, you will be forced to "change the tires on the car as it is going around the track" when you are pursuing growth. This is ambitious and risky for any company and, for a publicly traded company, can alarm investors, which complicates matters even further.

- PayPal knew its value and applied that to the changing market context. It wasn't about where it had been but rather where the market was taking it. It determined what customer segment it wanted to go after (millennials, and the next billion people coming online). As with **Customer Base Penetration**, if you don't know who your customers are today as well as who you expect, or want them to be, in the future, it won't be possible for you to continue to deliver the right products and the right experiences.

STORY

3

LEGO
COMING APART, BRICK BY BRICK

Belief in oneself is one of the most important bricks in building any successful venture.

—**LYDIA MARIA CHILD,**
American writer and activist

A S WAS THE CASE WITH Marvel, LEGO had an extremely valuable product in its bricks, providing the brand a strong and loyal customer base, which, since its founding, had become more popular than any toy in history. At one point it was said that "every second, seven new boxes of LEGO are sold; for every person in the world, there are 62 LEGO pieces; LEGO people—mini-figures, as they're known—outnumber real people." Between 1932 and 1998, the company had never made a loss.

Over the years, it diversified "beyond the brick," and new products were more frequent. However, in its quest to find new growth, it realized that it may have gotten too far away from its core by launching games, clothing, and theme parks. In 1998, LEGO faced its first deficit in its history. In 1999, LEGO decided to cut one thousand jobs. By 2003, net sales fell by 26 percent and play material sales slipped 29 percent. The company was facing its "most serious financial crisis to date" and dealing with a significant shift in market and customer context, including intense price competition and new consumer tastes.

For many, its pursuit of aggressive **Customer and Product Diversification** moved it away from the original brick into *very different prod-*

ucts, which was seen as one of the main reasons why LEGO was facing such tough times. Then 2004 came and with that a new CEO, Jørgen Vig Knudstorp, the first non–family member to head the company, and he devised a comprehensive restructuring plan. The idea was to once again have LEGO "become a financially well-founded, value creating business," one that switched its focus back to its traditional values, culture, and products.

Under his tenure the LEGO Group recovered from a significant growth stall that almost put the company into bankruptcy in the early 2000s. He was able to lead LEGO to a 600 percent increase in turnover from 2001 to 2016 when he became executive chairman. One of the most critical things LEGO did during this time was to get closer to its customers. It began to reimagine the experience children wanted and ultimately expected to have with its toys. You might even say, as LEGO refocused on its core, it also became far more interested in how it could improve the overall **Customer Experience**. It built labs, crowdsourced products, went "camping" in customers' homes—all in a quest to learn what it should be developing in the future. LEGO is said to have conducted the largest ethnographic study of children in the world. This ability to stay so close to its customers and stay ahead of their demands is what may have helped fuel its impressive growth over the past decade.

However, in 2017, following a decadelong sales boom, venerable global toy giant LEGO hit a growth stall (again), and it said it could not promise a return to growth in the next two years. This was a jolting acknowledgment for a group widely admired for embracing the digital era, especially with its LEGO Dimensions product and tying up lucrative franchises from Harry Potter to Minecraft.

What is most surprising about this particular growth stall and why I chose it as a lesson for *Growth IQ* is the fact that when LEGO ran into trouble back in early 2000, it was growing and growing fast, not just its revenue but its people (headcount), markets, customers, and products. It was pushing into the digital arena, launching movies, and codeveloping games. Although it had a strong **Partnership** strategy in place to outsource requirements outside its core, allowing it to work with other companies as it focused on what it did best—developing products—it still didn't allow for enough agility in the business. The organization had become overly

146

complex, inflated, and far too removed from the very customers it sought to serve. As Knudstorp said, "Suddenly the consumer, the shopper, the retailer is a bit too far from the top management."

In the PayPal story, when Dan Schulman decided to pursue new products and new customers, he began that transformation with a reconfiguration of the organization, including product development and customer segmentation. LEGO followed a similar sequence by tackling complexity in the business to help streamline people and processes. *The sequence of changes set them up for a higher likelihood for success.*

SPEED IS THE NEW CURRENCY

In its pursuit of **Customer and Product Diversification**, LEGO forgot about having the right internal capabilities and infrastructure to support the new business and product requirements. Pursuing one path without the necessary combination and sequence of efforts puts any company at a significant disadvantage. This time, it wasn't so much diversification as much as *LEGO being unable to respond to the changing demands of its customers fast enough.* The pace at which the market context was changing and the competitive landscape was intensifying for the attention span of kids—and that proved too much for a complex organization to handle. *Speed is the new currency in business, and if you can't keep up, you risk being left behind.*

> **LEGO has increased sales by an average of more than 15 percent per year in the last twelve years, with a 25 percent growth rate in 2015. But while sales in Asia and Europe, its most mature market, grew by double digits in the first half of 2016, there was no growth in the Americas.**

After recovering from its first growth stall in 2000, LEGO was able to regain revenue momentum. With its success came a combination of growth paths it began to pursue. It wanted to sell more into its base (**Customer Base Penetration**), it was expanding into new markets (**Market Acceleration**), it was enhancing existing products such as City and Space (**Product Expansion**), and it chose to pursue an aggressive digital strategy with LEGO Dimensions and LEGO Life. LEGO Friends, Ninjago, Mindstorms, and Nexo Knights were toys specifically built for a new market—girls, plus grown-ups with LEGO Architecture (**Customer and Product Diversification**). It was also capitalizing on lucrative **Partnerships**, helping it to deliver an amazing **Customer Experience**.

In September 2016 the company published its sales figures for the first half of 2016, announcing a 10 percent growth in sales from 2015. It experienced double-digit growth in Europe and Asia, whereas the Americas were flat year over year. Between 2012 and 2016, it added more than seven thousand new positions. But for the first half of 2017, LEGO growth slowed, with revenues down 5 percent and its growth rate just 6 percent. LEGO cut approximately 8 percent or fourteen hundred positions, many before the end of 2017. It also said that mid-single-digit growth rates were "more realistic for the years to come," but it has since revised those expectations downward. Knudstorp said, "We are not saying specifically whether we will grow the next two years or not."

The lesson in this story is that even when you are growing, even when you have one of the strongest brands in the world, you can't ignore what is needed to support the push into multiple paths . . . your people, and the ability for your company to respond, sometimes very quickly, to changing customer demands.

LEGO
KEY TAKEAWAYS

- *Past success, even past failure, is not always a good teacher*. In this case, LEGO had enjoyed decades of spectacular growth when it faced its first growth stall. As it refocused on its core, it cut underperforming products, reduced headcount, eliminated bureaucracy, and streamlined its product catalog—only to find itself back there again a little more than twelve years later. It took them sixty-eight years to hit their first growth stall, and then fifteen years to get themselves back to a fairly similar position.

- Beware of the organizational implications of **Customer and Product Diversification**. *New products won't just market, sell, and support themselves to a new customer base.* The more products you develop, the greater the customer insight you will need to stay on top of. Keeping up with the pace of the changing market context is hard in one product category or customer segment—multiplying that by two or three can overwhelm a company.

- **Customer and Product Diversification** is also a way to, metaphorically, keep from getting your feet wet. By that I mean that if one of your businesses is beginning to experience a slowdown, diversifying into a new business may enable you to step from the sinking deck of one onto the dry deck of the other without having to suffer the "swim" of slashed revenues. But you can't just do that on a whim. You need to have some process to keep your options open if the right opportunity presents itself in order to capitalize on a market opportunity.

PUTTING IT ALL TOGETHER

THE CUSTOMER AND PRODUCT DIVERSIFICATION path is one of considerable risk—not least because it can take you into areas in which you may have little experience. Some of these risks arise because this diversification requires you to develop new skills that you don't currently have—including new distribution channels, different relationships with a new population of retailers, and the servicing of products for which you haven't developed the requisite repair operations.

Given all of the risks, why diversify? Because if you can pull it off, diversification can help reduce your overall future risk. *A company operating in a single market or with a single product family is always at risk for discontinuities* (e.g., a technological breakthrough, a shift in the customer base, a breakdown of the supply chain, the failure of a strategic partner, a cultural shift) and is almost always doomed when a revolution happens. But a company with a bit of diversity in its customer base and product portfolio, while still not immune to a terrible shock, can survive by shifting its focus to its "other" parts of the business if and when it is necessary. Taking a smaller perspective, having more than one product, especially an adjacent one, a line extension, can also help companies smooth out seasonal or cyclical demand (summer and winter clothes, summer fruit and winter vegetables, school supplies and hobby supplies, etc.).

However, _diversification also presents potential cultural problems_. In particular, the more different the new product initiative is from the established one, the more likely the company will, over time, begin to pull itself in two. Senior management will need to keep the two efforts at the same table by constantly asserting the company's common goal to achieve sustained growth.

WHAT WORKS—AND POTENTIAL PITFALLS

In some innovation circles, it is suggested that to be considered an innovative company, at least one-third of a company's revenues should come from products developed within the last three years. Inge Thulin, president and CEO of 3M, projected that 40 percent of 3M's revenue in 2017 would come from products that did not exist five years ago.

There are a number of reasons why new product introductions fail; however, the one we see most often is lack of rigor behind sales and marketing planning and execution. Maybe the strategy was combined with the wrong path to support it—remember: _great products do not sell themselves_. So this path in isolation is much more destined to fail.

Some companies—big and old enough to know better—have attempted to enter new markets, especially new markets in new countries, with exactly the same products or services they used in their original markets. Because they don't know the "culture" of that market—its marketing channels, customer expectations, competitive history, pricing models, service, and quality standards, for instance—these companies

According to Harvard Business School professor Clayton Christensen, each year more than thirty thousand new consumer products are launched and 80 percent of them fail. A study by the Product Development and Management Association (PDMA) found that failure rates varied among industries, ranging from 35 percent for health care to 49 percent for consumer goods. Though lower numbers, the message remains the same: successful new product launches are not to be taken for granted.

find themselves blindsided by angry customers or retailers and end up making a bloody retreat.

Similar to **Market Acceleration**, the two most likely combination paths for **Customer and Product Diversification** are the two that pursue the process of teaming up with other enterprises (**Partnership and Co-opetition**), as well as **Product Expansion**. You can't do it all. In fact, when it comes to **Customer and Product Diversification**, the further you diversify, the less you'll likely be able to do it all on your own.

Look at your current, established business: How long did it take you to fully understand your market—to establish your supply and distribution channels, understand your customers well enough that you could create an effective sales and marketing campaign, establish a workable service and support system, determine the right coverage for warranties and return policies, and understand the financial cycles of your industry? I'm guessing years—and that's in a market that you built your company to pursue.

What makes you think you are going to be able to take on a new market of which you currently have little knowledge beyond that fact that it's a good target for your diversification? Because you are now big and successful? That's a common—and dangerous—mistake, because it assumes that your current operations can be readily transferred to this new challenge while you enjoy the same fit and economies of scale.

The truth may be just the opposite of that. A big, successful company diversifying into a new market is, at least at first, a small and unproven company. You may be a Fortune 500 company, or even a proven, successful small business, where you are right now, but the reality may be that *in your new market you are just the little unknown company you were twenty years ago.*

Even your brand, which may convey enormous prestige and power in your current market, may turn out to mean next to nothing—may even be a liability—in your new business. That's why **Partnerships**—in everything from product design to manufacturing to marketing to sales—can be a powerful new growth path once you've chosen your diversification strategy.

COMBINATION: PATH 5—
Customer and Product Diversification + Path 4—Product Expansion

This path requires expanding your product catalog. Diversifying can be a risky proposition, as you read with LEGO. You can push too hard and too fast after too many new products. Even with high demand, it doesn't mean your company can handle the increased volume without changes to the organization, sales models, partnerships, and marketing efforts.

COMBINATION: PATH 5—
Customer and Product Diversification + Path 8— Partnerships

The question here is: Do you develop products on your own or work with others? Do you go after new markets on your own or with others? There may be ways to minimize risks and costs if you work with partners in key markets to help you with sales and marketing coverage. Also, is there a way you could do joint marketing and selling to create a 1+1=3 multiplier effect? Entering new markets or new product categories may be better accomplished (especially if you are a small business) by working with others.

COMBINATION: PATH 5—
Customer and Product Diversification + Path 9— Co-opetition

Co-opetition—a relatively new concept that has taken on much more force with the rise of the global marketplace—involves partnering with one or more of your *competitors*. At first glance, this may seem counterintuitive. After all, why would you approach your customers arm in arm with a company you are trying to defeat? Moreover, why are you sharing information and strategy with a company that would love to find your weaknesses and use them to destroy you?

There's no denying that those are risks and that you must weigh them if you are going to enter into a **Co-opetition** type of agreement. The worst-case scenario described above has happened in this kind of partnership in the past. But it has usually occurred in a very unbalanced relationship between two unequal companies—often a hot new start-up and an aging and increasingly uncompetitive older company. The fact is, even without the partnership, the one company was destined to overrun the other.

PATH6

OPTIMIZE SALES

OPTIMIZE SALES

Work smarter . . . not harder.

**—ALLAN H. MOGENSEN,
the "Father of Work Simplification"**

WHY OPTIMIZE SALES MATTERS

- Sixty-four percent of consumers are willing to pay more for simpler experiences.
- Only about 22 percent of businesses are satisfied with their conversion rates.
- Forty-four percent of sales organizations list **Optimize Sales** as a top sales objective.
- Over half of sales organizations (54 percent) do not formally align their sales process, or other aspects of how they sell, to the specific journeys taken by their customers.
- Sales teams spend an average of 25 percent of their time on administrative tasks.
- Overall, 5 percent of shoppers who engaged with AI-powered product recommendations accounted for 24 percent of revenue on Cyber Monday.
- U.S. firms spend $15 billion per year training salespeople and another $800 billion on incentives. Yet estimates of annual turnover of U.S. salespeople run as high as 27 percent, twice the rate in the overall labor force.

THE LAST MILE

It was almost thirty years ago when I realized that my outgoing personality, insatiable curiosity, and competitive spirit would serve me well in the sales profession. Over the course of my career I was an individual quota-carrying sales rep, team leader, director of sales, and VP of sales. I finally ended my days of carrying a quota running a (sales) division at Gateway Computers (yes, the "cow" boxes). It has always amazed me how much misperception there is about the profession and the role that sales plays in a company's ability to grow. *Sales is the "last mile"—the moment of truth for any company.* All the sweat and tears that have gone into developing products, the pain of creating the perfect marketing campaign, the hard decisions made along the way hopefully lead to a sale. Otherwise, how can you possibly sustain a business without generating revenue?

> *Pretend that every single person you meet has a sign around his or her neck that says, "Make me feel important." Not only will you succeed in sales, you will succeed in life.*
>
> **—MARY KAY ASH,
> founder of Mary Kay
> Cosmetics**

Many years ago, I was advising one of the largest technology providers in the world on how best to optimize sales performance. This wasn't a global, boil-the-ocean assessment; rather, it centered on the U.S. region and large "enterprise" accounts it was targeting. A quick (I mean, like, two-minute) analysis of the coverage model exposed the first area ripe for improvement.

There were over 45,000 accounts under "management," and only 600 sales reps to cover them. All it took was easy math (45,000 divided by 600) to realize that 75 individual accounts per rep was completely unrealistic, from both a time and a customer value perspective. In addition, we found that existing sales resources were deployed by region (city, state) and spent more than 50 percent of their time in non-selling activities such as commuting, which meant that the company wasn't getting the full potential (revenue or otherwise) of its sales resources. *Leadership doesn't always take the time to review current sales practices on a regular basis,* so it was a bit caught off guard by the simplicity of this discovery.

This example, as basic as it might seem, should have been caught long before I showed up. The fact that the number of accounts assigned to each rep had reached a point of diminishing returns had gone totally unnoticed at the executive level. The point of this story is not to discuss how it solved this problem as much as it is about focusing on the basics, staying diligent on sales optimization, and rationalizing current sales efforts on a consistent basis. Isn't it true that pipeline reviews (a representation of where customer prospects are in the purchasing process) are weekly, maybe even daily? Quota attainment is a sales rep's score card. So, you must set them up for success. **Optimize Sales** is one of the ways to do that.

Indulge me for a moment in this vast oversimplification, but companies do two things: (1) they make stuff, and (2) they sell stuff. It's my belief that even the greatest products in the world can't market and sell themselves. *Companies have to be good at bringing customers to their products.*

With collapsing product life cycles, a more informed buyer, customer experience playing a greater role in buying decisions, and 24/7 access to online commerce, *companies can no longer count on products alone to be their sustainable competitive edge.* In addition to focusing on *what* they sell, companies are now placing more attention on *how* they sell. The goal? To meet customers where and how they want to buy, with the right products and services, at the right time, in a seamless, frictionless manner.

Easy, right? Not so fast. Sales optimization can be an amazing way to double down with existing (sales) resources, accelerate the effectiveness of another path by combining the two, and subsequently fund additional growth initiatives as revenue and cost of goods sold (COGS) improve. However, *many companies get trapped by the paradox of hitting numbers "now" versus improving sales for future quarters or years ahead.*

> What can get a CEO fired from a publicly traded company (besides an ethics violation)? Not hitting sales numbers, or missing sales targets over an extended period of time. There is tremendous pressure each quarter to perform, show quarter-over-quarter or year-over-year growth, and there are really only two ways to do that to improve revenue and profitability performance: sell more (top line) and cut costs (bottom line).

I coined the term "Seller's Dilemma" while at Gartner many years ago—playing off Clayton Christensen's *The Innovator's Dilemma*, to describe this paradox—and this concept still rings true today. Sales executives who exclusively own quota-bearing resources are the ones impacted by this dilemma. If they don't hit their numbers today, they won't have a job six months from now to worry about. So, they keep their heads down and push through each quarter to get revenue across the goal line. They are working harder, no doubt—nobody in sales would tell you otherwise. But could they be working smarter and not just harder to meet long-term performance goals?

Unfortunately, they rarely come up for air to reevaluate *how* they are selling. This means that current sales practices, processes, and organizational structure may in fact be hindering their growth more than any external factor they believe they are facing. This isn't a new issue. There wasn't a seismic shift in market context that made this more important today than it was a decade ago. But what has changed is the ease with which companies can now identify the areas to improve because of the advancements in technology. It used to be that we had to spend hours, days, and weeks analyzing the data, and by the time we uncovered an issue or even an opportunity, the reality had shifted.

Today's winners need to be much smarter sellers, leveraging the advancements of artificial intelligence (AI), machine learning, customer relationship management (CRM), marketing automation, and other sales enablement and digital capabilities. They need to be willing to disrupt the status quo and fully optimize sales resources (both human and online) around various sales channels.

It's a tall order. Companies are scrambling to keep pace with their customers' demands, especially when it comes to the way in which they sell across a multitude of sales channels (online, off-line, mobile, apps). This changing market context has given rise to the resurgence within companies to focus more on optimizing sales, not just developing new products—that is, increasing productivity and performance with current resources (number of salespeople and selling channels) that the company has in terms of its sales operations (tools, systems, CRM) and sales enablement practices—all while leveraging technology in new ways.

<u>What does that mean? It could be things like:</u>

- Adding more of what customers want (products available in new sales channels, promotions, recommendations, etc.).
- Getting rid of what is unnecessary (reducing steps required to place an order).
- Integrating online (digital) and off-line routes to market.
- Leveraging more of new (sales) enablement tools (digital signatures, payment methods, mobile order tracking, etc.).
- Defining the right size of a sales force (inside vs. outside, online vs. storefronts, insource vs. outsource).
- Rationalizing sales coverage models (by size, industry, region).
- Reorganizing around customers rather than products (like what PayPal did).
- Taking advantage of both online and retail (brick-and-mortar) storefronts.
- Improving training and hiring practices—just to name a few.

MIGHT NOT BE NEW—BUT IT'S STILL IMPORTANT

Why is **Optimize Sales** so important? *Companies do two things—make things and sell things*—and generating sales is the revenue engine that moves the business forward. Without sales, there is no revenue coming in, bills don't get paid, products don't get made, employees don't get their paychecks—and in big-business Fortune 2,500–size companies that are publicly traded, if sales aren't met, stock prices drop and executives, including the CEO, are at risk of being fired.

Optimize Sales is like the Customer Experience path in the sense that it should be a constant, underlying focus for any company that "sells" a product or service. There should never be a time when a company isn't focusing on increasing sales effectiveness—it ought to be as critical as reviewing financials. As a matter of fact, if you have decided to pursue one or more paths, such as **Market Acceleration, Customer Base Penetration, Customer and Product Diversification**, the first thing you should do is engage in a sales effectiveness assessment to make sure you have the appropriate sales models (people, processes, and systems) in place prior to launching a new growth path.

Unfortunately, when companies are experiencing strong growth, they begin to believe that their sales efforts are infallible, and they make the mistake of hiring more salespeople to increase revenue without first looking at overall productivity. This can be a slippery slope if you aren't careful. More headcount may in fact deliver you additional short-term value (revenue production), but it can also mask fundamental issues lurking below the surface, which ultimately manifest themselves in a growth stall. Pulling the same levers will only get you so far. Before you hire more people, you need to test and validate that your existing (sales) resources are actually performing at the optimal levels.

PATH 6 OPTIMIZE SALES

STORY

1

SALESFORCE
FOUR MEN AND TWO DOGS

*If I'm right—and I'm convinced I am—this on-demand
model will totally change the way technology is bought
and sold. In other words, it's the end of software as we
know it.*

—MARC BENIOFF, CEO of Salesforce.com

TODAY'S ENTERPRISE-CLASS TECHNOLOGY IS BEING sold in new ways (more self-service) and at far lower prices per unit. Shifting to a mass-market model dictates a fundamental change in how you sell things. A traditional IBM-type sales organization has almost become too slow and expensive to be competitive in this digitally driven, twenty-first-century world.

Using the old tactics to increase sales—cut prices, spend more marketing dollars, hire more salespeople—is no longer as effective as it once was. What works now is leveraging more and more of what new technology advancements offer to help improve salespeople's productivity—gaining greater sales with existing resources as well as improving predictable and measurable growth.

In the 1990s, CRM looked a lot different than it does today. Back then, CRM software vendors operated through a product model in which clients would make large up-front purchases to operate the systems on-site.

Then Marc Benioff, at the time an employee of Oracle, had a revolutionary idea: offer CRM as a service rather than as a product, allowing customers to pay lower monthly fees rather than spending millions at the time of purchase.

Salesforce started its life in a tiny one-bedroom apartment atop Telegraph Hill in San Francisco in March 1999. Four men—Marc Benioff, Parker Harris, Frank Dominguez, and Dave Moellenhoff—and their two dogs began the "No Software" revolution, disrupting an entire industry and forever changing the software and cloud landscape.

salesforce WAS BORN IN THE CLOUD and had no on-premise solution

amazon MADE IT SO EASY TO BUY BOOKS

salesforce wanted to do SAME THING FOR customer relationship management

LEVERAGED FREEMIUM

FREE FUNCTIONAL TRIAL FOR FIVE USERS FOR A YEAR

land and EXPAND strategy

ENERGIZE YOUR CUSTOMERS INTO A (MULTI) MILLION MEMBER SALES TEAM

REVENUES GREW 11000% SINCE SALESFORCE WENT PUBLIC IN 2004

PATH 6 OPTIMIZE SALES

Salesforce was betting on the future state of enterprise software. The increased demand to access CRM from various devices was the exact shift in market context it was hoping for. Salesforce had $5.4 million in revenue two years after launch, $22.4 million at three years, and $51 million after four years. But it was its "No Software" mantra and its extravagant marketing tactics that propelled the brand forward toward its now more than $10 billion run rate. Yes, its aspirations were big, but so was the market opportunity. Between 2012 and 2017 the CRM forecast netted a 56 percent increase in CAGR—that's a growth rate anyone would want to pursue. Also, CRM leads all enterprise software categories in projected growth, showing a 15.1 percent CAGR.

The fact that Salesforce was born in the cloud and had no "on premise" solution gave it a first-mover advantage for businesses looking to take advantage of any otherwise "too costly" investment. Salesforce was built around the one main idea—that software should be delivered 24/7 to people over the cloud by taking the benefits of the "consumer Web to the business world." _But being first doesn't always guarantee success._ Salesforce knew that it needed to be better not only at its technology but at the way it sold if it was going to win against market leader Siebel early on, and eventually Oracle (which purchased Siebel) and SAP. Benioff knew that if he was going to win against these much larger software companies, he needed to focus on building a high-performing sales culture, and he has never wavered from that philosophy.

The basic premise is that Salesforce summarily dismantled Siebel through its revolutionary software-as-a-service (SaaS) business model and its sales strategies, and it took so much market share away that by 2005 Siebel was forced to sell to Oracle. The proverbial story of "David defeats Goliath" played out in the high-tech industry.

Siebel Systems was founded in 1993 by Tom Siebel and Pat House. Within five years, the company went from little-known start-up to a nearly $2-billion-a-year powerhouse, with eight thousand employees

CRM continues to be the fastest-growing business application market and is expected to cross $36 billion by the end of 2017. The total SaaS market is expected to reach over $75 billion by 2020.

and a market cap of $30 billion. It was the leader of the CRM market. In 1999, Siebel Systems was recognized by Deloitte as the "Fastest Growing Company" in U.S. history, with 782,978 percent growth over five years.

By 2002, the company's top line had stalled, the stock had fallen to a fraction of its former stratospheric level, and on September 12, 2005, Oracle signed a definitive agreement to acquire the company. The transaction was valued at a little more than $6 billion. On March 1, 2006, Siebel Systems no longer existed as an independent entity, a rather inglorious end to a once unassailable company.

SALESFORCE ON SALESFORCE: THE SALES PLAYBOOK

Since the beginning, Salesforce has set its own counterintuitive course. With a single product focus, CRM (Sales Force Automation [SFA]), its cloud-based service allowed customers to learn about it, subscribe, and get it up and running with a few clicks on their computer. No long, drawn-out sales process full of customized demonstrations, scopes of work, and price negotiations. *Think about how easy Amazon made it to buy a book—Salesforce wanted to do that same thing to CRM.*

Making it easy was a great start, but in the beginning Salesforce went one step further: it leveraged a concept known in the software industry since the 1980s called "freemium," offering a free functional trial for five users for a year. It was a critical component to its "land and expand" strategy. While that seems like table stakes today, in 1999 it was unheard of. Giving away a fully functional version to five users was especially unheard of in the enterprise software market from the likes of Oracle, Siebel, or SAP. The benefit of taking this approach was threefold: it allowed prospective customers to try out the service, it got people talking about the product if they were using it for free, and it provided Salesforce with live customer feedback to help it improve its products going forward.

THE FIFTEENTH EMPLOYEE

As a start-up, hiring your first full-time sales rep is always a delicate balance. It wasn't until Salesforce had a handful of beta customers that it decided to hire its first dedicated salesperson to help acquire additional free customers and also to convert the existing (free) customers to paying customers. This was a classic **Customer Base Penetration** strategy, albeit on a very small scale. Salesforce had to be highly effective in its sales efforts early on—every move they made could have incredible impact to its early growth.

Salesforce, more specifically Marc Benioff, embraced the philosophy of "*How to energize your customers into a (multi) million-member sales team.*" That one sentence is at the core of a sales organization that now counts thousands of salespeople on its payroll. But the founding principle of making sure customers are successfully using the product has served Salesforce well. If the customers are happy, if its sales teams are more productive, if it is able to have better predictability in the business and greater pipeline visibility, then it is more likely to grow its own business. And if it does that, it will in turn need more CRM. It was a win-win.

However, it doesn't end there. Benioff believed that inside every customer "there was an unrealized potential." By offering training and support, it could build a sales army that was not limited to a finite number of Salesforce salespeople but could scale to hundreds of thousands, and, one day, millions of customers who would advocate and tell the Salesforce story to other companies. If you have ever attended the Dreamforce conference, Salesforce's annual customer event in San Francisco, which attracts over 170,000 registered attendees, you will totally understand what I am talking about. The extent to which customers advocate for Salesforce is unprecedented. It is a brand that has created tremendous loyalty among its customer base, and that loyalty has helped Salesforce grow to the size it is today—revenues have grown nearly 11,000 percent since Salesforce went public in 2004.

Optimize Sales isn't just about making sure your internal resources are optimized and enabled with the best tools and customer insights—you must never forget about your customers and the success they will gain from using your products and services. You can't get caught in the trap of internally focused processes and how you can constantly squeeze every last drop out of your salespeople. Instead, you must look from the outside in, so you can match customer expectations and their buying journey with how you organize, enable, train, and scale your sales force.

SALESFORCE
KEY TAKEAWAYS

- Improving sales performance isn't always about what you can do with your own internal resources; it may include your customers as well. _Look beyond your four walls to uncover unrealized potential._

- For small start-ups, hiring the first sales rep can be one of the biggest (early) decisions you can make. The sequence in which you do this can have implications for the business. This is a classic case of "need vs. want." Do you need a salesperson? Or do you want a salesperson? Depending on what you are selling, it may make sense for founders to do the initial selling, so they can understand the needs of the business and the customer, which will help define what skills will be needed when it hires its first salesperson.

- Great brands aren't just looking to make a quick sale—they want to make sure customers value what it is they are buying. You want to do as much as possible in the sales process to avoid having a problem later with **Churn**.

- In 1999, when Salesforce was founded, most software companies were using a freemium business model in a limited-time or feature-limited version to get prospective customers to try out its products. Why? So they could eliminate the cost as a barrier to entry. While Salesforce didn't invent the concept, it put its own spin on it, going above and beyond what its competitors were doing. It offered a free, fully functional trial for five users for a year. _Looking at an existing sales model from a competitor or even another industry can provide you with a starting point from which you can develop your product._ Using familiar sales models in an innovative way can help differentiate you from the rest of the pack and give your customers something to talk about.

STORY

2

WALMART
THE ULTIMATE RETAIL MATCHUP

The ideal way to win a championship is step by step.

—PHIL JACKSON,
American basketball player and coach

MPROVING SALES PERFORMANCE DOESN'T ALWAYS
mean that companies must have traditional "sales representatives"—
read: "humans with the title of 'sales representative'"—to optimize.
Optimize Sales operations now has an equally large component that focuses on the various sales, "routes to market," or channels that customers want to leverage and transact with.

No longer can companies strictly compete within a single buying channel (online or off-line) or sales model (face-to-face, retail storefront, phone, catalog, partners, etc.). Combining online and a retail storefront as an example is table stakes for many, if not all, companies that sell a "product." Remember, Sears owned the catalog channel and then combined it with storefronts, but it chose not to keep up with the changing market context to invest in online and e-commerce, at its own peril. It discontinued the catalog without thinking about the role it played for customers during their buying journey—albeit now online.

Given all of the technological changes of the last twenty years, it is easy to forget that at the end of the twentieth century, giant retailer Walmart was considered almost unstoppable. Through relentless expansion, revolutionary innovation in supply-chain management, and a tight focus on pricing, Walmart had all but destroyed many smaller retailers—and put considerably more buying power in the hands of America's lower-income and middle-class citizens. It was widely assumed that Walmart had established a new, hugely competitive, and operationally efficient retail paradigm that might be impossible to top for generations.

Yet, that dominance has lasted fewer than twenty years. Today, Walmart, even with its 2.3 million associates, 11,695 stores (as of January 2017), and clubs in twenty-eight countries, operating under sixty-three different names and having amassed 260 million customers, is beset by other, equally efficient giant competitors—notably, Amazon. It's not hard these days to find retail industry analysts making predictions about Amazon's impact on Walmart using the same language they used to use about Walmart's impact on "Main Street" all those years ago.

How is that possible? What happened was customer-facing technology; notably the Internet and e-commerce empowered a much more connected, demanding, and educated buyer, who was finding an easier sales experience and selection online than in brick-and-mortar storefronts. Now Amazon was knocking on Walmart's door—and the retail giant had to decide whether to hunker down and hold on to its market as long as it could, keeping the status quo (as we saw in Path 2 on Sears), or figure out a way to fight back and stay in the game. And if it was going to do the latter, having already perfected the supply side of its business, and carrying an immense brick-and-mortar inventory of more than eleven thousand stores worldwide, *any solution was going to have to come from rethinking how the company served its customers*. In other words, it would need a revolution in its *sales* practices.

AMAZON BUYS WHOLE FOODS

Walmart, unlike many of its own past victims, was showing every sign of being willing to fight—and, more important, to change. In fact, Walmart had been watching the Amazon threat since at least 2014 when C. Doug McMillon assumed the role of company CEO.

The Walmart-Amazon rivalry may have begun as one of brick-and-mortar versus online retail, but it wouldn't stay that way for long.

Walmart made its own foray into online retail when it bought online shopping site Jet.com for $3.3 billion in August 2016 and immediately put its CEO, Marc Lore, in charge of Walmart's e-commerce business. It was Lore who immediately matched Amazon by offering free two-day shipping (with no membership required) and tripled the size of Walmart's online offerings.

Across almost all categories, we're seeing growth. The food business, in particular, has accelerated.

—C. DOUG MCMILLON,
president and
CEO of Walmart

The success of this initiative likely saved the day, a year later, when Amazon announced its Whole Foods acquisition. News of Amazon encroaching on Walmart's physical turf, and its grocery business, which was Walmart's most valuable growth engine, caused Walmart's stock to drop 3 percent the following day. But Walmart was prepared. Within twenty-four hours of Amazon's announcing its Whole Foods deal, Walmart made an announcement of its own: it had acquired apparel retailer Bonobos for $310 million, which increased Walmart's inventory to sixty-seven million different items on its website. By the end of the week, Walmart's stock had bounced back and was 14 percent higher than at the same point the year before.

The most obvious part of the acquisition—Bonobos's extensive online operations—was actually the least interesting. As the *New York Daily News* noted: "Bonobos may have built its brand on the back of a successful online business, but it also has a chain of equally successful retail stores including a number of 'pop-up' stores in Nordstrom. Thus, the acquisition brings a unique capability to Walmart—*best practices in managing two very distinct channels* in tandem, not separately as has been the case for 99 percent of all retailers to date."

Bonobos's innovation was the "showrooming concept"—a men's apparel store that only had product to look at, and try on, but not purchase, requiring customers to complete their order online. Bonobos basically

Showrooming is the practice of examining merchandise in a traditional brick-and-mortar retail store or other off-line setting, and then buying it online, sometimes at a lower price.

built an industry-leading, "operationally efficient" supply chain for its brand, not stores—it eliminated the issue of overstock, inventory control, and expensive square footage. It was able to use this showrooming concept to its advantage, and Walmart wanted in on it.

CLICK AND COLLECT

Walmart's spending spree has been supporting its new "click and collect" grocery strategy, which is leveraging new technology capabilities to improve the **Customer Experience** and push toward greater **Customer Base Penetration**. Walmart has introduced geo-fencing to notify its store personnel when customers are in the store, to retrieve their orders, and twenty-four-hour kiosks that automate grocery pickup, all with the goal of optimizing its sales experience both online and off-line.

Walmart's strategy was becoming clear: even as Amazon was racing to build a greater brick-and-mortar presence, Walmart, with its forty-six hundred mega-stores (plus a few hundred more from other acquisitions, such as Bonobos), was already there—*an estimated 90 percent of all Americans live within ten miles of one of its stores*—and Walmart was going to put that giant footprint and sales capability to use in entirely new ways.

PATH 6 OPTIMIZE SALES

In particular, Walmart has embarked on a *new sales strategy*. If Amazon is targeting a future intersection of brick-and-mortar and online retailing, starting from its dominance on the online side, Walmart appears ready to win that race from its even greater dominance on the brick-and-mortar side combined with online and other innovative sales concepts.

COMBINATION + SEQUENCE

The first step was integration—sequence matters. Walmart has announced that it will combine, for the first time, its legendary buying process for its stores with the buying it does for its website—a significant undertaking when pursuing sales optimization.

Until now, the company has kept those two operations apart. This integration will not only reduce redundancy and cut costs, *but for customers it will make the interface between the physical and virtual Walmart experience nearly seamless.* It is also expected to attract vendors who have been wary of the smaller volumes on Walmart's website versus the stores. That may also help close the inventory gap with Amazon.

Speaking to analysts in August 2017, McMillon declared that Walmart's metamorphosis had just begun. Under a new motto of *"making every day easier for busy families,"* McMillon announced a number of new initiatives to **Optimize Sales**, including:

- More delivery of Walmart.com orders by staff from nearby stores.
- The construction of automated "pickup towers" at approximately one hundred Walmart stores around the United States, "where customers can pick up their orders within a matter of minutes."
- Further integration of store and online purchasing, including "Easy Reorder" to allow customers to view in one place all of their most popular purchases.
- A new program that enables parents and students to type in their zip code and teacher's name and find out their required class supplies.
- Walmart is expanding its online grocery delivery service to a total of 100 metropolitan areas by the end of 2018—a push that will help the retailer reach 40 percent of American households.

Will this be enough to take on such a fast-moving, innovative, and aggressive machine like Amazon? Only time will tell, but early signs show that Walmart is more than holding its own as other large retailers continue to struggle. In its third quarter 2017, its U.S. sales were up 2.7 percent and Walmart international saw sales rise 4.1 percent—its thirteenth straight period of growth driven by e-commerce and food. Online commerce, which now has about seventy million items (triple the number a year ago), rose 50 percent in the United States alone.

For a leviathan like Walmart to decide to revolutionize its entire sales apparatus in real time and attempt to race a company like Amazon into the future is a stunning decision. It was confronting the "Seller's Dilemma" head-on. While the Walmart story relied on mergers and acquisitions to modernize its technology, infrastructure, and operations, all were done in the spirit of optimizing sales and improving performance against a formidable competitor. Now, other industry players are upping their game to compete against Amazon and Walmart—in December 2017 Target acquired Shipt Inc.

Next up will be China and Walmart's moves against Alibaba, another formidable competitor like Amazon. A recent announcement by Alibaba to invest $2.88 billion for a major stake into Sun Art Retail Group—China's largest operator of Walmart-style superstores, shows once again the power of online and off-line sales to become more effective in meeting customers where they want to shop.

WALMART
KEY TAKEAWAYS

- This story is a great example of how Walmart was able to navigate challenges from competition and a shifting market context, but few other companies have the ability to make big M&A investments like this to fill out a product or capability portfolio. Even if you don't have the capital to use M&A in this way, *what you can and should take away from this is why it did it*. It was being hyper-focused on changing (context) desires of its customers. It was unwilling to lose to a competitor based on things within its control. It understood what needed to change and focused on the best way to get that done. In this case, it just so happened to be a combination of internal changes plus very specific acquisitions.

- Like PayPal, Walmart looked to the sequence in which it made changes to the business as a way to help it be more successful with its acquisitions. It took organizations, functions, and buying processes and modernized them to accommodate the new capabilities coming its way via its acquisitions.

- Although I was unable to cover all that Walmart is doing specifically to improve its sales performance and customer experience, the investments it is making are extensive. It continues a massive strategic and operational overhaul, designed not only to survive in an era of retail transformation and changing customer expectations but to fuel additional growth and attract new customers. Its investment in a seamless digital and physical shopping journey is to spur growth and to increase its U.S. revenue from online purchases to 40 percent.

STORY
3

WELLS FARGO
A RHYME IS NOT A REASON

Life imitates Art far more than Art imitates Life.
—OSCAR WILDE, "The Decay of Lying: An Observation"

GLENGARRY GLEN ROSS IS A 1984 Pulitzer Prize–winning play by David Mamet that was made into a film in 1992. One could argue that the movie is one of the most unflattering depictions of the job of being a salesperson Hollywood has ever made. A group of desperate Chicago real estate salesmen are driven to engage in any number of unethical, illegal acts—from lies and flattery to bribery, threats, intimidation, and burglary—to sell undesirable real estate to unwitting prospective buyers.

Alec Baldwin's character, Blake, a motivational sales trainer, gives an angry and verbally abusive speech to persuade them to close more sales or lose their jobs. "We're adding something special to this month's sales contest. First prize is a Cadillac Eldorado. Second prize is a set of steak knives. Third prize—you're fired!"

Baldwin's character may have been fictional, but he exemplified—and inspired—a cutthroat, unscrupulous sales culture that even found echoes in Bernie Madoff's infamous Ponzi scheme.

HIGH-PRESSURE SALES CULTURE GOES AWRY

Now, once again, the sales profession is challenged to defend its integrity from an example of life imitating art. Wells Fargo—founded in 1852 as a stagecoach express to carry valuable goods to and from the gold mines in the West—is now the world's second-largest bank by market capitalization. After a flurry of acquisitions and mergers in the 1990s and early 2000s, then company CEO Dick Kovacevich had a unique view on the role of banks and how best to "sell money."

Kovacevich looked for ways to make the banking experience similar to other business-to-consumer (B2C) businesses. In Kovacevich's mind, bank branches were "stores" and bankers were "salespeople" whose job it was to "cross-sell"—which meant getting "customers"—not clients—to buy as many products as possible. "Products" for the bank were things like checking/savings accounts, lines of credit, and mortgages.

While Kovacevich thought he was getting the company focused on **Customer Experience**, in reality his mandates created a high-pressure sales culture. He had launched an initiative called "Going for Gr-Eight," which meant getting the customer to buy eight products from the bank. Like at every other sales organization, there were status updates on daily goals. At Wells Fargo this one may have been a bit extreme. There was a

branch manager call in the morning about "how you were going to hit your sales goal, and if you didn't, you'd have a call in the afternoon to explain why and how you were going to fix it." This kind of high-pressure management practice never ends well: it either pushes good people out of the organization because the environment becomes a bit too toxic, competitive, and aggressive, or *people start gaming the system to meet the unrealistic goals*. In this case, both happened—and continued even after Kovacevich retired, multiple employees and executives complained, and a new CEO, John Stumpf, came on board.

Maybe one of Stumpf's greatest mistakes, which ultimately led to his downfall, was that he followed the practices that Kovacevich had put in motion. Even with the warning signs in the 1990s, nothing changed. The bad sales practices had become the new culture—and they ultimately came back to bite Wells Fargo. Stumpf never deviated from the sales practices Kovacevich had implemented—including those that were creating a less-than-ethical sales culture. There is no way to know for sure why these sales practices continued, but this statement made to investors unfortunately gives insight as to why management pushed for customers to get more products from them: *"customers who had five products with Wells Fargo were three times as profitable as those with three products, while those with eight products were five times as profitable. Additionally, the more accounts a customer had, the less likely it was that he or she would switch to another bank paying higher rates of interest."*

Fast-forward to September 2016. The consumer-banking giant (and the biggest U.S. mortgage lender) was facing its biggest scandal in its history. It fired 5,300 people, most of whom were low-level employees, as well as 10 executives. Other executives chose to step down or retire. One of them was Carrie Tolstedt, executive vice president of community banking, who oversaw over 100,000 tellers and other frontline employees at more than 6,200 Wells Fargo branches. She was paid $9.5 million in 2015 because of her "strong cross-selling ratio" and her work "reinforcing a strong risk culture." Wells Fargo CEO John Stumpf subsequently resigned under pressure. The board has since clawed back over $100 million in stock and executive compensation, paid $185 million to regulators, and settled a class-action suit for $142 billion.

What went wrong? How did Wells Fargo stray so far from its long-standing culture of integrity and putting the customer first? Wells Fargo has since acknowledged that its employees were under too much pressure to meet aggressive sales targets—sometimes as high as twenty banking products a day like a new account, a mortgage, a retirement account, or even online banking—whatever it took. During the investigation, regulators found that Wells Fargo had 3.5 million accounts that were potentially opened without the customers' permission between 2009 and 2016. It also found that "the Bank's sales practices were unethical; the Bank's actions caused harm to consumers; and Bank management had not responded promptly to address these issues."

According to Wells Fargo, its vision is to "satisfy our customers' needs, and help them succeed financially." The company emphasizes its mission: "Our vision has nothing to do with transactions, pushing products, or getting bigger for the sake of bigness. *It's about building lifelong relationships one customer at a time*. . . . We strive to be recognized by our stakeholders as setting the standard among the world's great companies for integrity and principled performance. This is more than just doing the right thing. We also have to do it in the right way." Unfortunately, they lost sight of this vision along the way.

This one story uncovers the unsavory tactics used when faced with a highly aggressive sales culture. It can happen in any industry, not just banking. The lesson here is: even when pursuing hyper-growth, never sidestep ethical behavior in pursuit of higher sales numbers and don't ever create a sales culture that rewards bad behavior or forces people to game the system just to maintain their jobs. *Do what's right by your sales force so that they can do what's right for your customers. Every time.*

WELLS FARGO
KEY TAKEAWAYS

- One of the biggest mistakes in reasoning made by Kovacevich was attributing causation to correlation when he noticed that customers with more accounts did more business with the bank.

- A high-pressure, top-down management sales environment is not the only reason sales organizations can find themselves on the wrong side of doing what's right for the customer and/or the business. Sometimes it can be the lack of training, tools, and processes, which are the reasons sales gets off track. Regardless of the reason, unethical behavior in sales must never be tolerated.

- It would be fair to say that Wells Fargo *wanted to deliver a better* **Customer Experience** than its competitors. It would also be fair to say that they were very focused on **Customer Base Penetration** and **Product Expansion** by trying to inspire existing customers to buy more products from them. All three of those paths plus **Optimize Sales** in combination can be a game changer if done well. However, Wells Fargo failed, and failed miserably, on the (internal) people side of those sales efforts. The pressure from above to hit unrealistic sales targets, coupled with a complacent management team, created the perfect storm for bad (sales) behavior. If you have a situation arise like Wells Fargo did in the **Optimize Sales** path and you ignore it, it can and will wipe out all of the efforts and progress you have made in the other paths.

- *Sometimes bad sales behavior follows bad sales management.* As leaders, it is our job to inspire people and help them realize ways that they can achieve their best performance. Overmanaging isn't one of those ways. Command and control tactics are bound to backfire, whether you are managing a team of two or a team of two thousand. The last-mile employees, those who are facing customers, are the voice of your brand.

PUTTING IT ALL TOGETHER

He don't put a bolt to a nut, he don't tell you the law or give you medicine. He's a man way out there in the blue, riding on a smile and a shoeshine. . . . A salesman is got to dream, boy. It comes with the territory.

—ARTHUR MILLER, *Death of a Salesman*

OPTIMIZING SALES IS THE DISCIPLINE of maximizing a sales team's performance by improving how it deploys its full set of available resources—systems, processes, people, technology, and capital—in closing the sale and then monetizing that customer relationship into the indefinite future. This requires perpetually assessing, rationalizing, evolving, and improving your company's sales operation and its underlying model, keeping it in lockstep with the customers you wish to serve.

At its core, sales is about relationships and trust. Ethics have become increasingly important to a company's reputation at a time when public opinion can go viral in an instant. Research from Mintel reveals that 56 percent of U.S. consumers stop buying from companies they believe are unethical. What's more, over one-third (35 percent) of consumers stop buying from brands they perceive as unethical even if there is no substitute available, and 27 percent stop purchasing even if they think the competitor offers lower quality. Overall, more than three in five consumers (63 percent) feel that ethical issues are becoming more important. If that doesn't reinforce how important it is to ensure that your sales teams are trained on best practices and ethical practices, I don't know what would.

There are entire books written on how to improve sales performance, and there is no way this one chapter could ever do this topic justice. The goal is to stimulate thinking about what you have at your current disposal and how this path is a critical "sequence" play. *The other paths will be far more difficult to execute if your selling function is ineffective.*

How can you sell more to your existing base if your resources are only compensated to sell to net new customers? How can you expand into new markets if you can't afford to hire more salespeople or recruit new partners? How can you build a profitable business if it costs you more to acquire a customer than the money you earn from selling your products?

While cost of sales is just one metric used to understand and analyze the health of a business, it also may be the most critical one. The modern buyer has wreaked havoc on the sales function, just like on every other part of twenty-first-century business. Whether it is business-to-business (B2B) or B2C, there is little that hasn't been impacted by digital technology. Even with all of the new capabilities at the fingertips of sales (social selling, Salesforce, LinkedIn, mobile phones), salespeople still struggle to "hit quota."

Despite all of the technology and training advancements, on average, only 50 percent of sales representatives met or exceeded quota. Furthermore, the average quota attainment still hovers around 60 percent—yes, that's right: *less than two-thirds of target is reached.* Most salespeople don't wake up every morning and think, "I'm going to shoot for hitting 60 percent of my quota." By nature, salespeople are highly competitive and expect to deliver their commitments every day, week, month, and quarter. *Even the best-laid plans don't guarantee success.* It's crazy to think that this statistic hasn't moved much over the past decade. While it hasn't gotten worse, by no means has it gotten much better.

WHAT WORKS—AND POTENTIAL PITFALLS

What if you could flip a switch and get your entire team to hit 100 percent of the assigned quota. Would your company grow? Of course it would.

So why is it that the level of rigor and planning that goes into sales improvements tends to be woefully inadequate compared with the rest of the business?

There is much discussion in those meetings about the revenue goals and expected growth in a given year. But that is the easy part, the "*what*" we are committing to. What's hard is the "how" we are going to get it done. Each growth path outlined in this book has the opportunity to improve growth in and of itself. Each will have a much greater impact if strong sales performance is combined with it. Would you ever allow your accounts receivable department to collect only 60 percent of the outstanding invoices? Would it be okay if your customer service department answered only 60 percent of all incoming calls? What if your products only worked 60 percent of the time? My guess: there's no way that would ever fly. Each alone could negatively impact growth. All together, it would be catastrophic.

Pause and consider—if you aren't selling anything, there are no products to "work," no accounts receivable to collect, no customers to call in. *The gasoline that powers a business is sales.* Without customers, you have no business. Without sales, you have no customers. So why would you ever accept substandard performance from your sales operation?

Improving sales performance, even by a small margin, can have a significant impact. If you have a large sales force, moving those middle performers even 2 to 5 percentage points higher in quota attainment can have a massive impact. Let's say you have one hundred salespeople. Each is expected to sell $1 million a year (for a total of $100 million) and today, to use the previous statistic, you are only able to achieve an average of about $75 million annually. If you could improve the average by, say, only 5 or 10 percent—you could add another $4.5 million to $9 million to the top line.

Imagine that you have five hundred or one thousand salespeople. You quickly see the value of this (**Optimize Sales**) path. *Improving the performance of existing resources without adding even one more salesperson can produce incredible returns.*

COMBINATION: PATH 6—
Optimize Sales + Path 1—Customer Experience

Thanks to your new and more powerful customer profiling and analytics capabilities, you now understand your installed base better than ever before. Now is the time to take that knowledge and put it to work crafting a more customized, personalized, and enriched customer experience, both to grow the range of your offerings to them and to deepen their loyalty to your company.

COMBINATION: PATH 6—
Optimize Sales + Path 2—Customer Base Penetration

Once you become more effective and optimize sales, there's every reason to take your powerful new sales machine out on the road and test it. "Optimization," of course, implies that your prior sales operation was not operating at peak performance—and that means that you likely missed a lot of potential customers, and even entire submarkets of potential customers, in your current market. Now is the time to go after them—with the advantage that gaining additional revenue from the existing base will be a lot less expensive than prospecting for new customers in an entirely new market.

PATH 7

CHURN

CHURN

*The well-satisfied customer will bring the repeat sale
that counts.*

—J. C. PENNEY

MANAGING CHURN TO MAXIMIZE GROWTH

- A 5 percent increase in customer retention can increase a company's profitability by 75 percent.
- Sixty-seven percent of consumers cite bad experiences as reason for churn and 11 percent of customer churn could be prevented by simple company outreach.
- Forty-two percent of companies invest in customer experience to improve customer retention.
- Retailers and publishers that increased their spending on retention in the last one to three years had nearly a 200 percent higher likelihood of increasing their market share in the last year over those spending more on acquisition.
- CMOs invested two-thirds of their budget in 2017–18 to support customer retention and growth.

MANAGE CHURN TO MAXIMIZE GROWTH

In 2001, I was an executive at one of the largest shared Web hosting companies in the United States (Interland, now Web.com), responsible for both sales and customer service. We were early in what is now known as the "cloud, infrastructure-as-a-service (IaaS)" space providing hosting solutions (domain names, shared and dedicated hosting) to businesses of all sizes. At a little over $100 million in recurring revenue, we were a leader in the space. We were also fortunate to be the beta clients for some of the early technology enablement tools commonly used today, such as Eloqua and Constant Contact. Being that we had 100 percent of our revenue tied to monthly recurring revenue (MRR) or annual recurring revenue (ARR), we knew all too well that _keeping our customers was just as important as gaining new ones_. We, of course, tracked the typical sales, marketing, and customer service metrics, but the first KPI we discussed at each quarterly review was *churn*.

> *Before going too wide, start with understanding your existing users: who is the high value highly loyal consumer that you would like to go after? . . . The smarter you are higher up in the funnel, the stronger you will be lower down in driving engagement, retention and ultimately lifetime value.*
>
> **—MAYUR GUPTA, global VP for growth and marketing at Spotify**

For many of us, it was uncharted territory and we were learning as we went along. All of our efforts on reducing acquisition costs, success in driving traffic to our website, and innovative solutions were for naught if we couldn't keep our customers long enough to make our acquisition cost back and turn a profit (per customer). It was my first exposure to lifetime value (LTV) and customer lifetime value (CLV). Unfortunately,

> **Customer churn rate is a metric that measures the percentage of customers (within the total customer base) who end their relationship with a company in a particular period."**
>
> **–JILL AVERY, Harvard Business School**
>
> **Companies typically track three churn metrics: customer churn, gross-revenue churn, and net-revenue churn. The most comprehensive of these three metrics is net-revenue churn, as it captures both the dollar value lost from churning customers and the dollar value gained from expansion revenue (which comes from both up-selling and cross-selling to existing customers).**
>
> **—McKinsey Report**

> In April 2017, subscription company websites had about thirty-seven million visitors. Since 2014, that number has grown 800 percent. Companies like Ipsy, Blue Apron, Dollar Shave Club, Home Chef, Stitch Fix, and Birchbox are some of the top subscription sites.

back then those LTV metrics were largely managed on Excel spreadsheets and Post-it notes—not ideal, to say the least, when you are trying to understand the account-level behavior of thousands of customers. We were trapped by limited technology capabilities, not by our lack of desire to gain a greater understanding of our business drivers. The reality was, we were more reactive than proactive or predictive.

Fast-forward sixteen years, with the proliferation of the Internet and cloud-based services and mobile apps—*there is now a more broad-based shift from a pay-per-product model to a more predictable subscription-based model.* Cloud services are probably the most often cited example of this shift. Gartner predicted that by 2020, more than 80 percent of software vendors will change their business model from traditional license and maintenance to subscription (software as a service [SaaS]). Beyond software, you may be noticing providers of utilites, financial services, education, farming, health care, and more, expanding into recurring services.

Even the prosaic razor has been transformed from a single transaction to a monthly subscription, with Dollar Shave Club (acquired by Unilever in 2016 for $1 billion). Welcome to the subscription economy and welcome to the importance of managing and controlling churn rates!

Whenever you can inspire a customer to join something and become part of your club, the concept of automatic recurring monthly billing is virtually assumed. Many industries have realized that a recurring revenue model is a better way to buy and sell for both consumers and businesses. Consumers get what they want, when they want it, for a price they expect, and are willing to pay for. This is one of the main reasons why subscription-based models are being applied everywhere as companies strive to build greater predictability into their business and cash flow. Plus, for those that are publicly traded, having recurring revenue is extremely attractive to investors and Wall Street.

However, *while the shift to this business model has lots of upside, it has also opened the door for an entirely new way in which companies can face an unexpected growth stall, even when the top line happens to be growing.* While that may sound counterintuitive, it is entirely possible that you can be growing your top line (getting more new customers in the door) with highly effective sales and marketing efforts, even though you are losing existing customers via churn after the fact. According to a 2015 study the average Google Play mobile app lost 77 percent of its daily active users within three months after "download"—and a whopping 95 percent of daily users within ninety days. There is no way to acquire and keep every single customer, but if you don't manage the balance between the two, it is entirely possible to put your company into a growth stall if churn wipes out all the gains you are realizing in sales growth. *That's why focusing only on top-line growth (customer acquisition) and not on the full lifetime of a customer, especially in a subscription business, is a recipe for disaster.*

When we discussed the **Customer Base Penetration** path, I talked about how companies put in disproportionate effort toward acquiring new customers and not in retaining those they already have. Some of it is internal inertia. Some of it is lack of understanding of the current state of churn in the business. Either way, as a result of not focusing on keeping the customers you already have and not working to reduce defection, churn leads to untold hidden revenue losses.

Managing churn as a growth strategy is understandably tricky, especially because it tends to be more of a defensive strategy. The very idea of reducing churn implies that you must be doing something wrong (the cause) to begin with to bring about customer defection (the effect)—if customers were thrilled with your product or service, there would be no risk of churn in the first place. It's the breakup we don't see coming (if only we'd seen the signs sooner!), and it hurts our businesses and our egos. *But churn is rarely caused by a single trigger.* If you are able to examine the timing and causes of customer defection (via your technology investments), you can come up with solutions that can stop churn in its tracks (and even reverse it).

Calculating churn for nonrecurring revenue business is a bit trickier but doable, and well worth the effort. For example, if a company knows (via data in its CRM system) that most of its customers who will make a repeat purchase do so within ninety days of their last purchase, it may choose to mark any customer who has not made a purchase in that time period as "churned." Whether you are a subscription or non-subscription-based business, maintaining a handle on your defectors (your churn rate) will help ensure the long-term growth and health of your business. *In retail, for example, returning shoppers spend a whopping 67 percent more than new ones.* Have you ever seen a cellular commercial where the provider offers up an amazing deal to "new customers only" and not to you, its current customer? What does that say about what they think about you? Does that provider value you or only the new account? This is not to say that sellers shouldn't go out and get new customers. But if you can extend the lifetime value (LTV) of the customers you have—and get them to buy more frequently—you can build a more effective growth business. *Churn is inevitable*: even if you don't lose customers to competitors, you will eventually lose them to other factors, including changing lifestyle, cultural shifts, and technological innovation. Therefore, *the goal is to minimize the "controllable" churn as much as you can.*

Why is the **Churn** growth path important? The proof is in the results. Management teams at companies that focus on retention are twice as likely to understand the impact of customer lifetime value (CLV) on revenue and growth. *In addition, companies focused on retention are nearly 50 percent more likely to consider projected long-term profitability growth when making decisions about customer strategy.*

Mayur Gupta, Spotify's global VP for growth and marketing, posits that churn can result from a "fragmented tunnel mindset [where] acquisition is assigned to a 'media team' that is measured on cost per action (CPA), the rate and volume of acquisition . . . [meanwhile] retention is managed by a separate team, or teams, across CRM, product management, lifecycle marketing and so on." Gupta advocates a more holistic approach to combatting churn, "controlling it all the way from awareness to acquisition and retention." This example wasn't about the products Spotify was developing, it wasn't about its customer service, it wasn't about its customer segment—it was about its organizational structure and the metrics used to manage every team. If functions are managed by different leaders, and metrics pull each group in a different direction, the result is a fragmented process.

PATH 7 CHURN

STORY

1

SPOTIFY
WINNING PLAYLIST

We don't think of people leaving the service as churn.

**—ROGER LYNCH, CEO of Pandora
and former CEO of Sling TV**

AFTER A DECADE OF DECLINE, the U.S. music industry is expected to see a compound annual growth rate of 4 percent from 2016 to 2021, led by the adoption of streaming services. This is a far cry from the doom-and-gloom predictions between 1999 into 2001, when Napster hit the scene and all but disrupted an entire industry into obscurity. In 2018, revenue in the "music streaming" segment amounts to $64 billion and is expected to show a growth rate (CAGR 2018–22) of 5.5 percent, resulting in $7.9 billion in 2022. User penetration is expected to hit 50 percent in 2022, providing lots more room for growth.

Sweden-based start-up Spotify launched for public access in October 2008 and had momentum like no other digital music service to date. As of January 2018, the music, podcast, and video streaming service had more than 140 million active monthly users and 70 million subscribers (up 20 million from the year before), triple that of Apple's music service.

In its most recently published financials, the company enjoyed more than $3 billion in revenue. Not bad for a company with a business model few people thought would work, after the challenges Napster faced when it hit the scene in the early 2000s. The key? *Spotify figured out not only how to grow its paying customer base but how to control its churn at the same time.* According to its SEC filing, Spotify's churn rate among premium subscribers was 5.1 percent in Q4 2017, a decrease from 6 percent in Q4 2016, and 7.5 percent in Q4 2015. The good news is that its churn rate is steadily decreasing, even as its user base continues to grow. Spotify is in one of the most competitive (consumer subscription) markets right now, going up against two of the largest brands in the world—Apple Music and Amazon. There was even a third competitor, Microsoft, with its Groove service. However, at the end of 2017, Microsoft closed its music store and streaming service and moved customers over to Spotify.

> *You never get a second chance to make a good first impression.*
> **—WILL ROGERS, actor**

So, what has made Spotify so successful? It's business concept was simple. The idea was that once you drove users onto the platform via a "freemium model"—like what Salesforce did in its early years—paid for by advertising revenue, and they saw the value of the service firsthand, they would be more willing to upgrade to a subscription-based, advertising-free service. Users would be able to search a seemingly endless supply of songs by artist, genre, album, even label, as well as share playlists on social media. And they could listen to the music for free in exchange for also listening to occasional advertisements, which today accounts for the quantity of content—Spotify offers access to more than thirty million songs.

This freemium model was nothing new to the music industry. After all, for nearly a century radio stations had employed this strategy of offering listeners free music that was subsidized by advertisements. Thus, for most users, using Spotify was anything but a radically new experience—it was comfortably like the radio experience they all knew . . . with the added appeal of letting them choose the music they wanted to hear.

In other words, by being ubiquitous, free, and familiar, Spotify made

"Freemium," a portmanteau of "free" and "premium," refers to products or services that a company gives away free of charge, then charges customers for additional features or continued use.

Spotify

LAUNCHED FOR PUBLIC ACCESS IN 2008 → IN JAN 2018 → 140 MILLION ACTIVE MONTHLY USERS

70 MILLION SUBSCRIBERS

CUSTOMER BASE PENETRATION

OFFER → TO GET VALUE

FREEMIUM

CONVERTED free USERS INTO PAID CUSTOMERS BY CREATING A MEMORABLE ONBOARDING EXPERIENCE

adoption almost barrier-free. Millions of customers responded. That was just the bait to hook potential customers to the service. Spotify cultivated loyalty by delivering a highly differentiated **Customer Experience**, through its curated playlists and personalized music recommendations. This encouraged users to spend more time on the service and eventually switch from the freemium offering to paying $9.99 a month to listen to music advertisement-free. Its ability to use **Customer Base Penetration** to convert free users into paid customers has been impressive—which is why Spotify's revenues jumped 80 percent between 2014 and 2015.

PLUG THE LEAKY BUCKET

Getting customers to pay is one thing. Keeping them paying is another. Spotify applied another industry's (cellular carriers) standard practice by using term contracts to "lock in" customers. That strategy not only helps stabilize revenue, but Spotify used it as another value-based addition to its service, a lateral **Product Expansion**, if you will. If you committed to a two-year contract, for example, you were protected from any price increases. Good for Spotify. Good for its customers.

Additionally, part of the attraction of Spotify's pricing model is that it has offered a range of price points for differentiated products, allowing its customers to decide what is best for them and their budget. That **Product Expansion** effort has resulted in reaching a wider range of customers, extracting value from those most willing to pay for a "premium" service, and even giving its customers an option to "downgrade" to a less expensive service. While this may sound like Spotify was doing the unthinkable—cannibalizing its own customer base—it was a great way to avoid customer churn altogether. A lower rate is better than having them go back to the free service.

*Here is an example of using the **Churn** path not as a "defensive" strategy but as an offensive strategy.* The alternative to this approach would have been to design a marketing "win-back" campaign, then wait until a customer leaves (churns), have customer service call or e-mail the customer—and then offer a discounted monthly subscription. The message that approach sends is: you can get a better rate, but only if you try to leave—which doesn't present a great customer experience. Instead, Spotify was proactively, preemptively getting ahead of the effect of customers wanting to pay less—and leaving.

Spotify has also invested heavily in customer service to ensure, if customers have issues, that they are resolved quickly, especially if they are shared on social media. Scaling this kind of model can be difficult, but Spotify has cut no corners in this area.

"Scaling Spotify's support function to match the customer base has been one of the biggest challenges of the last four and a half years of my life! When I started at Spotify [years] ago we had around eighty advisors, and the social team in its initial formation was like ten. Today the total number of advisors is well over one thousand and the social team is over two hundred," says Chug Abramowitz, vice president of customer support and social media and marketing at Spotify.

Like both PayPal and LEGO, if you want to pursue a particular growth path, you must ensure that you have the right organizational structure in place to support the effort; otherwise you might have the right strategy but it fails under the weight of internal dysfunction. This example wasn't about the products Spotify was developing, it wasn't about its customer service, it wasn't about its customer segment—it was about its organizational structure and the metrics used to manage each team. If functions are managed by different leaders, and metrics pull each group in a different direction, the result is a less-than-memorable experience for customers.

OFFER VALUE TO GET VALUE

Price is what you pay, value is what you get.

—BENJAMIN GRAHAM,
author of *The Intelligent*
Investor

Spotify has not only done a brilliant job of attracting new freemium and paid customers, but it has also reduced the churn of its entry-level customers by offering a free product so appealing that those customers stick around almost indefinitely . . . until they become so acculturated to the service that they are more willing to pay the fee to take the experience to the next level. Why? Because its conversion rate is about 27 percent from free to paying customers. So the more new customers it gets, the more paying customers it will enjoy. In other words, Spotify not only has figured out how to cast a very wide net to pull in prospective customers, but then also has a long test period to prequalify its most loyal users to determine how best to monetize the relationship over time.

One of the biggest challenges the company faces with these first-stage customers is to offer sufficient added value (such as exclusive artist content) to the subscription service to make the jump to subscription seem worth the price.

So far, Spotify has accomplished that by taking advantage of both technology (it offers a higher bit density, and thus higher-quality sound for subscribers) and content (removal of advertising) offering product and up-selling its massive customer base with other products and services. In November 2017, Spotify extended its merchandising **Partnerships** with its artists to allow them to sell products such as makeup via its arrangement with Merchbar. Although it will not earn direct revenue from this, the idea, instead, is to sweeten the deal for artists and give them more opportunities to make money via the platform and connect with their fans in multiple ways on Spotify. It will also get its subscribers coming back to do more on the platform (**Customer and Product Diversification**) than just listen to music, remaining sticky on both sides of its marketplace—ultimately another way to reduce churn.

These efforts, in combination, help Spotify differentiate itself from the likes of Apple Music, which is entering into exclusive deals with artists. Yet even as Spotify surpasses 170 million monthly active users, which includes 75 million paid subscribers, 99 million ad-supported monthly active users, and $5 billion in revenue, controlling churn will be critical to Spotify's long-term viability and profitability. Controlling **Churn** for Spotify means optimizing **Customer Experience**, offering greater product and service variety (**Product Expansion**) and fewer restrictions than its competitors, especially with its stated 10–20 percent YoY "fast growth mode."

SPOTIFY
KEY TAKEAWAYS

While it's impossible to eliminate churn entirely, it is possible to reduce it. There are three key actions Spotify did that help them manage and reduce the likelihood of churn:

- A good first impression is key. Whether you're on a date, at a job interview, or browsing Spotify for the next song to listen to, first impressions count a lot. When onboarding new customers, you should make it seamless, giving them a quick overview of your product and getting them started (using it) right away. This is critical. If you can get new customers to start using your product immediately after purchase, they are more likely to better understand all you have to offer, making your product much more desirable and hopefully indispensable. And if you can do that, you'll naturally reduce churn—proactively, I might add.

- Offer great value for the price. Value doesn't have to mean free or discounted offerings. Knowing your customers and their buying and usage habits can help you personalize the way you communicate to them and make them feel valued. Fifty-three percent of consumers want a totally personalized experience, in addition to instant savings and rewards based on past purchases. Customers now provide so much data to marketers and brands through online subscription services that they want something significant in return.

- Set, meet, and exceed customer expectations. One of the main reasons customers churn is because the product or service doesn't deliver on their expectations. As you have read in the previous chapters, customer expectations are increasing for both the brands they choose to do business with and the products they buy. Another great way to reduce churn is always to strive to meet or exceed these high expectations. Do that thing that makes your customers feel special or go the extra mile. Sometimes it doesn't require much, but it makes a huge difference when it comes to churn.

NETFLIX
TWENTY YEARS OLD (AND COUNTING)

There's no business like show business.

—IRVING BERLIN in *Annie Get Your Gun*

CCORDING TO CNBC, NETFLIX WAS one of the market's best-performing stocks of 2017. It brought in 8.3 million new streaming subscribers—including almost 2 million in the United States for the fourth quarter of 2017. Netflix expects the momentum to continue. For the first quarter of 2018, the company is forecasting 6.35 million new streaming customers (versus 5 million in the year-ago quarter), comprising 1.45 million domestically and 4.9 million internationally. Netflix has also announced that it will ratchet up marketing spending more than 50 percent in 2018, increasing it from $1.3 billion to $2 billion.

It has by far the greatest reach of all of the various streaming services in the United States, with Amazon reaching only half as many households as Netflix. It has grown steadily both its domestic and international

At the beginning of 2017, 19 percent of all broadband households and 29 percent of households subscribing to an over-the-top (OTT) video service had canceled one or more services within the past year.

subscribers over the past ten years and, in the process, has pioneered an entirely new way of delivering entertainment: *streaming OTT*.

Having a customer base the size of Netflix's has its advantages, but it can also plateau the growth of a subscription business if you don't keep churn under control. Losing 5 percent of your customer base when you have 1,000 customers means that the first 50 new customers you acquire only gets you back to even. When you have 104 million subscribers, as Netflix does, losing 5 percent of your customer base to churn means that it will take you 5 million new customers to just break even. What complicates matters even further for Netflix is that as Apple, Amazon, and Disney enter the streaming entertainment business, customers have more options to choose from, which increases both the cost of customer acquisition and the volume of "brand switching."

Parks Associates research shows that more than 50 percent of U.S. OTT subscription households subscribe to multiple video services. Of these, 81 percent use Netflix plus some other services or combination of services, typically Amazon or Hulu. To put that 81 percent number into perspective, there are over one hundred OTT video services available in the U.S. market as of March 2016. So, having that kind of dominance is a huge advantage Netflix doesn't want to squander. While that level of market share is an advantage, it also means that Netflix and its customer base becomes a prime target for the totality of the competition, looking to outmaneuver Netflix on quality, products, and price.

The nature of subscription video-on-demand services like Netflix, Hulu, HBO Now, and others makes it easy to cancel. Even if you've had Netflix for years and decide to leave for a few months (**Churn**), you can pick them back up easily at any time with the click of a mouse. Parks Associates also found that, apart from Netflix and Amazon Prime, OTT services are experiencing churn rates exceeding 50 percent of their subscriber base (both free and paying customers), whereas Netflix, Amazon, and Hulu have actually continued to reduce their churn rates. *This industry is a bit unusual because it has customers who simultaneously have multiple for-fee and free services in the same category*, with 63 percent of households subscribing to five or more services. So, while some of the churn is natural for those trying out the service and choosing not to upgrade to the fee-based service, the rest may in fact be due to paying customers switching providers.

How can a company build stronger brand loyalty and fend off competition when customers are perfectly happy using multiple providers, all for the same type of service, and they have a low barrier or no barrier to switching? Answer: *provide an original and unique product, keep customers from going elsewhere or leaving altogether (churning). How? For Netflix, it's content.*

HOUSTON, WE HAVE A SOLUTION: ORIGINAL CONTENT

Netflix plans to spend $8 billion to make its library 50 percent original by 2018.

When it comes to acquiring subscribers and keeping them, it appears that Netflix has found the right combination of product, quality, and price. Even as its business transitioned from DVDs via mail to online streaming, it has been able to stay in front of changing market context. Most of the company's recent growth has come from new subscribers as they pursued **Market Acceleration** across the 190 or so countries that it entered in 2016 alone and **Customer and Product Diversification** as it further develops original content. Netflix saw a 49 percent year-over-year increase in global subscribers, including 850,000 in the United States, taking its global total to 104 million during the third quarter of 2017. Both of those results are a testament of Netflix's comprehensive efforts aimed at acquiring new customers and keeping engagement high, price for value in line, and churn low.

What makes Netflix a "must-have" for so many households is its investment in original programming with a long-term goal of ensuring that nearly 50 percent of the content streamed on its platform will be original. From *House of Cards, Orange Is the New Black*, and its recent blockbuster grab—persuading Shonda Rhimes to leave Disney/ABC for an overall deal at Netflix—it now says it will spend $7 billion to $8 billion on (all) content in 2018.

Netflix was the top-earning app of 2017 that wasn't a mobile game, according to Sensor Tower's new year-end report on the most successful apps and publishers across Apple's App Store and Google Play.

NETFLIX has the right combination of

104 MILLION SUBSCRIBERS ACROSS 190 COUNTRIES

PRODUCT
QUALITY
PRICE

EVEN WHEN ← BUSINESS TRANSITIONED FROM DVD's TO ONLINE VIA MAIL STREAMING

By comparison, Amazon is expected to spend $4.5 billion and HBO spent $2 billion in 2016. Netflix believes "its future largely lies in exclusive original content." Switching becomes tough if you love a show on Netflix, or Drake on Apple Music. There is no question that Netflix will need its head start, because Disney recently announced plans to start its own streaming service, acquired a majority stake in BAMTech, another streaming and marketing service, and decided to end its partnership (for a subset of its content) with Netflix in 2019.

CONTROLLING CHURN

Customers choosing to leave your service because they just *don't want the kind of product you are selling* anymore is one thing. Customers *switching to another provider* for the same or similar service is a completely different challenge. And customers leaving you *because you discontinue the service* they were using, which is totally self-inflicted churn, is another. Netflix is facing all three of these challenges. Netflix Q1 2018 results showed noticable improvements in reducing churn rates between Q1 2017 and

Q3 2017 by 3.2 percent. However, as a direct result of a 10 percent price hike, overall churn rates increased by 1.9 percent . . . to 9.7 percent.

So far, the results from the effort to expand its product to include even more original content seems to be paying off. However, it doesn't come without some level of risk for future churn. Netflix has acquired customers since it began on a robust library and catalog of "other people's content"—that was its value proposition, which means that it must be careful not to alienate the subset of customers who don't want to watch original content. Just as when it expanded beyond DVDs in the mail to streaming, not all customers wanted to make the shift.

As a matter of fact, nearly four million people in the United States still subscribe to Netflix DVDs by mail. Even though the DVD service has lost nearly ten million subscribers over the past five and a half years, Netflix keeps it around because it remains tremendously profitable. The company makes an operating profit of roughly 50 percent on DVD subscriptions alone and doesn't even have a marketing budget dedicated to this business. In many ways, the DVD business has funded Netflix growth, both with international (**Market Acceleration**) and original content (**Product Expansion**). Unfortunately, there is no way to know how many of those ten million DVD subscribers that churned are now Netflix streaming customers. That puts pressure on Netflix to continue adding good content, including licensed Hollywood content and original shows, to keep subscribers happy. It will be the right mix of original programming and popular licensed content that will be critical for Netflix's growth strategy, both for top-line revenue and the reduction of churn.

NETFLIX
KEY TAKEAWAYS

- Price hikes don't always increase churn if the perceived customer value remains intact. You must be very careful not to use price increases to mitigate revenue loss because of churn. Otherwise you will find yourself creating an even greater trigger for churn.

- Offensive and defensive ways to mitigate churn: In any (monthly) subscription service, each new month gives Netflix subscribers a chance to cancel the service. The best thing Netflix can do to proactively keep customers and make them reluctant to leave or "switch" is to offer great content that people are willing to pay for. It does that by offering both licensed (via **Partnerships**) and original content.
- Netflix's churn playbook: Incentivize customer to commit to longer subscriptions with price breaks, always give your subscribers something they can't get anywhere else, leverage viewer data to provide a more personalized experience, and focus on your active subscribers—don't just chase new ones.
- When you pursue a **Product Expansion** growth strategy, you may in fact disrupt your current product with the new product. As Netflix expanded its offerings from DVD in the mail to online streaming, the latter absolutely disrupted the former. But as the context of the market changed, and customer entertainment habits shifted to mobile, Netflix was willing to lose 10 million subscribers in order to build a base of 104 million subscribers.
- Although it wasn't covered in this story, Netflix uses subscriber insights and preferences to help it shape which products and services to offer next. Its recommendation engine rivals Amazon's. It would be safe to say that its most powerful and competitive weapons are the insights delivered by big data to help it achieve greater customer engagement and retention. Without the data, the **Optimize Sales**, **Customer Base Penetration**, **Market Acceleration**, **Churn**, and **Customer and Product Diversification** paths all become much less effective.

STORY

3

BLUE APRON
TOO MUCH ON THE PLATE

Consumer preferences for food have changed . . .
changed radically. I call them seismic shifts.
—DENISE MORRISON, CEO of Campbell Soup Company

HOME-DELIVERED "MEAL KITS" ARE FORECASTED to have an annual growth rate of 25 to 30 percent over the next five years and become a $2.2 billion business—but that's still just a rounding error in the multitrillion-dollar food industry. Blue Apron didn't invent the ingredient-and-recipe meal kit service industry, but it drove it into the public's consciousness and took off on an impressive growth run. Unfortunately, that initial success masked a problem with customer defection—churn—that unexpectedly tripped up the company just as it was celebrating early victory.

Blue Apron was founded in August 2012 from a commercial kitchen in Long Island, New York. Working from the notion that the market context was shifting due to the nexus of the Web; fast, modern delivery infrastructure; and a growing population of consumers wanting gourmet food at home, the company's three founders (CEO Matt Salzberg, Ilia Papas, and Matt Wadiak) devised, packaged, and shipped bundles of ingredients and suggested recipes that consumers could cook by hand to create superior meals.

Blue Apron took off like wildfire—and within four years the company had shipped eight million meals. By that point, Blue Apron had grown sufficiently large to open its own fulfillment centers in Richmond, California (to serve the West Coast), Jersey City, New Jersey (the East), and Arlington, Texas (the rest of the United States). A fourth center, in Linden, New Jersey, was announced in early 2017.

In November 2014, in a quick shift (and in hindsight, maybe a premature move) to a new growth path, Blue Apron also began to pursue a classic **Customer and Product Diversification** strategy—opening Blue Apron Market, a cookware, merchandise, and cookbook store, and Blue Apron Wine, a subscription service that delivered to users six bottles of wine per month—to maximize customer acquisition cost by offering its existing base of subscribers more products to purchase. But was it too much too fast? As might be expected, there were setbacks: some health and safety violations at the Richmond plant reduced customer (experience) satisfaction because delivery times weren't met as promised, which could be blamed on the rush of such rapid growth. But all in all, Blue Apron seemed unstoppable.

It came as no surprise that on June 29, 2017, Blue Apron went public—thirty million shares that opened at $10 per share were sold. That made it the first public company dedicated to meal kit delivery—and worth an estimated $3 billion. The future seemed bright indeed.

That's when the dark clouds appeared. The first cloud came in the company's first IPO quarterly financials. The company reported revenues of $238.1 million, better than market expectations—yes, but it also suffered a loss of $0.47 a share, versus the Street's prediction of a loss of $0.30 a share.

Clearly something was wrong. By September, the stock price was off nearly 50 percent and hovering around $5 per share. Why the plunge? Two reasons: competition and *churn*. In the words of *Techcrunch*, investors were "concerned about customer retention and the looming threat of Amazon." Suddenly Blue Apron found itself hit by a class-action "stock drop" lawsuit—making three main claims:

1. The company had cut its advertising just before the IPO, damaging revenues;
2. Problems with the Linden, New Jersey, center had slowed deliveries; and the big one—

3. *The company was suffering diminishing customer retention—that is, greater churn—due to orders arriving late or incomplete.*

The first two could either be explained or fixed. But for many, the last was the kiss of death for a subscription-based business. *If you lose more customers than you gain each month, you don't have much of a business at all.*

According to an analysis, the company could lose 72 percent of its customers within six months, which puts a tremendous strain on the cost of acquiring new customers (CAC) fast enough and at an appropriate cost, especially in light of number 1 on that list above. As it stands, for Q4 2017, it reported 746,000 customers, down 15 percent versus a year earlier, and 13 percent from the prior quarter. In Q1 2018, customers decreased 24 percent YoY.

With revenues falling, the company was forced to institute a hiring freeze and, aggravating #1 in the class-action suit, further cut back on marketing, customer acquisition, and spending. In its latest earning, its marketing as a percentage of net revenue decreased as it continues to pull back on marketing. *This is a vicious cycle when churn gets out of control.* You end up cutting spending in areas such as marketing, sales, and customer service to save on costs, but those decisions will impact the company's top-line growth and put even further pressure on its stock price.

Going back to the premise of *Growth IQ*—it is never just one thing. *Diversifying and expanding a portfolio of products is a calculated risk,* but as is the case in many other examples you have seen thus far, *often companies forget about the interconnectedness of the decisions they make to other parts of the business.* In Blue Apron's case, the good news was that it was growing—the bad news was that it was growing so fast that it wasn't able to ensure that the rest of the company could keep pace. An example was when it announced the rollout of its expanded plan and menu options at the Linden facility it was opening.

At the time, it was only able to offer those new products to half of its customers, which negatively impacted the value of the monthly subscription. Since then, Blue Apron has completed the rollout, and now 100 percent of its customers have access to the expanded product offering. In its Q3 2017 earnings call, CEO Matt Salzberg said, "Our initial

FOUNDED IN AUG-2012

Blue Apron

HOME DELIVERED *meal kits*

GREW FAST TO OPEN ITS OWN FULFILLMENT CENTERS

CUSTOMER/ PRODUCT DIVERSIFICATION

OPENED **Blue Apron** *market*

COOKWARE, MERCHANDISE *and* COOKBOOK STORE

Blue Apron *wine*

A SUBSCRIPTION SERVICE FOR WINE

WENT PUBLIC IN JUNE 2017

IN SEP 2017

STOCK PRICE PLUNGED BY 50%

WHY?

COMPETITION *and* CHURN

GREATER CHURN

SLOWED DELIVERIES

CUT ITS ADVERTISING

indications, although early, show improvements in both order rate and retention when comparing customers who received the product expansion to those who had not yet received it." If products aren't consistent, if you don't meet and exceed customer expectations in a subscription business month after month, you will lose customers.

The fact that it had acquired so many customers so quickly should have been a huge competitive advantage. Why? It now had a base of customers that it could learn from. It could use purchasing habits, average sales price and "basket size," recipe choices, and average revenue per customer to help it design future products. Anticipating what your customers may want next has helped Netflix and Spotify stay ahead of churn and offensively mitigate customer defection. Blue Apron could have done the same thing, but didn't.

Meanwhile, attracted by Blue Apron's early success, the market was being flooded with other meal kit companies, including Chef'd, Hello Fresh, and Plated—while giants such as Unilever, Anheuser-Busch, and Coca-Cola were making investments in food-delivery service companies. Then, in the midst of all of this uproar, the biggest hit of all came: Amazon announced its purchase of Whole Foods.

Had Blue Apron used its early advantage to focus its attention on retaining its current customers, that is, reduced churn by developing a reputation for personalized, prompt, and quality service, instead of capturing new ones as quickly as possible, it might have found itself in a much more defensible position. In another move from Blue Apron as it tries to navigate its way back to profitability and growth, it replaced its CEO in December 2017, after reporting its third-quarter earnings.

BLUE APRON
KEY TAKEAWAYS

- Churn is the effect of decisions the company makes as it relates to product, product quality, customer service, customer experience, marketing, sales, and so on; it isn't just one thing. Blue Apron may have gotten too far ahead of itself. When it chose to move to a new highly automated facility, it caused the company's "On-Time, In-Full" (OTIF) rates to decline. That resulted in a cutback on marketing, so it wasn't onboarding more customers than it could handle, which resulted in slower new-customer growth. Put those two things together and you will find yourself in a growth stall, one because you aren't getting new customers, and two because customers you have are getting poor service and leaving. Now it has a brand perception problem and its competitors can market to Blue Apron's base and entice them to "switch."

- Instead of expanding its own distribution and taking on all of the associated expense to handle more customers, maybe it could have explored partnerships to outsource the fulfillment business. With tight quality controls in place, this may have given it the best of both worlds, allowing it to focus on what it did best—acquiring new customers, marketing, and selling—and letting someone else take over the logistics, which has proven to be challenging for it.

- With all of the expansion, Blue Apron left its core business exposed. Remember, *Growth IQ has three components: context, combination, and sequence.* Blue Apron was right on context and launched a product that the market and customers wanted. It could have done a better job on combination by ensuring that the internal infrastructure (people, systems, processes) could handle its rapid expansion, especially as it doubled down on **Product Expansion** and **Customer and Product Diversification**. Sequence is where it missed the mark completely. *Timing is everything,* and its push into new categories, new customer segments, new facilities, and new products for a new business proved too much to handle.

- As competition heats up in the meal delivery industry, the cost to keep customers loyal naturally is increasing, as is the cost of running the business. A company should take a bit more time to nurture its base, grow the average revenue per customer, and use customer purchasing patterns to learn what it should do next. Pulling back on expansion and focusing on what it currently has should be the focus. As you learned in **Customer Base Penetration**, it costs less to sell more to existing customers than to recruit new ones.

PUTTING IT ALL TOGETHER

The bitterness of poor quality remains long after the sweetness of low price is forgotten.

—ALDO GUCCI

IT MAY SOUND OBVIOUS, BUT the best way to beat churn is to never create it at all . . . *if only it were that easy.* Many struggle with figuring out how to acquire new customers while keeping current customers happy in order to minimize churn.

Over time, successfully navigating the **Churn** path can open the door to diversifying customer and product lines—as long as you don't do it to the detriment of service and **Customer Experience**, as was the case with Blue Apron. Measured moves are important in a subscription business. Churn can sneak up on you, forcing you to cut spending in areas you can't afford to cut.

The real power comes when companies begin to consider the long-term value of an acquired customer (LTV, CLV), not just the onetime sale. *Successful companies combine a focus on churn with a focus on LTV.* As big brands such as Adidas, with its Avenue A, Starbucks and its Reserve Roastery, and Procter & Gamble's Gillette on Demand continue to enter the new membership economy, there will be more and more focus on this particular path as another way to improve growth. *Before a business can fight churn, it's important to know why churn happens.*

The most basic cause is that the product isn't attractive, becomes less attractive over time, or loses value for the consumer. When consumers open their boxes and are underwhelmed by the product selection, are faced with lackluster quality, or discover that the price isn't worth the experience, logical subscribers will leave.

Another potential issue involves trial offers. We've all seen onetime trial subscription enticements offered for free or a steeply reduced price. The first order is a no-brainer for the customer and gets people to take the plunge. But is the actual product valuable enough, over time, to persuade customers to keep paying for future shipments at full price? About 80 percent of consumers should stay past the initial shipment. If the number dips significantly lower, the trial isn't inspiring members to remain for the next shipment. If you can't retain acquired customers, it puts an incredible strain on your sales and marketing efforts, especially the CAC.

Focusing on retaining existing customers offers the double benefit of lower costs and higher returns. The probability of converting a new customer falls in the 5–20 percent range; for existing customers, it's between 60 and 70 percent. Yet even with those numbers, 44 percent of companies still have a dominant focus on customer acquisition.

WHAT WORKS—AND POTENTIAL PITFALLS

An often-overlooked cause of churn is a company's inability to keep subscribers active when something goes wrong with their payment sources. Long-standing customers' credit cards can expire or be declined for multiple reasons, but that issue alone should not automatically make them miss a shipment or indicate that they don't want to continue the relationship. Sometimes bad things happen to good credit cards. Ultimately, churn is costly.

An unusually high churn rate will kill return on investment (ROI), making it tough for a company to recover losses from potentially higher acquisition costs. At the same time, when you experience a reasonable churn rate and the membership base stabilizes, you can expect significant cash flow from long-term subscribers. There will be recurring revenue and no acquisition cost against these cohorts.

If Netflix, Spotify, or another company with such a large customer base didn't spend any money to acquire more customers, reduced churn to 1 to 2 percent, and raised prices as custom content was targeted, while at the same time getting more free customers to upgrade, it would have a very profitable business. That is why recurring revenue businesses cost more to acquire (Dollar Shave Club: $1 billion), have higher valuations (recent IPO put StitchFix at a $1.4 billion valuation after only six years), and attract more investment. There is a point where additional sales and marketing spend is more of a science than an art.

COMBINATION: PATH 7—
Churn (Minimize Defection) + Path 6—
Optimize Sales Strategy

Reducing churn is, strictly speaking, less of an offensive growth strategy than a defensive one. You are working to preserve your current gains, not fighting to make future gains. Thus, it is an introverted strategy, not an aggressive one. It stands to reason that you can't just jump from reducing churn to, say, **Co-opetition** with your competitors. You need an intermediate step. And that is to once again turn your perspective outward, which means that you have to improve your sales operation.

This may surprise your salespeople. After all, they may say that they have been doing a great job at finding, qualifying, and closing new customers; that it is the company's fault if it hasn't been able to keep them. In some respects, that may be true. But even so, the fact that those customers were lost in churn suggests a general failure of perspective throughout the company. And now that the problem has been fixed, the successful processes and perspectives must be inculcated throughout the organization—and nowhere more than on the leading edge, in sales and customer service.

Inevitably, the sales force will need to see prospective customers differently, qualify them differently, and ultimately deliver a different group of new customers to the company. Otherwise, if the fight to reduce churn only occurs downstream, the company will continue to battle churn without much improvement. Ideally, changes in sales will start having an impact, churn will be reduced—and the company will be able to navigate on into the far more exciting paths of **Market Acceleration** and **Customer and Product Diversification** without the burden of losing customers unnecessarily.

Customer service is equally important, especially in a subscription business that "sells" online. Once customers purchase, any interaction they will have with the company going forward will be with customer service (billing and support). There are two sides to customer service as it relates to churn. One is when customers call in and have an issue. During those interactions, customers care about how quickly their issue is resolved, how long it takes to resolve it, and the "hassle level" of the time spent. This is where companies like Zappos have changed the game. Customer service and the people who work in that organization are the center of its success. They are empowered to do what's right by the customer first, expecting that the rest will follow.

The second side to customer service and churn is proactive communication with customers, anticipating their needs and predicting when they may need some help or want to purchase more from you. This latter example is where technology plays a huge role. _Don't forget that you can get in front of churn and create a more memorable experience that your customers can't get anywhere else._

The content streaming market is on an aggressive journey to transform the way we enjoy our favorite movies, music, and TV shows. The way service providers in this space interact with customers will go a long way in shaping future interactions between subscriber-based businesses and their customers. With the huge variety of choices available to customers, streaming service providers do not have any other options apart from upgrading their customer retention strategies. Retention is a direct result of an incredible customer experience and a quality product. Both are inherently linked, and neither exists alone. While this isn't the only combination path, I wanted to keep you focused on the one that can and will have the greatest impact. _If you are selling better, keeping and servicing your customers, churn may just take care of itself._

PATH8

PARTNERSHIPS

PARTNERSHIPS

Partnership is the way. Dictatorial win-lose is so old-school.

—ALANIS MORISSETTE

WHY PARTNERSHIPS MATTER

- Forty-eight percent of global CEOs plan to pursue a new strategic alliance to drive corporate growth or profitability.
- Organizations are increasingly leveraging partnerships to develop relationships for mutual gain, address business challenges, and drive bottom-line results.
- Two-thirds of CEOs expect to grow through collaboration.
- Eighty-five percent of business owners feel that strategic alliances are important or extremely important to their business, but most say that fewer than 60 percent of those partnerships are successful.

BETTER TOGETHER

In 1984, nineteen-year-old Michael Dell launched PC's Limited. He had funds totaling $1,000 and a game-changing vision for the technology industry. It began with a simple premise that challenged the status quo with its distinct supply-chain model and its sales of customized computers *directly* to customers to meet burgeoning PC demand. The context of the market was changing; consumers wanted a computer, not just at work but at home, too. Dell saw an opportunity and took it.

Fast-forward almost twenty years later to 2006—Dell found itself at a crossroads. It had used its direct sales philosophy, its focus on product development, customer experience, and culture as the blueprint for its success. Dell's revenue was $56 billion, it was shipping thirty-seven million systems worldwide, its **Market Acceleration** and **Customer and Product Diversification** strategies were in full swing, but the market context was once again shifting, impacting the prospect of future growth.

If you are not partnering, you are missing key opportunities to expand the brand.

—JOE GUITH,
president of Cinnabon

While Dell could still enjoy competitive advantage from customizing computers and selling them directly to consumers, the market for such offerings was beginning to contract, largely because customer needs and related supply-chain costs had shifted in the maturing PC business. What was needed now from Dell was a reevaluation of the way in which it went to market with its products. Selling directly to customers online had been the lifeblood of Dell, so much so that when Michael Dell wrote a book in 1999, he called it *Direct from Dell*, but the model was finally beginning to show its age.

In the spirit of full disclosure, I used to compete against Dell when I was hired to formally launch the indirect sales division at Gateway computers (2004–2006), right at the time when all of this was happening. We were facing the same dilemma at Gateway. There were 188 Gateway Stores across the United States that sold direct to consumers. If you wanted to buy a Dell computer, you had to do it through Dell online or over the phone. If you wanted to buy a Gateway computer, you could do it at a Gateway store, over the phone, or online. There were limited, at best, third-party "partnerships" available for customers to leverage. For both brands, it was time to move from direct sales to **Partnerships**, a hybrid model that would embrace both direct and value-added reseller (VAR) channels to more effectively compete against HP, Compaq, and IBM at the time. That is what both brands did. Gateway closed all 188 stores and instead chose to sell its products online and through other retailers—CompUSA and Best Buy. The move indicated Gateway's interest in leveraging partnerships and lowering operating costs to improve its competitiveness.

In 2007, Dell formally announced its PartnerDirect program. In a bit of competitive irony, I had since left Gateway and joined Gartner, where I was part of the advisory team that helped design and launch the Dell PartnerDirect program. I always knew that if Dell ever decided to make this shift, it would be a game changer, and it was. Dell technologies' global channel business is on a run rate to hit $43 billion under the newly formed Dell EMC partner program. While the Gateway story didn't end as well as it has for Dell, the moral of both of these stories is that *you must be willing to step outside your comfort zone when the customer and market context change—and partnerships can be one of those ways.*

TRUST, FAIRNESS, AND MUTUAL BENEFIT

The tenets of an effective partnership are trust, fairness, and mutual benefit to both parties. Companies can't always go it alone. The Internet's global expansion is entering a new phase, and it looks decidedly unlike the last one. New competitors and potential partners are ubiquitous. The next billion people who come online will avoid text, use voice activation, and communicate with images. They will come online for the first time thanks to low-end smartphones, cheap data plans, and apps allowing them to learn about products, services, and brands to shop in entirely new ways.

The response to all the changes in the market, in industries, and in consumer behavior requires businesses to work together much more closely than they have in the past, especially considering all of the advances in technology and new competitive threats. This is why partnerships have become so popular in recent years, squarely focused on additional avenues of growth, market coverage, and sales and marketing collaborations.

While partnering sounds great in concept, it often gets a bad rap for adding complexity to an already complex operation. You need to deal, intimately, with outsiders from another corporate culture. Executives worry it will cut into their potential margin and earning potential or that you give up some control and ownership of the customer relationship. Why do it?

The simple answer is that *rarely is a company able to do everything on its own*. Partnerships, collaboration, co-branding, strategic alliance—pick your term—can provide an important piece to the growth puzzle. If you choose to expand to a new region, you must ask yourself which would be more effective: hire a sales team, diverting marketing resources, leasing distribution facilities, and so on, in an expensive months-long effort, with a high risk of failure, or partner with a local company to augment its corporate-based efforts and to experiment with a new growth path without heavy capital investments?

The answer should be obvious. For example, an established company looking to expand into a new international market (**Market Acceleration**) would be starting from scratch if it pursued that strategy on its own. It may not want to take on too much initial risk, so it decides to partner with an independent local distributor who handles sales and maybe even marketing in country. Why? Because the local distributor has unique expertise and knowledge of the market context and understands the needs and wants of those local customers far better than the established company does. Plus, it already has the built-in advantage of a customer base.

When used correctly, partnerships can help companies avoid the costs and risks of entering new markets or going after new types of customers, and they can accelerate returns on investment in expansion efforts. *The result: both parties reap the benefits of the partnership.* However, don't kid yourself and underestimate what is required of your company if you choose to pursue this path.

Partnerships are more than a loose arrangement between two companies. *Partnerships should be proactive and have well-thought-out arrangements between the companies, with clear expectations and measurable results.* It can't only be about avoiding risk or costs but rather about capitalizing on a unique opportunity. **Partnerships** should be used in combination with other growth paths such as **Customer Base Penetration, Market Acceleration,** and **Customer and Product Diversification**— with an eye on increasing the potential *joint* revenue opportunity by combining sales and marketing efforts focused on predetermined goals.

STORY

1

GOPRO
ADRENALINE JUNKIES

Partners have been, and will remain, at the heart of this company as long as I'm here.

—CHUCK ROBBINS, CEO of Cisco

I N THE FIFTEEN YEARS SINCE Nick Woodman developed the first GoPro prototype, he has gone from sleeping out of his 1971 Volkswagen Bus to one of the fastest-growing camera companies in the world. Between 2004, when he was selling GoPro cameras on the Home Shopping Network, and 2011, when the company sought its first round of venture financing, it underwent a series of strategic changes to increase sales. The moves included **Customer and Product Diversification**—introduction of video, wide-angle lens, high-definition, and key messaging adjustments; **Market Acceleration**—taking its existing products global; and **Partnerships**—establishing joint marketing initiatives with key brands.

Fast-forward more than a decade and GoPro is the global leader in manufacturing and selling mountable and wearable cameras and accessories. How were they able to accomplish that? There is no question that GoPro used many unusual tactics to grow the business, such as aggressive marketing and social media campaigns. However, *the real boost to its success was in its ability to respond to the changing market context*, which was increased access to Wi-Fi and cheaper bandwidth, combined with millions of smartphone users who wanted to create and share videos from anywhere, anytime. How well would GoPro have done if there were no YouTube or if there was only limited Internet access? *The company was in the right place at the right time, with the right product.*

It was 2011, and Cisco Systems discontinued their Flip camcorder, which was the market leader at the time. That led Best Buy, a large U.S. retailer, to scramble to backfill the product in its consumer electronics category. It decided to make a bet on GoPro, *which at the time was a ten-person company*—yes . . . only ten people. It was a big bet for both companies: Best Buy working with such a small supplier, and GoPro having to deliver large demand from a massive retailer like Best Buy.

But, as you might have guessed, the stars aligned, and GoPro became one of Best Buy's fast-growing partners. As part of its "Renew Blue" strategy launched in 2012, Best Buy was very focused on "improving shoppers' perception of the store by building eye-catching merchandise displays," in hopes of increasing sales "by providing an experience that is unique to brick-and mortar channels."

GoPro merchandising was a perfect fit, and Best Buy's customers responded. They wanted to learn about the product, how to use it, and then purchase lots of accessories (similar to the Apple iPhone accessory windfall), but most notably, the new product provided Best Buy with an increased level of engagement and an enhanced **Customer Experience** from its existing base, at the same time attracting an entirely new demographic—extreme sports enthusiasts. The positive results, both for brand awareness and (sales) growth, built GoPro's partnering confidence—Best Buy would become the first of many.

Today, according to GoPro, its sales distribution channel *is one of its most valuable assets*. It does business with forty-five thousand retailers around the globe, which accounts for approximately 43 percent of its total revenue. But even after all of the subsequent partnerships, Best Buy remains its single largest partner, responsible for 17 percent of GoPro's 2016 revenue.

GoPro was experiencing enviable growth between 2011 and 2014. Revenue in 2011 was $234 million, 2012 $526 million, and 2013 $985 million. Then, in 2014, the company warned: "We do not expect to sustain or increase our revenue growth rates," suggesting that its sales growth had peaked—and it was right. GoPro found itself in a growth stall shortly after its IPO in June 2014. While its stock price initially shot up, slowing sales, failed ventures, and product issues hampered growth. But it was a series of partnering decisions, combined with shoring up its product issues, that helped GoPro get back on track.

> We've always felt a bit like Red Bull's younger brother.
>
> **—NICHOLAS WOODMAN,**
> **founder and CEO**
> **of GoPro**

According to Woodman, GoPro had been inspired by Red Bull—from producing action-packed videos to share on social media to sponsoring extreme sports events—but now, after years of an informal relationship, both companies decided it was time to make the relationship more formal.

In May 2016, in a deal that seemed surprising—and yet somehow perfect—camera maker GoPro and beverage giant Red Bull announced they were joining forces on a multiyear global partnership that included content production, distribution, cross-promotion, and product innovation.

The two companies found their common context in public events and their combination in attacking those events from different directions—beverages and image-capturing hardware. Remember, effective partnerships are built on trust, fairness, and mutual benefit—and this partnership had all the makings of a powerful combination.

> As partners, Red Bull and GoPro will amplify our collective international reach, the power of our content and the ability to fascinate.
>
> **—DIETRICH MATESCHITZ,**
> **founder and CEO**
> **of Red Bull**

An energy drink company and a portable digital camera company—odd couple? As this new co-branding, strategic partnership unfolded, the vision of the two firms emerged. The goal, seemingly, was to enhance the ability of both brands to create content to reach beyond their existing bases. For Red Bull, so dependent on its sports and adventure marketing, this meant a better presentation of those events. For GoPro, it got a crucial role in high-profile sporting events around the world—events it couldn't afford to get on its own.

These companies post content regularly on their YouTube channels, which is an important stat to review: between the two brands they have more than eleven million subscribers. On its fourth-quarter 2017 earnings call, GoPro even calls out social media statistics.

- GoPro gained more than 4.8 million new social media followers in 2017, growing its total following to 35 million across all platforms, a 16 percent increase.
- Instagram followers increased by 26 percent year over year in 2017, with the addition of 3 million followers, reaching a total of 15 million.
- GoPro content was viewed approximately 700 million times on social media platforms in 2017, up more than 25 percent year over year. GoPro content on YouTube saw a 93 percent increase in median organic viewership per video in 2017.

GoPro has made **Partnerships** a part of its growth equation for years. In 2014 it signed deals with BMW and Microsoft (Xbox 360 and Xbox One). In 2016 it expanded its 360-degree video partnership with YouTube, signed a live-streaming deal with Periscope, renewed its partnership with the National Hockey League, signed a patent licensing agreement with Microsoft, and inked a new golf deal with the PGA and Skratch TV.

While some of these deals are merely brand-building exercises, others, such as an exclusive partnership with Reliance Digital, India's largest consumer electronics retailer, will provide GoPro access to India's young consumer market. Tony Bates, former president of GoPro, said, "We view this as a strategic partnership that brings much more than just shelves for our products but a true partner to help with GoPro's success in India." My

GoPro
Be a HERO.

1971 ➤ NICK WOODMAN DEVELOPED FIRST GO-PRO PROTOTYPE

adrenaline JUNKIES

SALES DISTRIBUTION NETWORK

MOST VALUABLE ASSETS

45000 retailers across the globe

43% PARTNERSHIPS

BEST BUY

OF REVENUE

SINGLE LARGEST PARTNER

REDBULL and GOPRO HAD MADE THEIR PRODUCTS SYNONYMOUS WITH YOUTH, HEALTH and ADVENTURE. FORMING A PARTNERSHIP WAS NATURAL EXTENSION FOR BOTH BRANDS

guess is Red Bull is hoping to create a similar partnership with Reliance, as it was able to do with Best Buy in the United States.

Will GoPro's partnerships continue to help it penetrate new markets, develop new products, and reach new customers? That remains to be seen, but I wouldn't bet against these results. In its second quarter of 2017, its revenue was up 34 percent year over year, with over 50 percent of GoPro's revenue now being generated from markets outside the United States—which may not be a coincidence since Red Bull is such a strong brand outside the United States and now is seeing a total of 42 percent of its revenue generated from distribution partners.

For now, *the choice to pursue partnerships as part of an effort to re-ignite growth*, especially as it pushes into international markets and markets new products to its existing community, appears to be paying off. It won't solve all of its growth issues, but it's sure to help it move the brand, its product awareness, consumer adoption, and customer experience forward.

GOPRO
KEY TAKEAWAYS

- Many companies make the mistake of thinking that because they are "small" companies, bigger companies won't want to partner with them. GoPro, despite being a ten-person team, was able to fill a need that Best Buy had with a perfect product for both market context and the new **Customer Experience** orientation it was pursuing.

- You can obviously look for category partnerships that extend your reach and services into a similar customer or market segment. However, less conventional partnerships can be equally lucrative. GoPro worked with car companies, technology companies, sporting franchises, event organizers, and beverage companies in tightly integrated "brand-to-brand" partnerships. GoPro continues to stay ahead of the curve as it aligns itself across sports, technology, and entertainment to further develop meaningful relationships with its customers.

- GoPro uses partnerships to extend its brand and tap into new target markets. When it wanted to reach the customer demographic of cyclists, it struck a partnership with Tour de France.

STORY

2

AIRLINES
THE FRIENDLY SKIES

*It is literally true that you can succeed best and quickest
by helping others to succeed.*
—NAPOLEON HILL, Author of *Think and Grow Rich*

BEFORE THE PASSAGE OF THE Airline Deregulation Act of 1978, air transportation was tightly controlled under post–World War II regulations, and ten big carriers held 90 percent of the American market. At the time, airlines competed on service alone, as fares and where they could fly were controlled by the government.

As a matter of fact, the Civil Aeronautics Board (CAB) set fares that guaranteed a 12 percent return on flights that were 55 percent full. Many might remember these times as the *"golden age of aviation,"* when stewardesses carved prime rib on rolling carts and passengers could relax (and smoke) in piano lounges in the upper decks of Boeing 747s.

It was a time when there was a dress code in first class, Pam Am and TWA were major airlines, and the entire travel experience was glamorous and exciting. Leisure travel was a luxury back then, and not affordable for everyone—so the market context was: low volume, high cost, limited (customer) penetration.

The 1978 deregulation, which dissolved the CAB, led to the emergence of low-cost, low-frills airlines, looking for high-volume, mass-market penetration, which could now compete against the larger, national airlines.

In 1978, no one would have guessed that Southwest Airlines, which was originally a small regional airline forbidden by CAB rules to fly outside Texas, would just a few decades later become the largest domestic U.S. carrier in terms of passenger traffic.

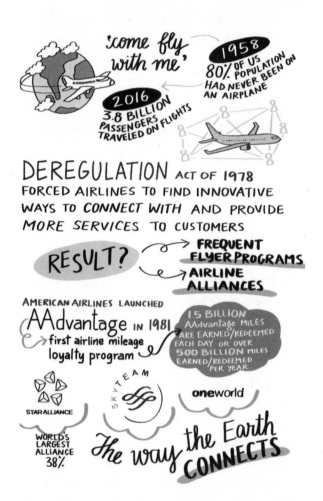

DEREGULATION ACT OF 1978 FORCED AIRLINES TO FIND INNOVATIVE WAYS TO CONNECT WITH AND PROVIDE MORE SERVICES TO CUSTOMERS

'come fly with me'

1958 80% OF US POPULATION HAD NEVER BEEN ON AN AIRPLANE

2016 3.8 BILLION PASSENGERS TRAVELED ON FLIGHTS

RESULT? → FREQUENT FLYER PROGRAMS → AIRLINE ALLIANCES

AMERICAN AIRLINES LAUNCHED AAdvantage IN 1981 → first airline mileage loyalty program

1.5 BILLION AAdvantage MILES ARE EARNED/REDEEMED EACH DAY OR OVER 500 BILLION MILES EARNED/REDEEMED PER YEAR

STAR ALLIANCE SKYTEAM oneworld

WORLD'S LARGEST ALLIANCE 38%

The way the Earth CONNECTS

Travel had been democratized overnight and, as anyone who has flown recently knows—good or bad—the level of comfort and "glamour" bears no resemblance to that of the regulated days.

Let's put this in context. When Frank Sinatra's "Come Fly with Me" was number one on the music charts in 1958, more than 80 percent of the United States had never been on an airplane. In 1965, it was about the same. By 2000, 50 percent of the country took at least one round-trip flight a year. The number of air passengers tripled between the 1970s and 2011. The IATA expects 7.2 billion passengers to travel in 2035, a near doubling of the 3.8 billion air travelers in 2016.

> **The International Air Transport Association (IATA) announced industry performance statistics for 2016 showing that system-wide, airlines carried 3.8 billion passengers on scheduled services last year, an increase of 7 percent over 2015, representing an additional 242 million air trips. U.S. and foreign airlines in the United States carried 932 million domestic and international passengers, a record number in 2016.**

Less expensive fares have increased the level of travel both domestically and internationally. Airline ticket prices have fallen 50 percent over the past thirty years, even though the cost of fuel, which accounts for more than a third of airfare costs, has gone up 260 percent between 2000 and 2013. Because of this, international airlines cannot survive with operational reach within just a few countries, especially with current cost structures in place. They must be able to extend their service and tap into more destinations than they can on their own. Unlike other industries, airlines cannot merge or acquire other carriers easily—the barrier of entry is high, but so is the cost associated with running an airline.

THE WAY THE WORLD CONNECTS

When the Open Skies agreements began to take shape in the 1970s, further allowing airlines the right to operate services from any point in the United States to any point in another country, multi-airline alliances were born. The United States began pursing Open Sky agreements back in 1972, and by 1982 it had signed twenty-three bilateral air service agreements worldwide. Now a global industry, commercial aviation was connected more than it had ever been in its history. In addition, the market context officially shifted.

While deregulations were supposed to fulfill two main goals—*spur competition and reduce airfares*—I would argue that it also forced airlines to innovate in ways to connect with, and provide more services to, its now global passengers. The result? *Frequent flyer* programs and *airline alliances*.

As the **Customer Experience** path outlined, customers now view "service and experience" as the product itself. They are voting with loyalty—and are willing to pay more, even sometimes to be inconvenienced, to stay with a brand, based purely on the loyalty points alone.

Just a few short years after deregulations, American Airlines launched AAdvantage, the first airline mileage loyalty program, in May 1981. In a recent American Airlines (AA) media and investor day, AA president Robert Isom said that *1.5 billion AAdvantage miles are earned or redeemed each day or over 500 billion miles earned or redeemed per year.*

The program generated $2.1 billion in revenue last year and accounted for much of the 3.9 percent growth in "other revenue" not derived from carrying passengers and cargo. American Airlines looks at the combination of its flight services and its loyalty programs as a key component of its growth.

This quote sums it up, in American Airlines' words: *"To ensure our best customers have the best access and experience that American and AAdvantage have to offer. All of our (program) changes are structured around that."*

Most people think of miles as a clever way for airlines to reward their best customers, a marketing technique designed to keep passengers coming back. But what many don't realize is that thanks to the ever-increasing popularity of credit cards with travel rewards, frequent flyer programs have become so profitable that some airlines may be making more money selling miles than they are from selling airfare.

Because of this, airlines have begun to leverage the partnership between airlines and credit card companies en masse. Initially for co-branding and cross-selling, it has been a game changer for both. Delta Airlines has a partnership with American Express (as do many other airlines), which hands out reward miles to cardholders for spending on flights or other expenses.

Yet another consequence of deregulations and other international arrangements was the need to better service international, multi-country travelers. There was no way to accomplish this without a strong partner network. Many years after the loyalty program was created, multinational airline alliances were conceived in the late 1990s and have become an important factor for the strategic growth of dozens of airlines. These alliances are a way for carriers to efficiently and profitably extend their networks through jointly operated flights.

The coordinated effort and global partnerships changed an entire industry. Founded in 1997, with the slogan *"The Way the Earth Connects,"* Star Alliance is the world's largest global airline alliance, with a market share of 38 percent. It was named the Best Airline Alliance by air travelers in 2017, followed by SkyTeam Alliance (33 percent) and OneWorld Alliance (29 percent).

Star Alliance has twenty-seven member airlines, including Turkish Airlines, Singapore Airlines, Air China, Air Canada, and United Airlines, that operate a fleet of approximately four thousand aircraft, serve more than one thousand airports in 194 countries, carry 637.6 million passengers per year on more than eighteen thousand daily departures, and generate $181 billion collectively.

Originally conceived as a small-scale partnership agreement between two airlines, there is no question air travel would be vastly different without these multinational alliances. Furthermore, the fact that airlines may compete and partner for the same set of customers (**Co-opetition**) highlights the fact that the benefits far outweigh the risks, even in the highly competitive and thin-margin business of air travel.

Why? The improved **Customer Experience** is undeniable and the value for **Customer Base Penetration** is priceless. These alliance programs offer passengers an extended network by which they can travel through code-sharing agreements, where two or more airlines share the same flight, listing it in both of their reservation systems. This makes booking easier and moving between connections more efficient. Flight times are reduced, operational costs are streamlined, ticket prices may be lowered, and the "passenger experience" is greatly improved. In an industry hampered by bad publicity for flight delays, lost bags, and occasionally rude staff—loyalty and alliance programs are bright spots.

AIRLINES
KEY TAKEAWAYS

- In this example of **Partnerships,** there were two major forces coming into play: (1) the context of the market shifted and airlines were in no way prepared or able to respond on their own, and (2) the airline industry is highly regulated and it is cost-prohibitive to capitalize on this opportunity using **Product Expansion** alone, that is, buying more planes and routes. If passengers were going to have a good experience with international travel, the airlines had to come up with a feasible solution: *a coordinated effort across competing airlines was the answer.*

- There can be situations where a **Partnership** is with someone who you compete with in some way (**Co-opetition**). Don't let that cloud your judgment, especially if a differentiated **Customer Experience** is what you are aiming for. *Customers aren't concerned with your internal hesitation; they care about the value they get for the money they pay you.*

- The airline alliances have been copied by almost every industry, especially those that are service- and loyalty-based: hotels, car rental companies, and retailers. Giving your customers a reason to stick with you (deter **Churn**), spend more with you (**Customer Base Penetration**), and choose you over lower-cost providers (**Customer Experience**) will always work to your advantage if you take **Partnerships** seriously and make them part of your value proposition.

APPLE
KILLING ME SWIFTLY

It doesn't matter how many times you fail, just have to be right once.

—MARK CUBAN

PPLE, ONE OF THE WORLD'S best-known brands, is known for many things: its innovative products, its focus on design, and its unwavering focus on The Apple Store experience. One area it is much less known for is **Partnerships**.

It was a 2015 open letter from Taylor Swift, one of the biggest pop stars on the planet, to Tim Cook, Apple CEO, that shined a light on how relationships—**Partnerships**, more specifically—can go woefully wrong. Apple was no stranger to working with partners, which is why I found this misstep to be such a surprise. They had worked with VARs (similar to Dell and Gateway) and brick-and-mortar retailers to sell and service their hardware products for decades before the Apple Stores opened, and it has recruited tens of thousands of app developers on its iTunes App Store.

In 2003, Apple launched iTunes, which changed the way consumers could purchase and listen to music. The service signed up ten million subscribers in just six months and thirty million since launch, who had collectively downloaded twenty-five billion songs by 2013. With the launch of iTunes, Steve Jobs, Apple CEO at the time, was focused on making the Napster experience better, more streamlined, and more user

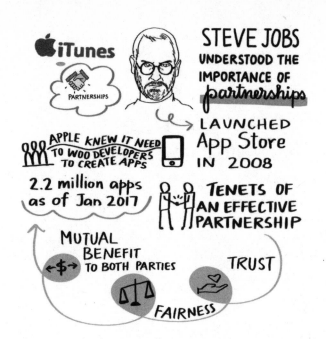

iTunes

PARTNERSHIPS

STEVE JOBS
UNDERSTOOD THE
IMPORTANCE OF
partnerships

LAUNCHED
App Store
IN 2008

APPLE KNEW IT NEEDED
TO WOO DEVELOPERS
TO CREATE APPS

2.2 million apps
as of Jan 2017

TENETS OF
AN EFFECTIVE
PARTNERSHIP

MUTUAL
BENEFIT
TO BOTH PARTIES

TRUST

FAIRNESS

friendly. He rightfully understood the importance of getting the record labels on board, because without a strong **Partnership** with them, iTunes would have found itself without much content. Jobs was able to win over the major record labels, which controlled the largest music catalogs on the planet. He allowed some digital rights management; in turn, they allowed Apple to price every song for $0.99. It was, at least in concept, a win-win partnership for both sides.

Another critical **Partnership** happened in 2008: the App Store launched, with only five hundred applications available for download. Apple knew it needed to woo developers to create apps for the iPhone, iPod Touch, iPad, and, further down the road, Apple Watch and Apple TV. As of January 2017, the App Store features 2.2 million apps. Those examples alone should show that Apple was no stranger to partnering. As a matter of fact, you could argue that much of its success has been *because of its partners*, who have made the usage of its products more desirable and valuable to a larger segment of the global market they were going after.

Back to Taylor Swift: in the note to Apple's CEO Tim Cook, she took the company to task for its decision not to pay artists during an initial three-month free trial of Apple Music, the new streaming service Apple was about to launch. Swift wrote: "I'm sure you are aware that Apple Music will be offering a free 3 month trial to anyone who signs up for the service. I'm not sure you know that Apple Music will not be paying writers, producers, or artists for those three months. I find it to be shocking, disappointing, and completely unlike this historically progressive and generous company."

Remember, the tenets of an effective partnership are *trust, fairness, and mutual benefit to both parties*. Swift clearly was calling Apple out on their lack of "partnership" with all artists—not just megastars like her but all artists who had their music up on iTunes. Keep in mind that her post was seen by her hundreds of millions of social media fans. It's estimated that Swift is the seventh-most-followed user on Instagram, the fourth-most-followed on Twitter (just under former president Barack Obama), the second-most-streamed female artist on Spotify—just to name a few.

How did this happen, especially from a company that clearly understands the value of "**Partnerships**"? Well, it ignored its musical artists (the actual product) in its Apple Music product launch. It was clearly focusing on "landing" (signing up) as many people as it could during the three-month free trial and then up-selling them to the subscription service—similar to what Spotify and Netflix have perfected: a good strategy, but unfortunately, in its aggressive push, poorly executed.

Apple CEO Tim Cook immediately responded and announced it would pay artists (albeit at a reduced rate) for their music during the free period. Swift's response: "I am elated and relieved. Thank you for your words of support today. They listened to us." (@taylorswift13) June 22, 2015.

This story would not have been so glowing if Apple had not already established strong partnerships with record labels, artists, and other component manufacturers in previous business ventures. It had a track record of the right intentions. Couple that with its "Swift" response— and Apple was able to stay on the right side of streaming music history this time around.

APPLE MUSIC
KEY TAKEAWAYS

- Defining the role partners play in any business is, of course, important. But if you have a product or service that is reliant on **Partnerships** to be successful, you better get that right. In this case, Apple Music, like Spotify, relies heavily on content partners to provide music that it can use to populate its "service"—otherwise it has a nicely designed but empty box. If **Partnerships** are a must-have for your business, <u>everyone better understand how the decisions they make about pricing, features, and availability will impact your partner ecosystem.</u>

- It isn't realistic to think that everything will always go right with a partnership, so you must plan for when things go wrong. The best thing you can do is fix it quickly, of course, but if that's not possible, then you must communicate with your partner(s) right away. Remember, strong partnerships require *trust, fairness, and mutual benefit*—if any of those three fall short, you risk negating all the progress previously made.

- Put in place the appropriate partner and change management systems to avoid issues like this from arising, or at least arising again. Case in point: The infamous open letter from Taylor Swift came in June 2015. Then it happened again in May 2017. Apple had announced that it was going to change the commission rates for iTunes affiliates (i.e., its partners). It was reported that all rates (for Mac and iOS app purchases, and for in-app purchases on both operating systems) would be cut from 7 percent to 2.5 percent. There was an immediate outcry from affiliate partners and Apple quickly backtracked. The good news is that Apple responds quickly when issues like this arise. The bad news is . . . they haven't fixed the underlying problem of how this could even happen in the first place.

PUTTING IT ALL TOGETHER

A strong relationship with your vendors will help keep
you at the forefront of changing market trends. . . . Our
dealer network generates extraordinary and timely
market intelligence. It's a rich source of information
that enables us to introduce new products and support
services successfully.

—DONALD V. FITES, former chairman
and CEO of Caterpillar, Inc.

NY EFFECTIVE PARTNERSHIP DEPENDS ON understanding where the value is. That comes from defining what each party brings to the table. Once you know that, you can begin to define what success looks like, what kind(s) of partners you may need, and what type of partnership arrangement you should form.

With the advancements of digital technology and the Internet, the emergence of powerful ecosystems has shaped entire industries and fueled growth for many companies. *Some partnerships are so critical to the success of a business that without them, the future of the business is totally at risk.* However, many companies lack the knowledge, connections, and management capabilities to realize the full potential of partnering. Others can capitalize on partnering in one part of their business and not know what to do in another. Or worse, they have strong partnership chops and forget those critical tenets of trust, fairness, and mutual benefit.

The unfortunate result is that *many partnerships are approached as an afterthought*, either because the company feels it doesn't need them because of its size or scale, or it'll launch and "fix it later." Either way, the challenges it will face aren't because the initial concept and intent weren't right. Rather, it comes down to overlooking the value of working with external parties (companies, people, ecosystems, etc.) because of its own inwardly focused agenda. It's all about what "they" want, not what's best for both companies.

Nonetheless, I don't anticipate the rate of partnerships slowing down anytime soon—especially as businesses struggle to react quickly to ever-changing customer expectations and growth demands. *Striving to out-maneuver competitors these days requires many more external partnerships to support evolving growth initiatives.*

WHAT WORKS—AND POTENTIAL PITFALLS

Any company choosing **Partnerships** as a growth path must understand that, regardless of the type of partnership it chooses to pursue, there is rarely a fixed destination. *Partnerships should continue to evolve over time, as new opportunities are uncovered.* While some partnerships prove to be fleeting encounters, lasting only as long as one partner needs the other, some partnerships become the very fabric of the two companies' success and can last for decades. The **Partnership** growth path, as you might imagine, offers opportunities beyond what a company usually would be able to create on its own and also offers a banquet of potential subsequent growth paths for the companies who pursue it. Here are three examples.

COMBINATION: PATH 8—
Partnerships + Path 3—Market Acceleration

The right partnership introduces you to a new market opportunity while saving you much of the expense of developing that market. The right partner has already competed in that market, undertaken the expense of prospecting it, staffed a team of developers, experienced all of the potential pitfalls, and developed a body of loyal users. Who wouldn't want that starting advantage? Of course, your partner is probably doing the same thing to you, so you had better make sure you are getting the deal you want.

COMBINATION: PATH 8—
Partnerships + Path 4—Product Expansion

The same is true with the **Product Expansion** path. Your partner has undertaken the expense and effort to develop a product specifically for its market. It has overcome various obstacles, perhaps failed on several occasions, and refined that product to be best suited for its potential customers. Why wouldn't you want to have access to that acquired wisdom? Something even more valuable can be access to your partner's intellectual capital, such as patents and copyrights, that you otherwise would not be able to use, much less duplicate. Indeed, saving the licensing costs may be worth the entire partnership.

COMBINATION: PATH 8—
Partnerships + Path 6—Optimize Sales

When we think about optimizing sales, it is usually as an internal activity. But with a partnership you can increase the size of your sales force and also its quality. Especially in a new market for you, your partner's sales operation can bring fresh talent, in-field experience, better lead generation, and specialty selling tools, and it can sometimes serve as a source of fresh best practices that you can implement in your own operation.

PATH 9

CO-OPETITION

CO-OPETITION

No one can succeed by themselves. . . . The only way you can achieve something magnificent is by working with other people. There is lots of co-opetition.

—REID HOFFMAN, venture capitalist and cofounder of LinkedIn

WHY CO-OPETITION MATTERS

- Creating partnerships or collaborative arrangements with other firms is the primary type of transaction that 50 percent of CEOs expect to undertake to increase shareholder value.
- Eighty-five percent of CEOs see such cross-sector coalitions and partnerships as essential to accelerating transformation, and a further 78 percent believe that these partnerships will help them deliver positive outcomes in the next five years.

WHAT'S OLD IS NEW AGAIN

Ever wonder why your USB cable works on any device, built by any manufacturer? Or your earbuds will plug into almost every device so that you can listen to music or take a phone call? You can thank the standards developed by the computer industry to ensure that customers have a more seamless experience using its PCs, smartphones, and desktops.

Co-opetition is a newly popular but actually quite venerable concept. The word itself is a portmanteau, combining "competition" and "cooperation." Logically, it is a contradiction, but in the real world it has been shown again and again to work, often brilliantly. It's a great survival strategy for small companies, especially if they find themselves in a growth stall, and a good expansion strategy for even the largest enterprises.

While the law may be sometimes hard for the individual, it is best for the race, because it ensures the survival of the fittest in every department.

—ANDREW CARNEGIE

The first known use of "co-opetition" dates back to the beginning of the twentieth century—but it is generally acknowledged that the modern principles of the field have evolved from game theory and from the Nobel Prize–winning work of John Nash (the subject of the movie *A Beautiful Mind*).

At the heart of the **Co-opetition** path is the notion that even competitors can *find ways to work together to accomplish ends that they would be unlikely to achieve alone.* Indeed, working with competitors can be *more* successful than traditional partnerships because, while the latter can often suffer from indistinct boundaries and mission creep, co-opetitive relationships, because they are based upon a "partial congruence" of interests, typically have both distinct boundaries and precise rules of engagement.

The most common form of Co-opetition is one in which two competitors work together in basic research and the development of applications, even product platforms to open or expand a market, while still competing with each other for customers and market share. One example is a memorandum of understanding (MOU), a non–legally binding partnership.

The most notable example of Co-opetition can be found in the technology industry, where hardware and software companies work together on standards and compatibility and form joint distribution (bundling) agreements with each other's competitors.

At the philosophical heart of *Co-opetition is a reaction against the notion that a particular market sector represents a "zero-sum" game:* an economic pie of fixed size from which competitors are reduced to cutting out slices of market share from their competitors, and vice versa, in a

For purposes of this growth path, we focus on the co-opetition aspect of partnerships, specifically product development and intellectual property (IP).

winner-takes-all scenario. By comparison, *the goal of Co-opetition is to find synergies and common ground between those competitors in the hope of growing the size of that pie*. If it can be done, everyone wins—and that makes it worthwhile even to work with your "self-proclaimed competitor."

FUTURE NEEDS REQUIRE FUTURE PARTNER MODELS

To sustain a population of 9.7 billion people by 2050, the world is going to need a different approach to innovation. Key industry sectors such as food, energy, water, agriculture, and transportation are already under pressure to move to more sustainable methods of production and consumption, and they are struggling to keep up with both consumer demands and the pace of technical change.

If we keep trying to tackle these big challenges with the same approach to innovation, we may find ourselves asking the same questions a decade from now, with little to no progress. One of the biggest opportunities for business lies in how it manages the creation and ownership of inventions and ideas. *A protectionist approach to IP is designed to protect and prolong the life cycle of existing technologies, allowing innovators to maximize returns on their investments*. While that may have been the preferred approach in the twentieth century, in the twenty-first century it makes it harder for new and more sustainable technologies to be developed and adopted quickly so that they can have the greatest impact.

Elon Musk, CEO of electric car manufacturer Tesla, "shocked" the world in 2014 when he announced that his company was joining the open source movement and giving away its patents for free. Admirable, but this was a change from its original philosophy about innovation. Originally Tesla developed a patent portfolio to protect its technology from its global car manufacturer competitors. Tesla was concerned that the production of electric cars was going to take off—and keeping its technology close to the vest was a competitive decision.

Instead, the electric car market hasn't gotten bigger than single digits. The stagnation led Tesla to rethink its approach. It changed its strategy from trying to prevent others from competing against it to using its technology as a catalyst to encourage and enable the market to grow faster.

Co-opetition was the path forward. Opening up its intellectual property could actually benefit Tesla with another product it has developed—batteries and charging stations. If more electric cars were manufactured, more batteries would be used; if more batteries were used, more charging stations would be needed. Whether it was a competitor or a Tesla vehicle, Musk wanted a larger piece of the total pie.

A shortsighted view can keep companies on their current path to growth and not think about how to approach the new market context in a different way. If more companies and more industries approached product level innovation with a cooperative mind-set, like Tesla, only then could **Co-opetition** flourish as a potential new growth path. Just as with **Partnerships** in the previous chapter, you have to believe that 1 + 1 = 3; otherwise, this path isn't for you. However, if you are developing technology, products, and services that could benefit a wider segment of the market if you were more collaborative, why not? All the better.

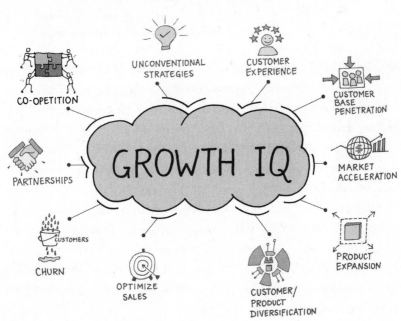

STORY

1

FIAT CHRYSLER, BMW, AND INTEL
JOINING FORCES

In order to advance autonomous driving technology, it is vital to form partnerships among automakers, technology providers and suppliers. Joining this cooperation will enable FCA to directly benefit from the synergies and economies of scale that are possible when companies come together with a common vision and objective.

**—SERGIO MARCHIONNE,
CEO of Fiat Chrysler Automobiles**

THE RESTORATION OF HARDWARE'S DOMINANCE in high tech has led to a renaissance in opportunities for companies to experiment with **Co-opetition**. The result has been some unlikely and unexpected partnerships. One of the most unlikely of such recently announced alliances is Fiat Chrysler Automobiles (FCA), BMW, Intel Corporation, and its newly acquired subsidiary, Mobileye, to develop autonomous cars.

After decades of battling it out with neighbor Mercedes-Benz, BMW was perhaps the world's most innovative automaker. From design to manufacture, business organization to driver experience, BMW was considered the model for every other car company. Even its headquarters facility in Munich was studied around the world as a paradigm for integration of operations and automation.

As early as 1998, BMW became one of the first of what became a tidal wave of carmakers setting up offices in Silicon Valley to tap into that tech center's expertise and to serve as a listening post for emerging new technologies that might be of value in transportation. BMW's office, located in Mountain View, was just a couple miles down the Bayshore Freeway

FIAT CHRYSLER AUTOMOBILES TEAMING UP WITH INTEL, BMW GROUP AND MOBILEYE TO DEVELOP AUTONOMOUS CARS

uncompromising EXCELLENCE in development

SCALABILITY of autonomous driving platform

auto and tech leaders

future of transportation → WORKING TOGETHER

COMBINATION of skills

HAVE ALREADY ACHIEVED SCALE they could never have achieved alone

from Intel's headquarters in Santa Clara. In retrospect, a partnership between these two legendary innovators seemed inevitable.

In July 2016, BMW, Intel, and Mobileye announced that they were teaming up to develop an autonomous vehicle, targeted for production by 2021. The immediate goal of the trio was to deploy forty autonomous test vehicles on the road by year end. But something was still missing from the co-opetitive relationship: *mass and scale*. BMW is a major carmaker, but it operates largely in the luxury market. Unlike, say, Mercedes, it doesn't make trucks or other mass-market vehicles. Its product line extensions have largely been other luxury vehicles featuring hybrid and electric motors, motorcycles, and niche vehicles such as the Mini and Rolls-Royce. What the team needed was one more partner, one targeted at the mass market, especially global customers—even if it meant that partner might be a potential competitor of BMW.

It found that partner in August 2017 with Fiat Chrysler, one of the world's largest automakers. According to Dean Takahashi of VentureBeat .com, "The companies are talking about creating both co-pilot driver assistance technologies and full-blown self-driving cars. They will leverage each other's strengths and resources to do so and will co-locate engineers in Germany to do joint work."

According to A. T. Kearney, all told, the apps, equipment, and vehicles related to autonomous driving will pull in $282 billion in revenues by 2030, which represents about 7 percent of the total automotive market. The numbers get much bigger from there. They expect the market to almost double to around $560 billion between 2030 and 2035 and represent 17 percent of the global automotive market.

Why would BMW let a company like FCA join the party? According to a statement by BMW AG chairman Harald Krüger, "The two factors that remain key to the success of the cooperation are uncompromising excellence in development, and the scalability of our autonomous driving platform. With FCA as our new partner, we reinforce our path to successfully create the most relevant state-of-the-art, cross-OEM [original equipment manufacturer] Level 3-5 solution on a global scale."

Just because they can agree to work together doesn't mean that, in practice, they actually do so. Automobile companies have traditionally wanted proprietary chips from their semiconductor partners—something a company with Intel's history will likely never agree to do. The same goes even for Mobileye: with the vast world of computer vision calling, it is unlikely to divert too much of its precious resources to this project only. But maybe with the moves from Tesla, other car manufacturers are seeing the benefit in being more collaborative in lieu of protecting technology that can move the entire market forward.

A new technology revolution—autonomous (self-driving) cars—was beckoning, and a new set of powerful players was spending huge sums to dominate it, companies like Google, Apple, and Tesla. And the traditional automobile industry—the sector most at risk from a new transportation paradigm—wanted in, if only for self-preservation.

Intel wanted in, too. As the microprocessor industry had evolved over the previous decades, Intel had long stayed the dominant player. It had supremely benefited from the dot-com boom, at one point becoming the most valuable manufacturing company in the world. But then Intel zigged when it should have zagged. It chose to throw its immense financial resources and technical skill in the pursuit of the networking business as the next big thing. That proved a huge mistake because the real game turned out to be in the mobile business. In other words, Intel had chosen to chase big, expensive chips when it should have gone after small, cheap, and low-power versions to stick in smartphones and laptops. Sharp new competitors such as ARM and Qualcomm were quick to fill the void left by Intel.

By the time Intel realized its mistake, those companies had largely tied up the mobile business . . . and mighty Intel was left only the crumbs. The company spent much of the early twenty-first century struggling to find its place in this new world. Now, autonomous vehicles seemed to offer Intel another chance at dominating the next great chip market. Under a new CEO, Brian Krzanich, it decided to go all in. To fill a perceived weakness, the company acquired computer vision specialist Mobileye for a whopping $15.3 billion. Said Krzanich, "The future of transportation relies on auto and tech industry leaders working together to develop a scalable architecture that automakers around the globe can adopt and customize."

Meanwhile, the most dangerous part of **Co-opetition** is not what competitors agree to do together but what they won't do—especially when it comes to proprietary tools and assets that they refuse to share, even hide from their erstwhile partners. In this partnership, it is BMW that appears to hold the upper hand when it comes to software acumen. Will it actually share with Fiat Chrysler—BMW a potential future competitor in small urban vehicles, Fiat Chrysler making moves on BMW's mid-range coupes—the proprietary code BMW develops to remain competitive with its more direct customers such as Mercedes, Lexus, Infiniti, and Jaguar?

That said, there may be even more powerful forces at work to keep this team together. In automobiles, the Japanese are known to be busy on autonomous cars. Tesla is already testing autonomy—which, with its leadership in electric cars, would quickly put it where the rest of the car industry wants to be a couple of decades from now. As for Intel, it knows that there are a lot of chip companies out there—from contract fabricators to successful direct competitors such as Nvidia and Qualcomm.

The long-term success of the BMW-Intel-Mobileye-FCA partnership is far from guaranteed, but in understanding the context and finding the right partners to create a combination of skills needed to tackle this potentially gigantic new market, the various players have already achieved a presence that they never could have accomplished on their own. Now, if they can just figure out how to work together long-term in their common cause.

The beginning of a wave of co-operative partnerships chasing the autonomous electric car market has begun. Not to be outdone, at Consumer Electronics Show (CES) in January 2018, Toyota announced that it has partnered with Amazon, DiDi, Pizza Hut, Mazda, and Uber to "collaborate on vehicle planning, application concepts and vehicle verification activities." This is an example of **Co-opetition** with Toyota and Mazda working together. It's also an example of using **Partnerships** to extend brands and gain access to a new customer set with a diverse group of brands such as these. The **Co-opetition** and **Partnership** paths, in combination, round out the narrow view of "IP being shared and used under the hood" (which only a handful of people are aware of) to more customer-facing experiences.

BMW/FIAT CHRYSLER
KEY TAKEAWAYS

- This **Co-opetition** alliance shows that global collaboration among companies, even with deep pockets, as is the case with FCA, BMW, and Intel, will become more commonplace as disruptive technologies threaten the status quo. FCA will benefit because it doesn't necessarily have the financial muscle to justify developing its own self-driving cars from scratch.
- The partners said they are working to develop a vehicle architecture "that can be used by multiple automakers around the world, while at the same time maintaining each automaker's unique brand identities." Maybe taking a cue from the Tesla playbook—if they can truly develop an architecture that can become the industry standard, like the USB or earbud, it could be a game changer for the next few decades.

STORY
2

WINTEL
ATTACK OF THE CLONES

Keep your friends close, and your enemies closer.
—MICHAEL CORLEONE, *The Godfather Part II*

WINTEL, THE ALLIANCE AMONG WINDOWS (Microsoft), Intel, and IBM, exhibited many of the aspects of **Co-opetition** long before the term was invented. For nearly three decades it remained, in the words of *Forbes* magazine, "the most powerful alliance in tech history." Even today, reduced to just two partners, Intel and Microsoft—and rapidly fading away—it remains a powerful force in the world economy.

The "Wintel" co-opetitive relationship was created almost by accident and ended as much by success as any other reason. In 1969, Intel developed a new kind of "computer-on-a-chip" called a *microprocessor* while working on a Japanese calculator company contract to produce a smaller, cheaper calculator circuitry. Despite its subsequent historic success, Intel

> Wintel is a computer trade industry term for personal computers based on the Intel microprocessor and one of the Windows operating system from Microsoft. The term 'PC' has often been used for this purpose.
>
> *— TechTarget*

didn't really know what to do with this new chip and briefly considered abandoning it.

Meanwhile, the world's biggest computer company, IBM, was looking to attack the exploding personal computer business. The company opened a secret research facility in Boca Raton, Florida, to design a "new machine."

In designing it, to be called the personal computer, or "PC," IBM decided not to use its in-house chip hardware or computer software operating system (OS) but to go externally for a "partner" who was already in the PC business.

IBM approached Bill Gates and said that it was looking for an OS to manage the PC and its software, Gates suggested DR-DOS, produced by a Monterey, California, company called Digital Research. But when Digital Research (for various reasons) wasn't responsive, Gates proposed to acquire the rights to a similar operating system, "DOS"—from Seattle Computer Products. IBM agreed. Microsoft bought the code, modified it, and renamed it MS-DOS. IBM then licensed it from Microsoft for its new PC.

Meanwhile, down in Silicon Valley, the microprocessor was doing sufficiently well selling to makers of large computer companies and the military to finally get Intel behind it—even to eventually turn it into its entire business. But despite its early start, Intel found itself losing business to Motorola, which had not only followed Intel into microprocessors but, with its latest product, had managed to pull ahead.

Intel was in a panic. It desperately needed to come up with a marketing team to try to figure out how to compete with its now second-rate product. The effort was called *Operation Crush,* one of the most famous marketing initiatives in the history of high tech. Over a long weekend, the team came up with a solution—*not to sell only its specific hardware chip but the "solution" represented by the chip, combined with its design tools and company support.* This trick, radically new at the time, caught Motorola flat-footed—and put Intel back in front.

Part of Operation Crush was to set new quotas for Intel's field sales, including sales calls on even the most unlikely potential customers. One of those targets was IBM. After all, why would Big Blue (that is, IBM) buy chips when it made its own? But when Intel's sales guy called on Boca Raton, he was astonished to find himself greeted with open arms. IBM was so secretive that Intel's technical people never actually saw the product. They had to do such bizarre things as reaching through black curtains to touch the machines. There may never have been such unlikely corporate bedfellows, but somehow it worked.

The great lesson of the Wintel story is that *you can't grow internally or through acquisitions fast enough to dominate a major technology revolution by yourself*. Not even the mighty IBM of the early 1980s could do so, despite having its own in-house software and chip hardware operations that were far bigger than either Intel's or Microsoft's at the time. Rather, you need to find the best companies out there in their respective industries to partner with—even if they had been, currently are, or potentially one day might again be, your competitor.

IBM in 1980, in its rush to catch up with industry leader Apple, opened its platform to hardware cloners. In other words, Big Blue invited direct competitors in to help Apple's opposition reach the critical mass to truly challenge Apple's hegemony. With this new arrangement, Intel was free to sell its microprocessor chips to those clone companies, as well, thereby enabling ever-greater competition to Big Blue. So, too, could Microsoft sell its new Windows software, the newly created upgrade to MS-DOS, to those same clone makers. Why did IBM agree to this? Because it was not just trying to sell personal computers; it was trying to drive a new industry standard, defeat Apple, and own the entire PC industry. It trusted its name and manufacturing prowess to keep it ahead of the competition. And indeed, with this strategy it very nearly did just that. And it was willing to let Intel and Microsoft also grow rich and powerful in the process.

IBM, along with its clones, quickly came to dominate more than 80 percent of the personal computer market. With Microsoft and Intel, this co-opetitive trifecta became the standard for the biggest new industry in the global economy and as a result became among the most valuable companies on the planet.

It was a high-risk game, with three hugely innovative and successful companies chained to one another, each one never fully trusting the other two, and all three driving one another forward to be the lead innovator. *The result was a virtuous growth and innovation spiral that changed the world*. Apple, meanwhile, isolated itself and refused to team with other companies, watched its market share drop from nearly 90 percent to un-

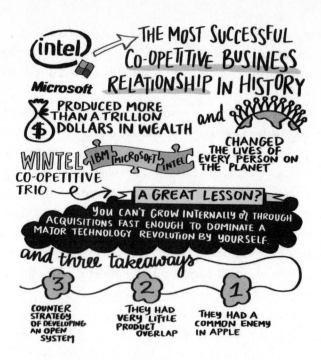

THE MOST SUCCESSFUL CO-OPETITIVE BUSINESS RELATIONSHIP IN HISTORY

PRODUCED MORE THAN A TRILLION $ DOLLARS IN WEALTH *and* CHANGED THE LIVES OF EVERY PERSON ON THE PLANET

WINTEL IBM MICROSOFT INTEL CO-OPETITIVE TRIO

A GREAT LESSON?
YOU CAN'T GROW INTERNALLY or THROUGH ACQUISITIONS FAST ENOUGH TO DOMINATE A MAJOR TECHNOLOGY REVOLUTION BY YOURSELF.

and three takeaways

3 COUNTER STRATEGY OF DEVELOPING AN OPEN SYSTEM

2 THEY HAD VERY LITTLE PRODUCT OVERLAP

1 THEY HAD A COMMON ENEMY IN APPLE

der 10 percent. It even missed the computer gaming boom, which buoyed the Wintel world even higher. This co-opetitive business relationship, the most successful in history, *produced more than $1 trillion in wealth and changed the lives of every person on the planet*. It has been the model for similar relationships ever since, especially in technology—for the value of industry standards and collaboration of multiple, and, sometimes, competing, brands.

Eventually, IBM left the hardware business to pursue enterprise consulting, software services, and the cloud, selling off its PC business to Lenovo. Now the trio was down to a pair, which continued to sell to the vast PC clone industry. Both companies continued to pursue new opportunities that might break the shackles that continued to tie them together. By the early twenty-first century, that chance came with mobile computing and the rise of the smartphone. Intel slipped and missed the birth of the former, freeing Microsoft to work with Intel's competitors, such as Qualcomm.

It was the end of an era. And yet, even today, a remainder of the old Wintel **Co-opetition** still survives: the most powerful Intel microprocessor chips are used in a number of Microsoft products.

WINTEL
KEY TAKEAWAYS

- *First, they had a common enemy.* Apple owned nearly 90 percent of the emerging personal computer business. And its business philosophy was to own every part of the process—hardware, operating system, and software applications. It had also designed its computers around the processor from a small, independent chip company.

- *Second, the three companies had little overlap.* Intel and Microsoft were still too small and targeted to compete with each other. But IBM was one of the biggest companies in the world—it could have easily decided to make its own PC processor (it already had others for its minicomputers) and it was the world's biggest writer of software. But because it had made the PC a stand-alone operation, it chose not to interfere with Intel and Microsoft. Besides, by the time these events were occurring, Apple already had a five-year head start. IBM had to move fast and needed to buy off-the-shelf parts and not wait for its own internal operations.

- *Third, there was an obvious counterstrategy to Apple.* By being so closed, Apple had forced itself to be excellent at every part of the process. IBM's revolutionary response was to be an "open" system—that is, to let private vendors design hardware for its products and software applications for MS-DOS (eventually Microsoft Windows). As a result, hundreds of companies sprang up to make Wintel-compatible devices, peripherals, and programs—not least the entire vast PC gaming industry. The other part of the strategy was to initially focus on the corporate world, where Apple had made few inroads, but where, as the saying went, "Nobody ever got fired for buying IBM."

STORY
3

CISCO-VMWARE-EMC
BETTER TOGETHER?

Cisco and EMC, together with VMware, are coming
together in an unprecedented way to help our customers.
—JOSEPH TUCCI, chairman and CEO of EMC

N NOVEMBER 2009, THREE UNLIKELY bedfellows—Cisco
Corporation (the world's largest vendor of networking hardware and
other infrastructure), EMC Corporation (a giant data storage provider), and VMware (at the time, a subsidiary of EMC, now owned by Dell
Technologies)—announced a co-opetitive venture to deliver a Virtual Computing Environment (VCE) operating system for their various customers.

For chief information officers (CIOs) and IT managers, cloud computing offers a more simplified way of managing information technology
so that the effort they've been putting into keeping the lights on can be
redirected toward innovation and driving value back into the business.
Converged infrastructure, like VCE, takes this a step further, having a
transformative effect on the data center that not only simplifies operations and management but is also packaged and delivers a solution in a
way that eliminates some of the complexity when deploying new systems.
The result is a promise of quicker infrastructure and application deploy-
ments compared to traditional approaches and, in the end, faster time to
market that enables customers to stay competitive.

For that reason, from the start, the venture had enormous potential, in part because there was a real need for such a solution: the cloud was just beginning to take off as a substitute for in-house data centers and the three companies involved each had a history of considerable success. The market context was shifting and customers wanted more flexible and cost-effective solutions. Cisco, in particular, was one of the biggest technology companies in the world, and it attributed more than 90 percent of its revenue to its various **Partnerships** (telcos [telephone companies], resellers, system integrators).

But events at the start of the venture should have been a warning to everyone involved. The coalition was unveiled in November 2009 at an

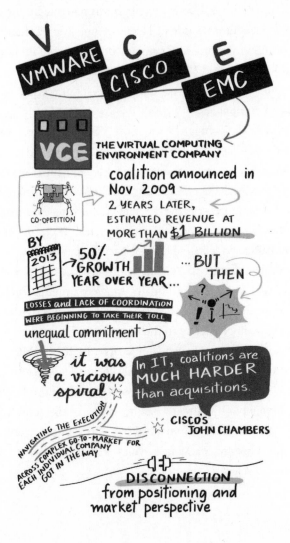

PATH 9 CO-OPETITION

EMC customer event, to be part of a long-term deal to create cloud computing platforms (called Vblock Infrastructure Packages). It should have been a big announcement, but at the same event, Cisco and EMC announced another joint venture—this one called Arcadia—also involved with the same Vblock Infrastructure Packages as VCE, the difference being that the latter was to perform development of the technology while the former created standardized products for customers.

The difference may have been clear to the folks at the various companies but not to customers. Thus, the announcement of such an important venture only managed to sow confusion among the customers it targeted. Eventually, in January 2011, the two programs merged, but by then some of the initial momentum was lost. The new company was named the Virtual Computing Environment Company. Initially based in Silicon Valley (Cisco and VMware) and Massachusetts (EMC), the venture was eventually based in Richardson, Texas, and management was divided between the two bigger companies.

At the time of the company formation, VCE had twelve hundred employees. Two years later, revenues were estimated at more than $1 billion. In other words, *it was a serious venture* and one enjoying considerable success. And yet, analysts deconstructing EMC and Cisco's financials—VCE didn't report separately—uncovered some disturbing data. In particular, even with those revenues, and now with a thousand corporate customers, the two companies were losing money. *Lots of money.*

One credible estimate had Cisco having lost a total of $460 million on the venture, EMC $430 million. There were other problems as well. For example, neither company, despite their huge respective investments, seemed to show much loyalty to the venture. In 2011, Cisco announced its own cloud framework, called CloudVerse. In 2012, EMC announced a joint venture with Lenovo that the market read as directly competing with the low-end VCE offerings. Cisco still said good things about VCE, but it sure seemed as if it already had one foot out the door. Cisco's CEO at the time, John Chambers, remarked at the VCE announcement that IT coalitions had a lower success rate even than acquisitions. In particular, he noted four problems:

1. **Misaligned quarter endings between Cisco and EMC.** This meant that one partner was just ramping up the selling process while the other was trying to close business.
2. **"Providing timely and organized delivery of the many different components from the different manufacturers."** The venture eventually solved this by opening additional facilities around the country.
3. **Unequal sales bonuses.** EMC reps received sizable uplift against quotas for Vblock sales. Meanwhile, Cisco reps received an additional bonus for a sale (sales performance incentive fund [SPIF]). VMware reps got nothing—other than being warned (or so many believed) not to sell VMware products through VCE. The inevitable result was that EMC enjoyed most Vblock sales, Cisco second, and VMware negligible.
4. **Discounting.** "A single manufacturer such as IBM or HP has the flexibility to discount any component they deem to be particularly price sensitive knowing they can make up the lost margin on other components. The VCE players, of course, don't have this option."

VCE in 2012 reached a 57.4 percent market share, according to Gartner, largely because of its pioneering work. The press, initially skeptical, was starting to come around, too. By 2013, it was achieving 50 percent year-over-year growth. But the losses and the lack of coordination were beginning to take their toll. The unequal commitment the two big companies had exhibited toward the venture from the beginning now began to tell in their respective willingness to continue to throw money at it.

Despite the venture's visible success, Cisco allowed its ownership stake to fall to 35 percent, while EMC's rose to 58 percent. It was a vicious spiral—from now on the two companies would be moving in opposite directions regarding this partnership.

Within a year, Cisco dropped its stake to just 10 percent and EMC announced that it acquired majority control of VCE. Three months later, in January 2016, VCE disappeared into EMC as its new "Converged Platform Division." Within the year, in September, EMC was acquired by Dell. Cisco's John Chambers had been right: in IT, coalitions are much harder than acquisitions.

VCE
KEY TAKEAWAYS

- The disconnection out of the gate from both a positioning and a marketing perspective should have been an early warning sign that all three companies needed to ensure they were heading in the same direction with the same expectations.
- Each brand individually was a powerhouse at partnering. Cisco had close to 90 percent of its total revenue from its indirect channel, VMware was roughly fifty-fifty at the time, and EMC was similar to VMware. The point of those stats was that they knew how to partner. They understood what it took. Each of them have successfully partnered in huge alliances with telcos, cloud providers, and other technology companies in co-marketing efforts. This **Co-opetition** agreement had all the makings of a winner. Early returns, while bumpy, were positive. Navigating the execution across the complex go-to-market for each individual company—coupled with their own growth aspirations—got in the way.

PUTTING IT ALL TOGETHER

O F ALL OF THE GROWTH paths, the **Co-opetition** path may be the most fraught with peril. That's why, in entering such an agreement, _it is incumbent that you see the potential for great rewards in order to justify the risk taken._ The good news is that identifying that reward becomes easier in the era of shared platforms, open systems, and interconnected IT. Still, if a company is not careful, it can find itself not with a mutually beneficial relationship with a "frenemy" but instead with a ferocious enemy inside its walls that has access to its proprietary knowledge. Potential failure lurks at every step of the **Co-opetition** life cycle. _Proceed with caution._

WHAT WORKS—AND POTENTIAL PITFALLS

Under what conditions is **Co-opetition** a good idea? If "the partners' strategic goals converge while their competitive goals diverge . . . the size and market power of both partners is modest compared with industry leaders . . . [and] each partner believes it can learn from the other and at the same time limit access to proprietary skills."

COMBINATION: PATH 9—
Co-opetition + Path 8—Partnerships

This is a bit obvious but worth noting. Maybe the way to first engage with a current competitor is via a partnership that is focused on leveraging both brands to sell and market in a new way. See how that goes and then push the relationship further.

COMBINATION: PATH 9—
Co-opetition + Path 6—Optimize Sales

This particular growth path involves the top levels in the organization. It is highly strategic in nature; don't underestimate the level of pushback you may get from your front lines. The various sales teams at a minimum have competed against each other, maybe even for the same accounts. And legal departments may have been embroiled in contentious, long court battles. You can't expect, beyond the C-suite, the rank and file to understand why you would strike such a deal "with the enemy." The communication needed, both internally and externally, to ensure that sales are *not* impacted for the worse is key.

COMBINATION: PATH 9—
Co-opetition + Path 5—
Customer and Product Diversification

Because this growth path focuses on the product development side of partnering, using strategic partnerships to help with R&D costs, manufacturing capabilities, and leveraged IP is the ideal combination for **Customer and Product Diversification**, especially if you are in an industry with high up-front costs.

PATH 10

UNCONVENTIONAL STRATEGIES

UNCONVENTIONAL STRATEGIES

Swim upstream. Go the other way. Ignore the conventional wisdom.

—SAM WALTON, founder of Walmart

WHY UNCONVENTIONAL STRATEGIES MATTER

- Seventy-nine percent of consumers prefer to purchase products from a company that operates with a social purpose.
- Eighty-one percent of business executives said purpose-driven firms deliver higher-quality products and services.
- Sixty-six percent of consumers are willing to spend more on a product if it comes from a sustainable brand.
- Social capital is achieving a newfound status next to financial and physical capital in value . . . 65 percent of CEOs rated "inclusive growth" as a top-three strategic concern, more than three times greater than the proportion citing "shareholder value."

More than any other generation, millennials see a company's commitment to responsible business practices as a key factor in their employment decisions:

- Seventy-five percent say they would take a pay cut to work for a responsible company (vs. 55 percent U.S. average).
- Eighty-three percent would be more loyal to a company that helps them contribute to social and environmental issues (vs. 70 percent U.S. average).

- Eighty-eight percent say their job is more fulfilling when they are provided opportunities to make a positive impact on social and environmental issues (vs. 74 percent U.S. average).
- Seventy-six percent consider a company's social and environmental commitments when deciding where to work (vs. 58 percent U.S. average).
- Sixty-four percent won't take a job from a company that doesn't have strong corporate social responsibility (CSR) practices (vs. 51 percent U.S. average).

DO WELL BY DOING GOOD

I once posted on Twitter and LinkedIn about how the focus of my career has changed over the years. It received almost thirty thousand views, five hundred "likes," and dozens of comments. I must say that I was a bit surprised by the reaction. While brief, even a bit simple, it was a profound lesson to reflect on. I tried to capture how I felt at each big-age milestone and realized how I had not only grown as an executive in business but as a human being. The reactions and comments I received were a testament to how each of us tries to balance it all. Make a living. Raise a family. Make a difference. Be successful. Be happy.

If you want to grow, find a good opportunity. Today, if you want to be a great company, think about what social problem you could solve.

—JACK MA, founder and executive chairman of Alibaba Group

However, what was most inspiring was how many of those who left a comment were way ahead of my four-decade journey. People were quick

The most important questions for my career by age.

20s > What do I really want to do?

30s > How to make more money?

40s > What does all this hard work mean?

50s > How can I pay it forward and make a difference?
#dreamjob

PATH 10 UNCONVENTIONAL STRATEGIES

to say that even now, in their twenties and thirties, they were trying to pay it forward, engaging in social causes, and working at companies who share their values. While I was always personally engaged in social issues, mentoring, and donating time and money, that never factored much into my decision of where I wanted to work, that is, until my most recent job change.

Having spent twenty years in the technology space, I have been to hundreds of tech conferences all over the world, but there was one that always stood out to me. Dreamforce is an annual conference hosted by Salesforce every year in San Francisco. I have attended Dreamforce twelve years in a row, first as an analyst at Gartner and now as an employee of Salesforce, and I can tell you, without question, that it is *the* only conference I have ever been to where I left feeling inspired to be a better human being. I was changed. I wanted to do more.

When I was crafting the outline for *Growth IQ*, I originally intended the **Unconventional Strategies** path to be about how companies were using unique, unorthodox ways to stimulate growth. However, the past two years have exposed me to a different interpretation of what "unconventional" really means, as I've had the opportunity to meet executives who are passionate not only about growing their business but about leveraging their platform, voice, products, employees, partners, and even shareholders to bring about social change.

So much of *Growth IQ* covered the big disruptions happening in business. But successful businesses are embracing their human side and reaching for something deeper; a new value system that has inspired a new Zeitgeist: "*A desire for purpose and mission. An emphasis on positive impact over material gain. A preference for sharing and giving over owning and taking. A willingness to break down silos and connecting the dots in new ways. An urgent, enthusiastic desire to find new solutions to the world's most pressing problems.*"

> **Zeitgeist** is a powerful force embedded in the individuals of a society. The German word *Zeitgeist*, translated literally as "time mind" or "time spirit," is often attributed to the philosopher Georg Hegel, but he never actually used the word.

THE FINAL FRONTIER

This final growth path—**Unconventional Strategies**—is, in terms of cost and labor, not particularly expensive to execute. It cost almost nothing for Steve Jobs to get onstage at the annual Apple convention and inspire thousands of people to want (and buy) his products. He was masterful at making his speeches and product launches about more than just the hardware and software it developed but rather *what people can do with the technology*. Reflect back on some of Apple's most memorable ad campaigns—"Think Different," "Here's to the crazy ones"—all focused on people, not the technology. Whereas the costs may not be prohibitive, in terms of emotional fortitude and courage, this path can be the most demanding of all.

What makes **Unconventional Strategies** so appealing as a growth path is that it has the potential to be a gigantic breakout, making an end run around the competition—and even to pioneer a vast new market. What makes it scary is the potential for catastrophe. Under conventional growth strategies, if your new product line or market entry goes awry, you can usually cut your losses and escape. But by definition, **Unconventional Strategies** represent an embarkation into the unknown. It is hard enough to know when you are successful; it's even harder to recognize when you are in trouble. You are making new rules as you go, so predicting the future can be almost impossible.

This becomes particularly difficult when the new path you take is different from your current business, even orthogonal to it. Choosing to rebrand your business around a charismatic leader or enlisting customers to help design your next generation of products is one thing; building your marketing campaign around an entire twin operation delivering shoes to poor children in the developing world—like TOMS Shoes did, while at the same time making money—is a whole different matter.

Why even try it? If you're a bootstrapped early-stage company with limited time and resources, it can be easy to dismiss corporate social responsibility as something you formalize when you're more established. But giving back can (and should!) be done at every stage of your company's growth. The key is to make sure that doing the right thing is part of your culture and business model from the beginning. Done right, it can create a spectacular breakout against well-established competition, creating a whole paradigm that could take competitors years to catch up. For a mature company in a mature industry, it can shake up the status quo, revitalizing the business, its employees, and its customers and resetting the game—with the innovator enjoying a head start and a second chance to capture a new wave of growth and an entirely new set of customers.

That's the big picture. Less obvious, but often just as important, is the impact an **Unconventional Strategies** approach can have on your most important constituents—employees and customers. Making both proud to be part of such a company—especially if it is work for social good— can improve morale, help with employee retention, and make customers excited to be part of the crusade. Who wanted to work for Apple in the 2000s when it was announcing entire market sector–creating products every couple of years, or Hewlett-Packard in the 1960s when it was considered the most enlightened company on the planet, or Amazon in 2010 when it was reinventing retailing? Or Tesla today? This pride is even greater when you know that your employer is involved in "conscience capitalism," using some of its resources and profits to help the world's needy.

As I've mentioned, when I made my latest change on my career journey, I decided where I wanted to go for very different reasons than I have historically. I wanted to work for a company that was committed to providing quality products and services, of course, but even more so, a company where doing good was part of its core DNA. I have been fortunate to have found both a company and a CEO that fit the bill. *"There's all this incredible energy in your company and you can unleash it for good,"* Marc Benioff, CEO of Salesforce, told Fast Company. *"All you have to do is open the door."*

For Salesforce, that means creating a company with a *purpose beyond profit*. Says Benioff, *"My goals for the company are to do well and do good. The most important thing to me is that we bring along all our stakeholders with us. We had a vision from the beginning that not only would we have a new technology model, which was the cloud, not only would we have a new business model, which was subscription, but we'd have a new philanthropic model, which is 1-1-1."*

When a business like Salesforce gets to scale, with more than thirty thousand employees and customers all over the world, it has an opportunity to influence them in a positive way. There should be no question that it is having a huge positive impact. You can see it in the [widespread] "Pledge 1% campaign," where the 1-1-1 idea has spread to thousands of companies around the globe. It's amazing to think that Salesforce supports more than thirty-two thousand nonprofits and NGOs around the world that use Salesforce for free or at a discount—an extraordinary number matched by very few governments. Salesforce has given more than $170 million in grants and donated 2.3 million hours of Salesforce employee volunteer time. Employees are even given seven days a year to perform volunteer work.

Toward the last, Salesforce commits 1 percent of its equity, employees' time, and product to nonprofit work. "*Not only are we building a great product, but we're building a great company that is trying to create a great world.*" Certainly, it's a source of great talent. People come to the company and stay because of the incredible opportunity and impact that the collective Salesforce *Ohana* ("family" in Hawaiian) has on cities and causes around the world. In 2018, Salesforce was ranked #1 on *Fortune*'s "100 Best Companies to Work For" list.

THE NEW SENTIMENTALISTS

This attitude has spread to a number of business executives, most of whom are hardly sentimentalists. They recognize that it really is possible to do well by doing good. But many are also discovering that it is a lot more complicated than it looks, not least that you sometimes must endure the doubts of skeptics who still believe in the Harvard Business School rule of maximizing shareholder value at the expense of everything else.

One figure who created considerable controversy for his stance regarding his company's larger duty in society is Unilever's CEO, Paul Polman. One of Polman's first moves was to stop Unilever's quarterly financial reporting—in order to free the company from short-term thinking. The market howled, and company stock fell 8 percent. But Polman was unfazed:

What we said was, *in order to solve issues like food security or climate change, you need to have longer-term solutions*. You cannot do that on a quarterly basis. They require longer-term investments. It's the same for companies. A lot of companies are driven by the short-termism of the markets. [They] make short-term decisions that often go against the long-term viability of the company. . . . It's very easy to show more profits, if that's what you want, by cutting investments in training and development of your people or your IT systems. And you can do that for a few years but in the long term, you erode your company. So what I said when I came here is I need to create this environment for the company to make the right longer-term decisions.

Needless to say, many stock traders were upset. Polman's response? "I also made it very clear that certain shareholders were not welcome in this company. . . . I don't have any space for many of these people who really, in the short term, try to basically speculate to make a lot of money. We want people who want to be long term with us and build this company over the long term."

Not many executives have the guts of Paul Polman. He has an **Unconventional Strategies** approach—changing the entire valuation model of corporations—at its most extreme. But any company, if it is careful and systematic, can try a fundamentally new growth path. As the following stories show, it is possible to take a different direction—one congruent to your beliefs and passions—and turn it into the ultimate competitive differentiator—and, in the process, make the world a better place.

BlackRock's chief executive officer, Larry Fink, has posted a 2018 letter to CEOs, cautioning them that the world's largest asset manager won't support companies that fail to make positive contributions to society.

CO-OPETITION

UNCONVENTIONAL
STRATEGIES

CUSTOMER
EXPERIENCE

CUSTOMER
BASE
PENETRATION

PARTNERSHIPS

GROWTH IQ

MARKET
ACCELERATION

CUSTOMERS
CHURN

OPTIMIZE
SALES

CUSTOMER/
PRODUCT
DIVERSIFICATION

PRODUCT
EXPANSION

PATH 10 UNCONVENTIONAL STRATEGIES

STORY
1

TOMS SHOES
HEART AND SOLE

Goals are only wishes unless you have a plan.

**—MELINDA GATES, American philanthropist and
cofounder of the Bill & Melinda Gates Foundation**

CARING CAPITALISM

Some companies come to this **Unconventional Strategies** growth path
after they have become so safely successful that they can risk taking a
long shot on a real breakout strategy. Others try it as a brand "recovery"
plan after a social faux pas or corporate embarrassment. But the third,
and most interesting for our purposes, are the companies that make this
growth path part of their founding design. Some may be small and we'll
never hear about them; others have gone on to become household names
that others aspire to mimic. From organic candy that promotes world
peace to coffee beans for puppy rescues, there's no category that should
be off-limits. *These companies that have made it part of their DNA may
actually offer lessons for those already established brands interested in
pursuing this as both a social and an economic boost.*

One of the first, and most successful, companies to incorporate "social
entrepreneurship" with traditional market capitalism was TOMS Shoes.
Its story gives an interesting glimpse into how taking a nontraditional
growth path not only can pay off on the bottom line but can gain considerable goodwill by benefiting mankind.

TOMS Shoes was founded in 2006 in Playa Del Rey, California, by Blake Mycoskie, a Texas entrepreneur who had successfully founded and sold several companies. Exhausted, he and his wife moved to Southern California, rented an apartment, and took a sabbatical to ponder how to spend the rest of their lives.

A few years before, Blake and his sister, while contestants on the TV show *The Amazing Race*, visited Argentina. He fell in love with the country and, on a return visit in early 2006, noticed that the country's polo players were wearing a unique shoe, the alpargatas, that was a simple slip-on with rope soles. During the visit, while doing volunteer work in Buenos Aires, he noticed how many of the city's poor were without shoes or were wearing castoffs of the wrong size. He resolved to find a way to use the first to solve the second.

Returning to Southern California, he founded TOMS (the name is derived from "Tomorrow's Shoes") with $500,000 in seed money made from selling his online driver training company in Texas. The business plan—to make alpargatas with rubber soles for the North American market—had an interesting added wrinkle: *to provide a new pair of shoes free of charge to youths from Argentina and other developing countries for each pair sold, a for-profit company based on the buy-one, give-one idea.* He received moral support from Bill Gates, who told him the lack of shoes was a major contributor of childhood disease.

Despite being designed as a mechanism for "one-for-one" conscious capitalism, TOMS quickly enough achieved considerable commercial success. Mycoskie initially had commissioned Argentine cobblers to make 250 pairs of shoes of the simplest, "minimally viable" quality and finish to test the concept. Soon after sales officially began in May 2006, the *Los Angeles Times* ran a story on the company. Within days, the company had received two thousand orders.

By the end of the company's first year, it had sold ten thousand pairs. A matching ten thousand free pairs were delivered to Argentinean children in October 2006—news of which only adding to the company's good image. Soon celebrities, among them Tobey Maguire, Keira Knightley, and Scarlett Johansson, were being photographed wearing TOMS. And it was getting lots of positive press from *Vogue*, *People*, *Time*, and *Elle* magazines.

TOMS didn't stop with what it could do on its own—in 2006, with sponsors including AOL, Flickr, and the Discovery Channel, it launched an annual *One Day Without Shoes* event, which encouraged people not to wear shoes for one day in order to raise awareness about the impact shoes can have on a child's life. By 2011, TOMS had an annual growth rate of 300 percent and had *given away its ten millionth pair of shoes*. Similar to other companies showcased in *Growth IQ* (Kylie Jenner, Red Bull, GoPro), TOMS spent little on traditional advertising early on, instead relying on its five million social media followers to create word-of-mouth buzz on its behalf.

By 2012, TOMS had grown from an apartment-based start-up to a global company with $300 million in annual revenues. It used its momentum and growth in its shoe business to fuel the additional growth paths of **Market Acceleration** and **Product Expansion**. While it maintained its core philosophy, it now was pursuing **Customer and Product Diversification** when it decided to expand into eyewear (part of the profit going to save or restore eyesight to the nearly three hundred million people who are visually impaired in developing countries), apparel, and handbags. TOMS Bag Collection supplies funds to train midwives and distributes birth kits for safe childbirth.

But having a strong brand (awareness) for social capitalism doesn't guarantee success if you decide to expand beyond your core products and services. In 2012, Mycoskie sensed something was wrong, despite the fact that TOMS was now a giant company, growing 300 percent per year and having distributed ten million shoes. He stepped down from the CEO position, moved back to Texas with his wife, and took a sabbatical. During that hiatus, Mycoskie pondered the fate of his company and its philosophy. He realized that the company he founded had become more focused on process than purpose. It had lost its way. During the years of hyper-growth

Brands That Use the TOMS Model for One-for-One Giving:

Warby Parker	Smile Squared
Bombas	SoapBox
One World Play Project	Figs
Bixbee	Better World Books
Roma	State

it became disconnected from its greatest competitive advantage: "use business to improve lives."

Mycoskie returned to TOMS revitalized—*and with a plan*. He did not assume the CEO position. Until that point, he owned 100 percent of the company. He decided to sell 50 percent of TOMS, which at the time was valued at $625 million, to Bain Capital in mid-2014, and at the same time he agreed to bring in a more seasoned CEO. It was quite fitting that TOMS hired Jim Alling, who understood socially conscious companies better than most, having been an executive at Starbucks working with Howard Schultz for eleven years.

Next up: TOMS Roasting Company in 2013, and TOMS Bags in 2015. In keeping with the one-for-one promise, purchases of these products help improve the lives of people in need by helping restore sight, providing safe water, supporting safe birthing practices, and aiding bullying prevention programs. Mycoskie was going back to first principles. "*My mission was clear: Make* TOMS *a movement again*"—and improve lives.

When it was time for TOMS to celebrate its anniversary, it did it the best way it knew how: by giving back. On the tenth anniversary of its One Day Without Shoes awareness campaign, it encouraged social media users to take a picture of their bare feet or their TOMS and tag a photo with a **#withoutshoes**. Every photo shared counted toward giving up to one hundred thousand new pairs of shoes to children in ten countries.

Today, after a decade in business, TOMS enjoys annual sales of an estimated $400 million, employs 550 employees, and has five products, each with its own one-for-one offer combined with additional give-back programs such as eye exams, medical care, and sometimes even surgery based on the various needs of a particular country. Its products are sold by hundreds of retailers around the world—including Whole Foods (Amazon), and it partners with over one hundred NGOs and other nonprofit partners in more than seventy countries. Just as important, *it has distributed more than seventy million free shoes and delivered 175,000 weeks of clean water to the developing world*. Not least, TOMS's concept of "one-for-one" support has become a model to socially conscious companies around the world.

Writing in *Harvard Business Review*, Mycoskie said, "I feel more energized and committed than ever. As far as we've come, I still see tre-

UNCONVENTIONAL STRATEGIES

IN TERMS OF COST and LABOR NOT PARTICULARLY EXPENSIVE TO EXECUTE

DOING GOOD *by* DOING GOOD

One for One.

TOMS

FOUNDED IN 2006

BLAKE MYCOSKIE VISITED ARGENTINA ON THE TV SHOW *The Amazing* RACE

MANY OF CITY'S POOR WERE WITHOUT SHOES

NOTICED THAT POLO PLAYERS WERE WEARING *a unique shoe* THE ALPARGATAS — *but*

BUSINESS PLAN

MAKE ALPARGATAS FOR NORTH AMERICAN MARKET AND

to provide a new pair of shoes free of charge for each pair sold

buy-one, give-one **IN 2006**

ONE DAY WITHOUT SHOES ANNUAL CAMPAIGN

Step 1

click a picture of your feet #WITHOUTSHOES

Step 2

POST TO instagram with hashtag #WithoutSHOES

Step 3

TAG YOUR FRIENDS TO JOIN THE MOVEMENT

YOUR PHOTO COUNTS TOWARD GIVING 100,000 NEW PAIRS OF SHOES TO CHILDREN IN 10 COUNTRIES

it has distributed more than 70 MILLION free shoes and delivered 175,000 weeks of clean water to the developing world.

mendous opportunities to grow our movement. The 'why' of TOMS—using business to improve lives—is bigger than myself, the shoes we sell, or any future products we might launch. . . . Now that

Being an inspiration is gratifying. Being a catalyst is satisfying.

—BLAKE MYCOSKIE

I have a clear purpose and amazing partners supporting me, I'm ready for the company's next 10 years and the many adventures ahead."

TOMS SHOES
KEY TAKEAWAYS

- Mycoskie has built a company that is winning both sales and hearts by giving away a pair of shoes for every one that it sells through its business. While not every company is able to start with this one-for-one model, look for ways you may be able to use this concept within a single product line or during certain promotional events. This model has been emulated by some of the most disruptive and hot companies, such as Warby Parker and Bombas (recently purchased by Walmart).

- The line is blurring between nonprofit and for-profit organizations. TOMS just happened to catch the context of the market perfectly. It was able to intersect with the rise in consumers who have become more conscious about their spending. They are willing to spend on consumer goods that also do some good in the world. Using a value proposition like that for positioning and messaging—"cause-related" marketing—can help a company improve its brand reputation as good corporate citizens, but only if the message is authentic to who and what the brand is.

  - Attach a story to your product.
  - Give customers pride in wearing/using your product
  - Make efforts sustainable via one-for-one.

- TOMS's success was fueled by one product, shoes. When it began to branch out into new product and customer categories

277

(**Customer and Product Diversification**), it got distracted and began to lose its way. Let's, for a moment, reflect on Starbucks, another brand that had lost its "soul" as it started to expand its products and services. Starbucks became disconnected from its greatest competitive advantage—**Customer Experience**—but found its way back. Both CEOs took time away, and when they came back, they returned with a renewed sense of clarity. You could even add Steve Jobs to the mix. Time away provided him with an entirely new sense of purpose. It unleashed another level of "vision" that he applied to Apple. *Taking a step back, pausing, and hitting reset is sometimes the best way to move forward.*

STORY
2

LEMONADE INSURANCE
WHEN LIFE GIVES YOU LEMONS

We have to execute our purpose objectives in order to deliver performance. It is not Performance and Purpose; it is not Performance or Purpose; it is Performance with Purpose.

—INDRA NOOYI, chairman and CEO of PepsiCo

THE WILLINGNESS TO TAKE AN Unconventional Strategy path is right there in the name—*Lemonade Insurace*. In any industry, the name would be fun; but in the staid old insurance industry, where companies are named after cities and Founding Fathers, it was obviously designed to raise eyebrows. The two men who founded Lemonade in April 2015 had no previous insurance experience other than buying policies. They were, in fact, serial technology entrepreneurs. Looking for new opportunities, they spotted in the insurance industry a nearly $5 trillion market ripe for a technological, digital revolution.

- **"Eighty-one percent of millennials even expect their favorite companies to make public declarations of their corporate citizenship"**
- **"Eighty-three percent of junior staff would prefer to work for a company that operates with a social purpose"**

As mentioned earlier, millennials are looking for brands that contribute to a greater purpose. *More than a third have said they would spend more on a brand that supports a cause they believe in.* While many industries are starting to take note and take more socially progressive stances, the insurance industry may in fact be held back by its long legacy and established business models.

That was the context from which Daniel Schreiber and Shai Wininger launched their company. The insurance business in the United States suffered from poor customer satisfaction (i.e., a poor **Customer Experience**) and was far behind in the application of the latest information technologies, notably big data analytics and social networks (**Customer and Product Diversification**).

The pair set out to attack those weaknesses with a combination of behavioral and digital technology, social media, and a new sales and service model—and to roll them in rapid sequence to create an integrated and unique **Customer Experience**. The goal was to create a brand-new insurance user experience that realigned the customer with the insurer in regard to coverage, ease of use, and incentives—in other words, an almost complete break with hundreds of years of insurance company history. Focusing on ways to **Optimize Sales** as a growth strategy is good, but not necessarily a game changer. However, combining that with the most **Unconventional Strategies** part of the start-up was its promise to *"give back up to 40 percent of premiums to a cause its customers want to support."*

Wait, what? Yes, you read that correctly. Lemonade will ask its customers to "nominate a charity when they first buy a policy." It then collects the premiums of everyone who has chosen the same charity and puts it into a single pool, which pays claims. *Anything left over goes to their chosen charity.* That, and that alone, was by far the most profound break from other insurance carriers, many of which follow a much more traditional path of social responsibility, such as Allstate and Insurance Australia Group, both on *Fortune* magazine's 2017 "Change the World" list.

The basic financial model was comparatively simple and straightforward. Lemonade charged a 20 percent flat fee on the customer's premium. The company used the remaining 80 percent to pay claims and purchase reinsurance (typically through Lloyd's of London). This was already a new paradigm.

Traditionally, insurance companies earn their money through a "float"—that is, by investing customer premiums—then (when everything goes right) paying out less in claims and expenses than they took in from premiums and earning an underwriting profit. Lemonade instead not only simplified the process but, in the process, removed itself from being in an adversarial role with its own clients. But it didn't stop there—it got even more interesting: *any unclaimed premiums were then to be awarded annually to a nonprofit of the user's choosing in a program titled "Giveback."*

> *Giveback* is a unique feature of Lemonade, where each year leftover money is donated to causes our policyholders care about. We treat policyholders who care about the same causes as virtual groups of "peers." Lemonade uses the premiums collected from each peer group to pay the group's claims, giving back any leftover money to their common cause, and uses reinsurance to cover for cases where the group's claims exceed what's left in the pool.

Beyond the obvious difference in business models with its Giveback program, Lemonade is taking advantage of new technology such as artificial intelligence, in particular machine learning and chatbots (programs that can talk directly to users in a conversational language) to work with its customers in policy creation and claims handling.

What the claimants didn't know was that their entire interaction with Lemonade had been carefully orchestrated from the start to convince them not to try to defraud the company—including signing a pledge of honesty at the beginning (instead of at the end) of the claims process. They also spoke directly into their computer or phone's camera to make their claims—psychologically more supportive of honesty than merely filling out a claim form.

By the same token, the Giveback program not only enhanced Lemonade's reputation as a good company to belong to (it is officially, and legally, a "social benefit corporation") but also reinforced honest dealings. After all, cheating Lemonade on a false claim is as good as taking money from your favorite charity—it's not just a big, anonymous company you

are ripping off but people in need. And not any people, but ones the customers actually nominated when they first bought their policies.

Giveback essentially puts "unclaimed money" out of reach of both the company and its customers. Further solidifying this message for customers and prospects alike is the knowledge that Lemonade is one of the few insurance companies in the world to receive B Corporation certification

As of December 2017, Lemonade has raised a total of $180 million in investment capital from a blue-ribbon list of investors that includes Japanese telecom giant SoftBank and Silicon Valley venture giants Sequoia Capital and GV (Google Ventures).

The customers who are joining largely fit the same profile—younger, educated, tech-savvy, above-average earners, passionate about giving back—and almost a fifty-fifty split of male and female policyholders.

for its commitment to social and environmental justice—the equivalent of being a "fair trade" food or coffee vendor.

While the company still has a comparatively small footprint—in August 2017, Lemonade Insurance had forty-eight employees and $2 million in revenue—it has signed up more than fourteen thousand customers. That's minuscule compared to the industry titans. Still, *in fewer than two years, Lemonade had become the largest insurer of first-time buyers (many of them millennials) of renter's insurance—surpassing such insurance titans as Allstate, Geico, Progressive, State Farm, and USAA.* It has been able to secure $325 million of reinsurance protection from two of the top three global reinsurers. All of those accomplishments have made it one of the hottest—and most honored—new start-up companies in America.

Lemonade knew that its Giveback program would help it attract a certain type of customer, but as you have learned throughout *Growth IQ*, it is the combination of efforts that provides the competitive advantage. In this case Lemonade used **Unconventional Strategies** approaches with **Optimize Sales** and **Customer Experience** in combination as its secret sauce.

This approach has allowed Lemonade to buck another industry trend—selling insurance to women. To put that statement in context, in the United States, a man is 50 percent more likely to buy a home insurance policy than a woman. But at Lemonade, a woman is 50 percent more likely to buy a policy than her male counterpart. The unintended consequences of the various growth paths Lemonade has chosen to pursue in combination has been attracting an "underrepresented" segment of the market: *women.* Lemonade didn't intentionally target female customers; rather, it focused on its core mission and value proposition of giving back, ease of use, and aligned values. Male or female, *that is* the target demographic it is attracting.

Lemonade is the most exciting and innovative company the insurance industry has seen in a long time. It has managed to do what was considered impossible until now: form a huge community of like-minded people in insurance, while maintaining growth at a historic pace. As consultant Miguel Ortiz told the *Economist*, the big bet for Lemonade is that "it can stay ahead of a sleepy industry by doing standard insurance processes better than everyone else." For now and into the foreseeable future, Lemonade is winning that bet. John Sheldon Peters, Lemonade's chief insurance officer, wrote: *"We love our customers, think they fit well with Lemonade's values and mission, and are thrilled each time another member joins the Lemonade family."*

LEMONADE INSURANCE
KEY TAKEAWAYS

- Lemonade Insurance used the historic preconceptions and poor customer experience in the insurance industry to its advantage. *Market intelligence was its road map.* When developing its product, it looked to significantly improve customer experience across the key pain points current insurance customers were complaining about. First, it began with the idea that it would give unclaimed premiums to charity via the company's Giveback program. Next, it launched on Product Hunt—a website that lets users share and discover new products. It was the first insurance company to be featured on the site. Then it was very clear about its target demographic. And finally, and maybe most important, it focused on user experience, meaning: everything from buying insurance to making a claim can be completed via the app, with no human intervention: It "takes as little as 90 seconds to get insured and just three minutes to get paid."

- Lemonade prides itself on its transparency. It uses its blog *Transparency Chronicles* to share metrics and performance data—information that other insurance companies don't freely share. Providing this information creates a brand that is open and socially conscious, which appeals to its customer base.

- Lemonade Insurance knows its target demographic and uses technology to constantly monitor changes in its customer base. Its customers are "25–44 and 87% have never bought insurance for their homes before." The millennial generation is more socially conscious and technically savvy, so Lemonade's giveback philosophy and technology investments resonate well. The technology investments specifically have proven to be a huge industry differentiator.

STORY
3

GRAMEEN BANK
IN BANGLADESH
ON PURPOSE

*Purpose is that sense that we are part of something
bigger than ourselves, that we are needed, that we have
something better ahead to work for. Purpose is what
creates true happiness. . . . To keep our society moving
forward, we have a generational challenge—to not only
create new jobs, but create a renewed sense of purpose.*

—MARK ZUCKERBERG

THROUGHOUT *GROWTH IQ,* **EACH PATH** chapter included a
"Story 3" emphasizing *"what not to do."* Path 10, **Unconventional
Strategies,** lives up to its name by breaking from that tradition and
ending with a positive Story 3. Social entrepreneurship comes in as many
forms as there are human needs in the world. Hunger, exploitation, il-
literacy, deep poverty, and disease still threaten the lives of hundreds of
millions of people around the world. Traditionally, helping to alleviate
this suffering has been the work of charities and nonprofit institutions.
But beginning *at the turn of the century a new philosophy, a new business
model, began to emerge: social enterprises, as they are called.*

In their original incarnation, these enterprises were almost always
nonprofit. There were two differences between them and traditional
charities. First, they weren't targeted at a single group, location, or project
but were designed to create sweeping societal change. Second, they were
designed to emulate existing commercial entrepreneurial start-ups. That
is, they were designed to be scalable up to millions of people, they would
eventually become self-sustaining, and their impact would be measurable
and comparable.

A classic example of great social enterprise is Grameen Bank in Bangladesh, for which its founder, Muhammad Yunus, was awarded the Nobel Peace Prize. As their website explains, "The origin of Grameen Bank ('Grameen' means 'rural' or 'village' in Bangla language) can be traced back to 1976 when Professor Muhammad Yunus, head of the economics program at the University of Chittagong, launched an action research project to examine the possibility of designing a credit delivery system to provide banking services targeted at the rural poor."

THE GRAMEEN BANK PROJECT CAME INTO OPERATION WITH THE FOLLOWING OBJECTIVES:

- Extend banking facilities to poor men and women;
- Eliminate the exploitation of the poor by money lenders;
- Create opportunities for self-employment for the vast multitude of unemployed people in rural Bangladesh;
- Bring the disadvantaged, mostly the women from the poorest households, within the fold of an organizational format that they can understand and manage by themselves; and
- Reverse the age-old vicious circle of "low income, low saving & low investment," into virtuous circle of "low income, injection of credit, investment, more income, more savings, more investment, more income."

Grameen pioneered micro-loans: tiny, no-collateral loans to the very poor that depended on social pressure to guarantee their payment. He did so in the belief that capital is a friend of the poor and that its accumulation by the poor represents their best means of escaping the abject poverty that the welfare state and wasteful, corrupt, and incompetent international aid organizations have failed to combat. Yunus's concept not only had a major impact on Bangladeshi society but has been duplicated with great success around the world.

SOCIAL ENTREPRENEURSHIP

Part of the impetus behind social entrepreneurship came from foundations, which found themselves unable to turn off the money spigot for ongoing legacy causes, often for years—even while new programs clamored for their support. The idea was that these programs could, through thoughtful product and service development, financial discipline, and good business practices, eventually become self-sustaining—either through covering their costs or, as in the case of the Red Cross, gaining sufficient support of the general public.

The pursuit of this goal led, two decades ago, to the creation of important new institutions, including the Skoll Foundation and Ashoka, dedicated to investing sizable sums to get the kinks out of this new model and educate the first generation of social entrepreneurs. They have had mixed success—too often, these programs fail to become self-sustaining and fall back onto the rolls of perpetually requiring institutional support.

More successful has been the arrival, in the Internet Age, of crowdsourcing: the use of the scaling powers of the Web to present charitable (as well as commercial) opportunities in front of millions of private citizens. Crowdsourcing can claim credit for the support of thousands of social enterprises in its first decade.

But an entirely unexpected revolution in the support of social entrepreneurship has been the arrival of for-profit commercial companies—such as TOMS Shoes and Lemonade Insurance—on the scene. At first, most of these initiatives were seen as the product of a softhearted senior executive or as positive public relations for a company caught in a scandal . . . but in recent years, that has seen a radical change.

Today, an increasing number of companies have recognized social enterprise investment—from a company foundation to setting up an independent entity to integrating social entrepreneurship directly into company operations—as an important new way for a company to combine its current operations with an **Unconventional Strategies** approach. *Not just as a way to look good but actually as a way to grow the organization.*

For that reason, *social entrepreneurship can be considered one of the most compelling forms of Unconventional Strategies paths*—one that can not only bind existing customers (who want to be part of such a positive

Grameen Bank

PIONEERED
MICRO-LOANS

CAPITAL IS A FRIEND OF
THE POOR

Founder
Muhammad Yunus's
belief that

FOUNDER
MUHAMMAD YUNUS
WAS AWARDED
NOBEL
PEACE PRIZE

SOCIAL
ENTERPRISE

NOT JUST A WAY TO LOOK GOOD BUT
A WAY TO GROW THE ORGANIZATION

CONSCIOUS
CAPITALISM

☑ CREATE A HEALTHY CULTURE
☑ ATTRACT TOP TALENT
☑ LONG-TERM PURPOSE

crusade) but also attract new ones (who are attracted to the company's image). It can also discipline a company in special ways, create healthy corporate culture, attract top-notch new employees, and give the company a higher, long-term purpose beyond simply short-term profits.

Pioneers in this work have been The Bill and Melinda Gates Foundation, notably in their work fighting malaria in Africa. Though, strictly speaking, theirs is an extremely well-funded charitable organization, the presence of one of the most successful commercial entrepreneurs in history at its helm, with his tough, empirical discipline regarding investments, has been a signal to other business leaders to investigate taking the same step.

A growing number of companies are experimenting with different forms of "conscious capitalism," ranging from direct donations to the matching of employee donations, setting aside a fixed percentage of quarterly profits, one-to-one matching between sales and donations, creation of independent foundations, sponsorship of training schools, and even supporting a shift to social entrepreneurship through new value measurements (intellectual capital audits, carbon offsets, etc.). In classic fashion, these companies are experimenting with new models in a way that nonprofits rarely do—all disciplined by customers, investors, and the marketplace.

The good news: *"Doing well, by doing good" is not only possible—done right, it can be an authentic way to connect with your employees, customers, partners, and shareholders in a meaningful way.* But more important, it goes a long way to make all the hard work have greater impact than just dollars earned.

When we know better, we do better. When we get, we should give.

THE "GOOD-IFICATION" OF BUSINESS

UNCOVENTIONAL STRATEGIES
KEY TAKEAWAYS

■ Looking for an unmet need in the market and aligning that with a socially conscious business model can be a compelling combination. It can reshape an entire town, city, country, or demographic. Like what PayPal is trying to do by bringing the "un-banked" into the fold: giving access to money, financial tools and loans can lift people out of poverty and give them a chance for a better life.

■ Ideas can come from even the briefest of encounters. As with TOMS and with Grameen Bank, a single interaction transformed an entire "microlending" movement. Looking for a market "need" may be as simple as—well, experiencing a market need. When you see an opportunity to make a difference, and you have the means, wherewithal, and capital to do so—do it!

PUTTING IT ALL TOGETHER
"WALK THE WALK"

When you sacrifice [corporate culture] all on hyper-growth, it has a price on human capital.

—ARIANNA HUFFINGTON

ONE OF THE BIGGEST ADVANTAGES of pursuing an **Unconventional Strategies** growth path is that, when it works, it draws considerable attention from customers, the media, the markets, and competitors. Get it right and you can help change the world even as you reward your shareholders. *"Mission-driven" companies tend to have 30 percent higher levels of innovation and 40 percent higher levels of retention.*

Companies with highly engaged workforces outperform their peers in earnings per share by 147 percent. Growing a great company can be immensely satisfying, but saving millions of lives is a supreme achievement for you and every employee and stakeholder in your company. What greater legacy?

■ ■ ■

WHAT WORKS—AND POTENTIAL PITFALLS

COMBINATION: PATH 10—
Unconventional Strategies + Path 8—Partnerships

As we showed in the chapter on this path, **Partnerships** are a very powerful growth tool, as they enable you to reduce the risk of taking on some higher-risk strategies, including entering into new markets, developing new products, marketing and promotion, and filling in blanks in your company's skill portfolios. One of the advantages of having pursued the **Unconventional Strategies** growth path is that it expands your universe of potential partners beyond the conventional choices pursued by your competitors.

COMBINATION: PATH 10—
Unconventional Strategies + Path 9—Co-opetition

We stand on the brink of a technological revolution that will fundamentally alter the way we live, work, and relate to one another. In its scale, scope, and complexity, the transformation will be unlike anything humankind has experienced before. We do not yet know just how it will unfold, but one thing is clear: the response to it must be integrated and comprehensive, involving all stakeholders of the global polity, from the public and private sectors to academia and civil society.

—KLAUS SCHWAB, founder and executive chairman of the World Economic Forum

The idea of finding common cause to work in targeted areas with your competitor is appealing. But it usually runs into one big problem: your competitors usually have pretty much the same strengths and weaknesses that you do. Otherwise, they would have either fallen behind or raced ahead to industry dominance. The chances that you can find a scenario where you can slot together to produce something greater than the sum of your two operations are likely pretty slim.

On the other hand, if you are successfully pursuing one or

more **Unconventional Strategies** approaches, it is likely that you now really *are* different from your potential partner/competitor in important and valuable ways. The result is a chance for an industry "hat trick"— success in pursuing an **Unconventional Strategies** growth path that sets you apart from the competition that segues into a **Co-opetition** growth path with one of those competitors that slingshots into a position of defensible industry dominance.

KNOWING WHEN TO JUMP

TEN GROWTH PATHS—IT'S COMFORTING TO think that's all there are: a manageable number of options for how to proceed into the future. But I also suspect that a thought has been growing in your mind as we've marched through the descriptions of these paths: *How do you know when one path is ending and it's time to jump to another?*

This may be the most important question of all. Even if you choose the right path to take, if you do so too early or too late, it may all be for naught. The analogy is trying to cross a stream by jumping from boulder to boulder . . . except that the rocks are moving. Time it wrong and you may find yourself falling into the water.

You can understand the context of your business, you can determine the combination of actions you need to take, and even execute in the right sequence. You may even accurately pick the next growth path you need to take. But if you jump too soon, you may leave money on the table from your current growth path (and maybe land in a still-unformed opportunity), and if you jump too late, you may miss altogether the window to that opportunity. Jumping from one growth path to the next requires the orchestration and precision of a military campaign.

In other words, to context, combination, and sequence, we need to add one more factor: timing. That kind of timing is not an instant in time. No company should ever identify a need to change a current growth path and then instantly take the leap. Rather, *there are three crucial factors that must be addressed: monitoring, preparation, and execution.* Let's look at each in turn.

MONITORING

The key to operating any of the ten growth paths is to ride them until you have wrung out every ounce of revenues, profits, and market development and then make the (next) leap—that is, when the growth curve of the path begins to plateau, when you still have the maximum momentum, not when the financials have begun to flatten—or worse, to fall—and the company starts to stall, lose customers, and see the departure of key talent.

How do you know if your current growth path is about to stall, before it does? If you wait for two quarters of flattened or falling revenues, you may be too late.

The answer? *Establish metrics for your company's health and put systems in place to monitor those metrics.* Doing so is more possible than ever before, thanks to complex algorithms, artificial intelligence, CRM, analytics, information processing, and big data. Some companies are even establishing the new position of chief data officer (not to be confused with chief information officer), whose task is to continuously gather data from operations throughout the company, process it, and deliver it in a cogent way—often some kind of user-configured control panel—so that

> *Not everything that can be counted counts, and not everything that counts can be counted.*
>
> **—WILLIAM BRUCE CAMERON, novelist**

management can monitor the "vital signs" of a company in real time. Short of that, smaller companies can use the Web and internal networks to constantly poll existing operations and assemble the equivalent overview.

In either case, the goal is to create a fast-enough feedback loop to identify new trends within a company before they fully emerge and have a major (and incontrovertible) impact. Sometimes the more dangerous of these trends (a jump in customer returns, a decrease in product yield rates) can be fixed, but others, such as a growing amount of discounting or a failing number of patent filings, may not be fixable and signal that it is time to find a new growth path.

What metrics should a company be measuring? There are actually two answers:

- The first is simple *company health*. Thus: orders, shipments, returns, product repairs, market share, employee turnover, profit margins, cost of goods sold, salaries, and so on.
- The second is more complicated: every growth path has its own set of *metrics*. Thus, entering a partnership has its own measures, such as sales contribution, customer acquisitions, market coverage; whereas churn includes rate of customer replacement, cost of acquisition, and LTV. That much should seem obvious. Perhaps more surprising is that you also need to begin monitoring key factors in your company related to your next growth path.

How do you do that? It is more straightforward than you may think. *Chances are that when you do make the leap, there are a handful of follow-up paths, which are more likely to be the right combination decision for you.* That should make your task a whole lot easier—you only have to begin measuring the key metrics of the most likely of those follow-up paths. Or, test your next most likely jump by monitoring certain metrics to find any hidden gotchas or opportunities in advance of adding another path.

This doesn't have to be done as assiduously as your primary metrics, but it should be done consistently—both to make sure that the new growth path is still desirable when you do jump and to give you a running start on your new "vital signs" when you get there.

HERE IS A QUICK LIST OF THE MAJOR METRICS YOU MAY WANT TO MONITOR FOR EACH OF THE TEN GROWTH PATHS:

- Path 1: **Customer Experience** > Net Promoter Score (NPS)
- Path 2: **Customer Base Penetration** > RFM (recency, frequency, monetary)

- Path 3: **Market Acceleration** > New logos acquired
- Path 4: **Product Expansion** > New product usage, mix against current portfolio
- Path 5: **Customer and Product Diversification** > Adoption rates within new customer/product categories pursued
- Path 6: **Optimize Sales** > Quota attainment
- Path 7: **Churn** (Minimize Defection) > Churn rate and customer defection trends
- Path 8: **Partnerships** > Joint sales/revenue brought in
- Path 9: **Co-opetition** > New joint product development and market launches
- Path 10: **Unconventional Strategies** > Volunteer hours of employees

PREPARATION

If you were to abandon your current business and lead your company into a brand-new one, wouldn't you want some time—months even—to do so? Why would think you would need less time to jump from one growth path to another? Ask yourself: What do I already know about the nature of those most likely combination paths? How best can I prepare my company and my people, and what do I need to set myself up for success?

> *Success is where preparation and opportunity meet.*
>
> **—BOBBY UNSER,**
> **auto racer**

For a start, you already know what metrics in the new growth paths you should be monitoring. You should also be thinking about creating a market intelligence team (even if it's just one person) who consistently monitors competitor intelligence, product intelligence, market/context understanding, and changes in customer behaviors, buying habits, and expectations. The team should have "an ongoing, holistic knowledge of all aspects of the marketplace." The output of that group would be a (real-time) complete dossier on the industry, customers, and your future competitors. And if you are really interested in learning, look outside your industry to what others are doing that would be applicable in your business.

Most of your preparation will be internal. Nearly every department in your company will be affected by the jump to a new growth path. This is not a piecemeal change done over time—the sequence of efforts may happen everywhere simultaneously, but maybe not at the same pace. That can only happen if you develop a battle plan that identifies what needs to be done in each department and how that plan will be executed, including deadline dates (days after the green light is given for the jump) by which the transformation must be completed.

If this plan is to succeed, you will have to put some teeth into it—*all employees in the organization need to understand how vital their roles are.* The plan also must be decisive: each department needs to determine in advance which employees have been rendered superfluous by the change or are needed elsewhere. New talent needed for this new growth path will have to be characterized, and the departments need to be prepared to begin recruiting when given the green light.

EXECUTION

Any company, regardless of size, can have the greatest ideas—*but the best ideas will only be as good as its ability to execute.* You have determined through the market intelligence team you have put in place, the new metrics you are now monitoring, and an enhanced understanding of changes in the market context that it's time to jump to a new path. Now it all comes down to execution.

So when it's time to execute, what can you do to improve the likelihood of success?

Improve communication, for one thing. *Those companies that have been successful at navigating themselves out of a growth stall or have increased top-line growth have developed a strong internal and external communication engine.* They have processes in place to begin the communication and education process internally. Remember, *the most important resource you have when embarking on growth is preparing your people,* since they are the ones who will actually make

> *Execution is not just tactics—it is a discipline and a system. It has to be built into a company's strategy, its goals, and its culture.*
>
> **—RAM CHARAN,**
> **coauthor of *Execution***

it all happen. If you don't have them on board, it will all be for naught. They will either just go through the motions, doing the minimum to keep their job, or they will sabotage the efforts, consciously or unconsciously, by resisting changes that need to occur.

Next, you may want to consider creating two different working groups within the company. One team would be focused on bringing in new revenue (via the current growth path[s]) and protecting the existing business from an unwanted decline. This team would have the responsibility of continuing to maximize returns from previous investments and looking for opportunities to enhance current efforts. Otherwise, the decline in the existing business will put too much (additional) pressure on the new path to deliver quickly. *Basically—make the current business the best it can be!*

The second is what I like to call a "pop-up team," which is a group within the company focused exclusively on the planning and execution of all new growth path(s). Those who are part of this second team will be relieved of their day-to-day duties, freeing them up to focus on the task at hand—*the successful planning and execution of a new growth path.*

Dividing and conquering in this way reduces the risk of unnecessary distractions, benefiting the company. One is tasked with making sure the business keeps running as smoothly as it possibly can, while the other is totally dedicated to looking forward to the future—where the company needs to be going. The downside of creating a pop-up team is if a company is too small, carving out even a few resources cuts too deep into current efforts. It also puts another layer of complexity into the business for the leadership team, especially since it will most likely have to stay involved with both groups to ensure coordination on critical cross-functional decisions. This goes back the "Seller's Dilemma" I introduced earlier. Keeping the car going around the track while you're changing tires is tough, whether you're a big or a small company.

Ultimately, success may come not from putting into place the right new tools and processes to operate efficiently on this new path but from changing the culture and attitudes and operating philosophy of the employees who will execute that philosophy. And that represents a far greater challenge to management. Thus, a fiercely independent and insular company may recognize the value of a **Partnership,** or even a **Co-opetition,** relationship with another company and simply not find the resolve or commitment to pull it off. By the same token, the innovative product-oriented company may recognize the need to finally monetize its success with a new commitment to marketing and sales but is temperamentally incapable of transforming the company to that new direction.

What this means is that following a strategy of pursuing optimal growth paths may not be as simple as it looks. Sure, the good news is that there is a finite number of paths available, and the number of viable new paths available to a current path amount to only a handful . . . but in the real world, the number of options for your company in its current configuration (culture, resources, key employees, etc.) may be even fewer than that.

A great leader can lead the kind of shifts in attitude and practice that not only make all potential new paths possible but a greater degree of success in the one chosen. That's why the right growth path only makes successful continued growth possible. *Making it real requires the right combination and sequence, and strong execution, as well as* vision and great leadership. That is why preparation is so important. The most successful companies in the world regularly change direction—and do it with such confidence and coordination that it looks almost effortless. As you now see, it is anything but.

WHAT'S NEXT

Staying endlessly on your new path is ultimately as deadly as sticking to your first one. In time—months, years, if you're lucky, decades—you will again find yourself at a crossroads—either facing an amazing opportunity to accelerate growth or an impending growth stall. And in the fast-moving world of twenty-first-century business, that next jump will likely need to occur sooner rather than later. And so it begins again.

Here is a fact that the best leaders understand, but everyone else wrestles with: *growth needs to be countercyclical. The best time to create the next big opportunity is when things are going well, not when you are struggling.* Too often I have seen situations in which sales are booming, growth is accelerating, a company is crushing it, and most leaders tend to get a bit overconfident in their future and their existing growth strategies. As the saying goes, they make hay while the sun is shining. But then the rain comes. The economy slows. The once reliable products or services have begun to lag. There are unexpected new competitors. Customers are going elsewhere. . . . You know the list.

> *When we do something in the course of the day matters almost as much as what we actually do.*
>
> **—DANIEL H. PINK, author of *When: The Scientific Secrets of Perfect Timing***

Only then does leadership realize that the company is in a full-blown growth stall. Leadership springs into action, awoken by a true sense of urgency. It begins to assemble a team to dig into what is going on. It pulls its best and brightest to come up with a plan once it understands what is going on. Then it looks to execute that plan quickly—even if ill-prepared. *But by this point, it is too late.* Here's why.

Unfortunately, your company is perfectly engineered to create the outcomes it is currently creating for yesterday's market context. In other words, it doesn't have the internal fortitude or capability to change quickly enough. So, under the pressure of slowing sales or waning market relevance, your perfectly engineered machine will tighten its grip on the past. The well-meaning changes will focus relentlessly on your past success formula, spending more marketing dollars, hiring more salespeople, and cutting expenses—thus accelerating your demise because what worked in the past will no longer work in the future. Making a better buggy whip, a faster film camera, a quieter typewriter, or even cleaner coal won't keep the stagecoach operators, film processors, typesetters, or miners employed.

AMAZON CASE STUDY:

STAYING IN DAY ONE

If we have a good quarter, it's because of the work we did three, four, and five years ago. It's not because we did a good job this quarter.

—JEFF BEZOS

PERHAPS NO COMPANY IN OUR time has more successfully navigated the *Growth IQ* paths, in all their nuances and complexities, than **Amazon**. In less than a quarter century, the company has grown from just a dream in the imagination of founder Jeff Bezos as he drove across the United States, to one of the world's most valuable companies, the first to realize a market cap of $1 trillion—and Bezos himself is one of the world's richest men. The company currently employs more than half a million full- and part-time employees around the world and has annual revenues of nearly $180 billion. That makes it the largest Internet retailer in the world as measured by revenues and market value, and if its revenue were a country's GDP, it would be the world's fifty-fifth richest nation.

Amazon has been so successful, has grown so quickly—and dominated so many new markets—*that the entire business world perpetually waits in nervous anticipation of its next move.* Those moves—successful or not—are often unexpected. AWS, Kindle, Whole Foods . . . who, outside Amazon's executive row, saw these moves coming?

But looking through the lens of *Growth IQ*, it's not only possible to understand Amazon's moves but appreciate their inevitability. In little more than two decades the company has sprinted through all of the ten growth paths, some of them more than once. Seeing how quickly Amazon navigated its way in and out of certain growth paths and combined efforts in the right sequence can only leave one in awe. Amazon isn't so successful—and feared as a competitor—because of the paths it has taken, but how deftly it has identified each new path to jump to and quickly made the move.

It is a strategy that every company should emulate, if only on a smaller scale and over a longer time frame. Let's take a look, through the lens of *Growth IQ*, at how Amazon did it:

A PHILOSOPHY OF PERPETUAL CHANGE

Jeff Bezos founded Amazon in July 1994. The idea for the company came during a cross-country trip from New York, where he'd just resigned as vice president of a brokerage, to Seattle, where he intended to start a new company. Amazon was the result.

Amazon introduced itself to the world as a seller of books online. It seemed a modest ambition—and few noticed the new firm at first.

But Amazon had much, much bigger plans. Bookselling was just its beachhead strategy—pursuing Growth Path 1: **Customer Experience**. It set out to give those early book-buying customers the best possible service—even if it meant six years of unprofitability—including four years after the company went public—that made it something of a joke on Wall Street.

But Amazon had the last laugh. It was, after all, the dot-com boom, and Amazon was awash in cash . . . which it spent on that **Customer Experience**, including warehouses, fulfillment technology, vast inventories, and one of the most efficient delivery systems. The result, for most customers, was that Amazon matched the buying experience of neighborhood bookstores, delivered books quickly enough to challenge the experience of commuting and store shopping, and offered a collection of products unmatched anywhere.

It took a while to put all of these pieces in place, then operate them to perfection—but when done, customers began to flock to Amazon by the millions. Profitability came soon thereafter, in 2001.

Meanwhile, the company set about perfecting an ordering system that made purchasing books easy—even impulsive: "one-click" with a powerful "recommendation engine." This next move was all about Growth Path 6: **Optimize Sales**. Both innovative online (customer-focused) processes have been copied by almost every other online retailer ever since. To put this into perspective, the importance of the recommendation engine can be gauged by the fact that 35 percent of all sales are estimated to be generated by this one investment.

Amazon furthered this optimization by introducing a premium purchase and delivery system, Amazon Prime, in 2005. Everything was now in place. Amazon had revolutionized the book-selling industry. Thousands of smaller bookstores were struggling—and even the big retailers were facing an uncertain future. Amazon now made its next jump.

A decade before, as he developed the Amazon business plan, Bezos listed twenty potential markets waiting to move onto the Internet. Now, the company was ready to realize all of them, and more. It pivoted to Growth Path 2: **Customer Base Penetration**. Starting in 2006, it signed numerous merchant partnerships, including ones with Toys 'R Us, Borders, Target, and Marks & Spencer, among others. The bookstore to the world was about to become the future department store to the world; and the company began to fulfill the promise of its logo, showing that it would offer customers products from "A to Z."

Concurrently, Amazon also pursued another growth path—this time, Growth Path 5: **Customer and Product Diversification**. Bezos is a fan of innovating—not just to succeed in the market but also to fail quickly if he must fail. While there have been several less-than-stellar results, such as the Amazon Fire Phone, Amazon Destinations, and Amazon Local, they have been long since forgotten in the grand scheme of things.

There have been four significant product launches, which have driven huge change within two industries ripe for disruption: First was book publishing. Second was IT services. The third was a Blue Ocean strategy, with "voice" leading the way. The fourth was taking subscription services to retail shopping: Amazon Prime.

IT services were in the middle of a transformation in 2002 when Amazon pushed itself into the fast-growing cloud services business with its introduction of Amazon S3, now known as **Amazon Web Services (AWS)**, as "a simple storage service that offers software developers a highly scalable, reliable, and low-latency data storage infrastructure at very low costs." In its first quarter of 2018, Amazon generated $5.44 billion in sales, up 40 percent, and _AWS remains its profit engine_ even though it only accounts for only 10 percent of the company's total revenue.

Following up with **Amazon Prime**, which gave customers access to free two-day delivery for a recurring annual fee—since its launch in 2005, it has exceeded 100 million paid members globally in more than 8,000 cities and towns. The program has recently been extended to its business customers, called "Business Prime Shipping."

The next happened in 2007 when it introduced **Kindle**, the electronic reader, thus not only offering its own platform for special digital versions of its physical books to make delivery even faster than traditional bookstores, but also an accompanying platform for authors to circumvent traditional book publishing. Ten years later, ebook sales are on fire, literally kindled. _Amazon's U.S. customers read four times more digital books than physical books, and in India, the ratio is ten to one._

In recent years, Amazon has expanded its dedicated hardware/software offerings to include home **"assistants" Echo and Alexa**, which represent alternatives to traditional Web searches (and thus Apple and Google). According to Mary Meeker, partner at venture capital firm Kleiner Perkins Caufield & Byers, voice is becoming more popular than typing in online search. Twenty percent of mobile searches were made using voice in 2016.

In all four of these examples, Amazon needed to pursue Growth Path 8: **Partnerships** and Growth Path 9: **Co-opetition**, to see massive adoption and success in combination. The universe of products and services surrounding all these product introductions has enabled the company to pursue Growth Path 4: **Product Expansion**. As it introduced more subscription-based products, it now had the opportunity to pursue Growth Path 2: **Customer Base Penetration**, up-selling and cross-selling customers who chose to buy one-off purchases, which until now had characterized its business—even with the addition of millions of retail products. Yet with the benefits that recurring revenue brings the business, it also opens the door to Growth Path 7: **Churn**, which until then had been a hard metric to track.

Now, with tens of millions of loyal users, Amazon continued to work on improving, expanding, and accelerating its delivery systems (**Optimize Sales**). For years it has used UPS and Federal Express, but now even those carriers were being strained by the sheer volume of Amazon deliveries. In 2013 it signed a **Partnership** agreement with the U.S. Postal Service (which benefited that perpetually troubled institution—and even was rumored to be experimenting with delivery by drones).

Until this point, Amazon was primarily a U.S. operation, with a presence in Europe and other developed parts of the world. Now, in 2014, Amazon set out to expand its global markets, starting with a $5 billion development investment in India—Growth Path 3: **Market Acceleration**.

In April 2018, Amazon launched the "International Shopping" experience within the Amazon Shopping app, making the shopping experience on mobile devices even better and more convenient for customers who live outside the United States. The International Shopping experience offers shopping in five languages, including English, Spanish, Simplified Chinese, German, and Brazilian Portuguese, with the ability to shop in twenty-five currencies and ship more than fifty-five million products to over a hundred countries around the world.

Just a year later, having captured a sizable portion of capital goods sales and distribution in the United States, Amazon set out again on Growth Path 4: **Product Expansion**. This time it was to reverse the history of the company by turning away from the virtual world back into bricks and mortar—into consumer disposables (Amazon Go convenience stores), and most shocking, fresh food, with the purchase in 2017 of Whole Foods.

Meanwhile, Amazon continues to grow its core business. It already had thousands of small manufacturers and retailers using Amazon as their primary retail channel. Now, the company set out after bigger game through Growth Paths 8 and 9. That is, through **Partnerships**, when possible, and with bigger, and more established firms, through **Co-opetition**. Among the latter were Kohl's and Nike, the latter having once promised that it would never sell products through Amazon. By 2016, even it had seen the writing on the wall. In 2017 it struck a deal with Sears to sell Kenmore appliances and followed that up with DieHard batteries and tires. And in 2018 Amazon and Best Buy entered a partnership to sell Smart TVs.

Amazon today is a juggernaut that has had few equals in business history. In 2015 it even surpassed Walmart as the most valuable retailer in the United States. Traffic on its website approaches one billion visitors per month. In November 2017, Jeff Bezos's personal wealth surpassed $100 billion.

What's next? The only growth path that the company hasn't pursued is Growth Path 10: **Unconventional Strategies**, though you can make the case that its blistering pace through the other nine growth paths is itself an unconventional approach. However, it is interesting to note that Jeff Bezos tweeted a "request for ideas."

He wrote: *"I'm thinking about a philanthropy strategy that is the opposite of how I mostly spend my time—working on the long term. . . . But I'm thinking I want much of my philanthropic activity to be helping people in the here and now—short term—at the intersection of urgent need and lasting impact. If you have ideas, just reply to this tweet with the idea (and if you think this approach is wrong, would love to hear that too.)"*

And so, it would seem, Amazon has pursued all ten possible growth paths in little more than two decades. Given that precedent, one can only wait in anticipation for what the company will do in the next two decades. Amazon is the very embodiment of *Growth IQ*.

Amazon, Inc.
2016 Letter to Shareholders

April 12, 2017

"Jeff, what does Day 2 look like?"

That's a question I just got at our most recent all-hands meeting. I've been reminding people that it's Day 1 for a couple of decades. I work in an Amazon building named Day 1, and when I moved buildings, I took the name with me. I spend time thinking about this topic.

"Day 2 is stasis. Followed by irrelevance. Followed by excruciating, painful decline. Followed by death. And *that* is why it is *always* Day 1."

To be sure, this kind of decline would happen in extreme slow motion. An established company might harvest Day 2 for decades, but the final result would still come.

I'm interested in the question, how do you fend off Day 2? What are the techniques and tactics? How do you keep the vitality of Day 1, even inside a large organization?

Such a question can't have a simple answer. There will be many elements, multiple paths, and many traps. I don't know the whole answer, but I may know bits of it. *Here's a starter pack of essentials for Day 1 defense: customer obsession, a skeptical view of proxies, the eager adoption of external trends, and high-velocity decision making.*

ACKNOWLEDGMENTS

'A'OHE PU'U KI'EKI'E KE HO'A'O 'IA E PI'I
No cliff is so tall it cannot be climbed.

THEY SAY A JOURNEY OF ten thousand miles begins with a single step, or, in my case, a single whisper. Welcome to step 3,107 of my *Growth IQ* journey. The journey of writing this book began in 2013 while I was speaking at an event. I found myself on stage with a number of bestselling authors and people who I had admired over the years. It was at that moment that someone said to me, "Hey . . . why don't you have a book?" That one single question I took as my first sign, *my first whisper*. Then it happened again, and again and again. By that point it was a loud scream in my head that I couldn't quiet down. So I did what I had always done when I faced a professional crossroads: I reached out to my amazing network (my tribe) and asked what they thought. But I didn't just reach out to anyone. I reached out to those who had set a high bar for me to aspire to achieve.

I stand on the shoulders of giants: The first call was to **Seth Godin**. We had been acquaintances since 2000 and shared the stage a number of times. Without hesitation, Seth was quick to respond, sharing some great advice. Then I reached out to **Dan Pink, Josh Linkner, Nancy Duarte, Naomi Simson, Guy Kawasaki, Whitney Johnson, Geoffrey Moore**, and so many others who were willing to share their invaluable wisdom with me. And I can't forget my full-circle moment. From writing one of the first business books I ever read (*In Search of Excellence*), to giving me a quote for my book, **Tom Peters**, I'm so glad we met. I am humbled and forever grateful to each of you for your willingness to support me and this book. Thank you!

My Team: Getting a book like this done is never just the hard work of the author—it takes a village.

First, **Mark Fortier**. With his amazing lineup of clients, business authors, and thinkers, I knew he was who I wanted as my publicist. He just didn't know it yet. After I relentlessly hounded him, he at last gave me fifteen minutes, which turned into an hour, which turned into him becoming the most pivotal person on this journey for me. I am forever grateful to you, Mark!

My literary agent, **Jim Levine**, who is the best agent a book author could ask for. He can leap NYC subway turnstiles in a single bound, while holding on to his briefcase and getting me on the right train (really) to meet publishers without missing a beat. Beyond his transportation creativity, he was masterful in getting to the heart of the book I was contemplating. His guidance was just what I needed to structure my thought process, and, more important, protected me from my own self-doubt. Thank you, Jim!

Penguin Portfolio: To the Dream Team of **Adrian Zackheim**, **Will Weisser**, **Margot Stamas**, **Taylor Edwards**, and especially **Kaushik Viswanath**, for your patience, guidance, and the amazing editing with such an aggressive publishing schedule. To the graphics team who made my book brilliantly come to life on every page—thank you!

My Collaboration Team: I'm sure each of you had no idea what you were getting into when you started working with me. But make no mistake . . . all of you helped me find my voice and create something we all can be proud of. **Peter Smith**, what can I say? You are a star in my life's constellation. **Mike Malone**, you were patient, understanding, and a calming force in all the madness. And finally, **Tanmay Vora**, who used his amazing talent to create the perfect sketch notes to visually bring my stories to life. All of you made this possible, so, thank you!

Work: My colleagues and friends at **Gartner** for teaching me what it meant to get compelling and sometimes complicated thoughts down on paper in an engaging way, especially **Hank Barnes** and **Christine Adams**. You challenged me to bring my A-game no matter the circumstances. I learned so much from each of you and you should recognize many of these lessons as ones we learned together. **Salesforce** for being a #DreamJob—what an amazing company to be part of. Each and every day I am inspired by what the entire Salesforce Ohana, especially our customers, can accomplish when we are all focused on the same goals. And, of course, **Marc Benioff**, for being a CEO that has taught me that "doing well by doing good" is what it's really all about. Mahalo!

My Tribe: For those who were supporting me behind the scenes. I feel so lucky to be surrounded by people who never thought for a minute that I couldn't do this. There are so many I could thank, but I hope you know who you are. I appreciate each and every one of you and the role you have played in this book and my life.

My Family: Finally, I am so grateful my parents left Boston in 1957 and moved to Hawaii, where I was born and raised. I couldn't have asked for a better place to call home. My mother who has always been my rock and lifelong teacher even if she didn't know it. She showed me that strength comes from within, you just have to find it. My grandfather, who visited me from Boston each year for three months, for fifteen years, until he passed away. During that time, he took me on trips around the world and exposed me to different cultures and ideas, shaping my perspective of humanity and spurring my curiosity. He was my hero and my best friend—I just wish he could have seen me grow up. To my father, I'm so glad we were able to reconnect, play some golf, and spend time together before you were gone. IDLR, for your enduring love and support. You never hesitated to pick me up when I slipped on a banana peel, when I doubted myself, didn't think I could get it done, or felt defeated by the process. This book would not have been possible without you.

Me Ke Aloha Pumehana.

NOTES

THE ONE THING IS—IT'S NEVER JUST ONE THING

1   **"it's a combination of many things"**: Jeff Bezos, Amazon 2018 letter to shareholders, www .sec.gov.

2   **"Be prepared to spot"**: Valentina Zarya, "15 Powerful Women Share the Best Career Advice They've Ever Received," *Fortune*, October 2, 2017, http://fortune.com/2017/10/02/most-pow-erful-women-advice/.

3   **"Success is a lousy teacher"**: Bill Gates, *The Road Ahead* (New York: Viking, 1995), p. 50.

3   **87 percent of all companies:** Matthew S. Olson and Derek van Bever, *Stall Points: Most Companies Stop Growing—Yours Doesn't Have To* (New Haven, CT: Yale University Press, 2008).

4   **85 percent of the executives surveyed:** Chris Zook and James Allen, "Barriers and Pathways to Sustainable Growth: Harnessing the Power of the Founder's Mentality," Bain .com, Bain & Company, Insights, July 20, 2016, www.bain.com/publications/articles/founders-mentality-barriers-and-pathways-to-sustainable-growth.aspx.

7   **"Growth is never by mere chance,":** Attributed to James Cash Penney. Original source unknown.

8   **"Follow effective action with quiet reflection":** "High Time for 'Think Time,'" Drucker Institute, February 16, 2011, www.druckerinstitute.com/2011/02/high-time-for-think-time.

PATH 1 CUSTOMER EXPERIENCE

12   **"start with the customer experience":** Biz Carson, "Steve Jobs' Reaction to This Insult Shows Why He Was Such a Great CEO," *Business Insider*, October 22, 2015, www .businessinsider.com/steve-jobs-reaction-to-insult-2015-10.

12   **three thousand business-to-business (B2B) companies:** *B2B Customer Experience: Winning in the Moments That Matter*, KPMG Report, May 2017, https://home.kpmg.com/content/dam/kpmg/uk/pdf/2017/05/b2b-customer-experience-report.pdf.

12   **Sixty-eight percent of C-suite executives:** "Incumbents Strike Back," report, IBM Institute for Business Value, February 2018.

12   **spend more for a better customer experience:** Vala Afshar, "50 Important Customer Experience Stats for Business Leaders," *Huffington Post*, October 15, 2015, www.huffingtonpost .com/vala-afshar/50-important-customer-exp_b_8295772.html.

12   **how customers feel:** Marc Beaujean, Jonathan Davidson, and Stacey Madge, "The 'Moment of Truth' in Customer Service," *McKinsey Quarterly*, February 2006, www.mckinsey.com/business-functions/organization/our-insights/the-moment-of-truth-in-customer-service.

12   **revenues 4–8 percent above their market:** Frédéric Debruyne and Andreas Dullweber, "The Five Disciplines of Customer Experience Leaders," Bain.com, Bain & Company, Insights, April 8, 2015, www.bain.com/publications/articles/the-five-disciplines-of-customer-experience-leaders.aspx.

12   **spend an average of 13 percent more :** "Good Service Is Good Business: American Consumers Willing to Spend More with Companies That Get Service Right, According to American Express Survey," American Express, May 3, 2011, http://about.americanexpress.com/news/pr/2011/csbar.aspx.

12   **customer service is a draw:** Ibid.

14   **"Gillette has lost U.S. market share":** Robert Hetu, "Product Is No Longer King," Gartner Blog Network, January 3, 2018, https://blogs.gartner.com/robert-hetu/product-no-longer-king/; and "Gillette, Bleeding Market Share, Cuts Prices of Razors," FoxBusiness.com, April 4, 2017, www.foxbusiness.com/markets/2017/04/04/gillette-bleeding-market-share-cuts-prices-razors.html.

15   **Gartner predicts that:** "Gartner Reveals Top Predictions for IT Organizations and Users for 2016 and Beyond," Gartner.com, Newsroom, press release, October 6, 2015, www.gartner.com/newsroom/id/3143718.

16   **Zappos campus to attend:** "School of WOW Customer Service Training," ZapposInsights.com, www.zapposinsights.com/training/schoolofwow?gclid=EAIaIQobChMIuOGdr7C12AIVXrbACh0_SgBcEAAYASAAEgK0cPD_BwE.

16   **"Whatever you do, do it well":** Attributed to Walt Disney. Original source unknown.

18   **"In today's retail environment":** "SEPHORA Pioneers New Retail Innovation with Launch of First Small-Format Concept Store," *Business Wire*, July 17, 2017, https://finance.yahoo.com/news/sephora-pioneers-retail-innovation-launch-110000943.html.

18   **More than a hundred stores:** Jennifer Calfas, "T.J. Maxx and 5 Other Stores That May Actually Survive the Death of Retail," Time.com, Money, June 29, 2017, http://time.com/money/4835442/retail-apocalypse-tj-maxx-zara-dollar-general.

19   **43 percent of consumers:** TimeTrade, *The State of Retail Report 2017*, TimeTrade.com, https://www.timetrade.com/resource/state-retail-report-2017.

19   **brands that create personalized experiences:** Mark Abraham, Steve Mitchelmore, Sean Collins, Jeff Maness, Mark Kistulinec, Shervin Khodabandeh, Daniel Hoenig, and Jody Visser, "Profiting from Personalization," BCG.com, Boston Consulting Group, May 8, 2017, www.bcg.com/publications/2017/retail-marketing-sales-profiting-personalization.aspx.

19   **Sailthru first annual Retail Personalization Index:** "Sailthru Ranks Top Retail Brands with First Annual Personalization Index," *PR Newswire*, Cision, September 14, 2017, www.prnewswire.com/news-releases/sailthru-ranks-top-retail-brands-with-first-annual-personalization-index-300519303.html.

22   **"We constantly challenge":** "Viva Technology: Innovation at the Heart of Sephora," LVMH.com, June 24, 2016, www.lvmh.com/news-documents/news/viva-technology-innovation-at-the-heart-of-sephora/.

24   **"We're not in the hamburger business":** "The Rise of a Fast Food Empire," *Pressreader*, The Week, February 18, 2017, www.pressreader.com/uk/the-week/20170218/281487866108533.

25   **"You may think":** "The Secret Ingredients of Hospitality—as Told by Danny Meyer," Maines.net, Fresh Ideas, http://freshideas.maines.net/secret-ingredients-hospitality-told-danny-meyer/, accessed April 6, 2018.

25   **"which is more or less":** Carolyn Cutrone, "Danny Meyer to 'Treps: Put Your Employees First, Customers Will Follow," *Inc.*, Know How, January 28, 2014, www.inc.com/carolyn-cutrone/danny-meyer-speaks-at-inc-business-owners-council.html.

26   **"Put us out of business":** Rob Brunner, "How Shake Shack Leads the Better Burger Revolution," *Fast Company*, Innovation Agents, June 22, 2015, www.fastcompany.com/3046753/shake-shack-leads-the-better-burger-revolution.

28   **"The damage was slow":** Kate Taylor, "Here's What Happened the Last Time Howard Schultz Stepped Down as Starbucks CEO," *Business Insider*, www.businessinsider.com/last-time-schultz-stepped-down-as-starbucks-ceo-2016-12.

28   **an industry-leading Net Promoter Score:** Net Promoter Score (NPS) is calculated based on responses to a single question: How likely is it that you would recommend our company/product/service to a friend or colleague? It is a customer loyalty metric developed by Fred Reichheld, Bain & Company, and Satmetrix that can be used to gauge the loyalty of a firm's customer relationships. NPS can be as low as −100 (everybody is a detractor) or as high as +100 (everybody is a promoter). An NPS that is positive (i.e., higher than zero) is felt to be good, and an NPS of +50 is excellent.

NOTES

28 **77 against an industry average:** "Starbucks Net Promoter Score 2018 Benchmarks," Customer Guru, https://customer.guru/net-promoter-score/starbucks.

30 **"The most serious challenge":** Nichola Groom, "Schultz Back as Starbucks CEO," Reuters, January 7, 2008, https://www.reuters.com/article/us-starbucks/schultz-back-as-starbucks-ceo-idUSWNAS581320080108.

30 **"We became less passionate":** Andy Serwer, "Starbucks Fix: Howard Schultz Spills the Beans on His Plans to Save the Company He Founded," *Fortune,* January 18, 2008, http://archive.fortune.com/2008/01/17/news/newsmakers/starbucks.fortune/index.htm?postversion=2008011805.

30 **"Live and breathe Starbucks":** Ibid.

31 **in February 2008 Schultz closed:** Aimee Groth, "19 Amazing Ways CEO Howard Schultz Saved Starbucks," *Business Insider Australia,* June 20, 2011, www.businessinsider.com.au/howard-schultz-turned-starbucks-around-2011-6#in-february-2008-starbucks-closed-7100-us-stores-for-3-12-hours-to-retrain-its-baristas-on-how-to-make-the-perfect-espresso-1.

31 **"Your premium brand":** Erika Andersen, "23 Quotes from Warren Buffett on Life and Generosity," *Forbes,* December 2, 2013, www.forbes.com/sites/erikaandersen/2013/12/02/23-quotes-from-warren-buffett-on-life-and-generosity/#11412450f891.

32 **stock's total return was 551 percent:** Maggie McGrath, "Howard Schultz Stepping Down as Starbucks CEO," *Forbes,* December 1, 2016, www.forbes.com/sites/maggiemcgrath/2016/12/01/howard-schultz-stepping-down-as-starbucks-ceo/#194e07525347.

34 **"customer who pays the wages":** Attributed to Henry Ford. Original source unknown.

PATH 2 CUSTOMER BASE PENETRATION

38 **Acquiring a new customer:** Amy Gallo, "The Value of Keeping the Right Customers," *Harvard Business Review,* October 29, 2014, https://hbr.org/2014/10/the-value-of-keeping-the-right-customers.

38 **It costs six to seven times more:** Bain & Company/Mainspring, "The Value of Online Customer Loyalty and How You Can Capture It," Bain.com, eStrategy Brief, n.d., www.bain.com/Images/Value_online_customer_loyalty_you_capture.pdf.

38 **Seventy percent of companies:** Luke Brynley-Jones, "70% of Companies Say It's Cheaper to Retain a Customer Than Acquire One," OurSocialTimes.com, n.d., http://oursocialtimes.com/70-of-companies-say-its-cheaper-to-retain-a-customer-than-acquire-one.

38 **The probability of selling:** Patrick Hull, "Don't Get Lazy About Your Client Relationships," *Forbes,* December 6, 2013, www.forbes.com/sites/patrickhull/2013/12/06/tools-for-entrepreneurs-to-retain-clients/#35d40a772443.

38 **Repeat customers, on average:** Bain & Company/Mainspring, "The Value of Online Customer Loyalty."

38 **Loyal customers are:** "ROI of Customer Experience," *Customer Experience Matters* Blog, January 18, 2018, https://experiencematters.blog/category/roi-of-customer-experience.

39 **Netflix spent more than twice:** Timothy Green, "Netflix Has a Problem That No One Is Talking About," *Motley Fool,* July 22, 2017, www.fool.com/investing/2017/07/22/netflix-has-a-problem-that-no-one-is-talking-about.aspx.

40 **60–80 percent of customers:** Brooks Barnes, "How Black Label Media Became Hollywood's Hottest Indie Producers," *Town & Country,* October 16, 2017, www.townandcountrymag.com/leisure/arts-and-culture/a12838536/black-label-media/.

40 **The likelihood of success:** Hull, "Don't Get Lazy About Your Client Relationships."

41 **spend 67 percent more:** Bain & Company/Mainspring, "The Value of Online Customer Loyalty."

43 **"We don't bring the product":** Gerhard Gschwandtner, "The Powerful Sales Strategy Behind Red Bull," SellingPower.com, March 1, 2012, www.sellingpower.com/2012/03/01/9437/the-powerful-sales-strategy-behind-red-bull.

44 **sixty-two billion cans sold annually worldwide:** "The Company Behind the Can," RedBull.com, n.d., http://energydrink-us.redbull.com/en/company.

NOTES

45 **a market share of 1 percent:** "Red Bull Company's Market Share in the United States from 2004 to 2015," Statista.com, n.d., www.statista.com/statistics/225452/us-market-share-of-the-red-bull-company-since-2004/.

46 **Red Bull's marketing and emotional branding:** Craig J. Thompson, Aric Rindfleisch, and Zeynep Arsel, "Emotional Branding and the Strategic Value of the Doppelgänger Brand Image," *Journal of Marketing* 70 (January 2006): 50–64, https://zeyneparsel.files.wordpress.com/2010/06/thompson-rindfleisch-arsel1.pdf.

47 **"Taste is a barrier":** Bruce Horovitz, "Red Bull Targets Taste with Three New Flavors," *USA Today,* October 7, 2012, www.usatoday.com/story/money/business/2012/10/07/red-bull-energy-drinks-taste/1615351.

48 **$84.8 billion by 2025:** "Energy Drinks Market Report 2017: Key Vendors Are Red Bull GmbH, Monster Energy & Rockstar," *Markets Insider,* press release, August 22, 2017, http://markets.businessinsider.com/news/stocks/Energy-Drinks-Market-Report-2017-Key-Vendors-are-Red-Bull-GmbH-Monster-Energy-Rockstar-1002276239.

49 **Red Bull Stratos Jump:** "Felix Baumgartner's Supersonic Freefall from 128k—Mission Highlights," October 14, 2012, https://youtu.be/FHtvDA0W34I.

51 **McDonald's sells more than:** Jana Kasperkevic, "How Many Burgers Has McDonald's Actually Sold?," Marketplace.org, May 26, 2017, www.marketplace.org/2017/05/26/business/ive-always-wondered/how-many-burgers-has-mcdonalds-actually-sold.

51 **McDonald's menu swelled:** Luke Lango, "McDonald's Corporation (MCD) Stock Thrives in the Intersection of Health & Price," *InvestorPlace,* July 25, 2017, https://investorplace.com/2017/07/mcdonalds-corporation-mcd-stock-health-price/#.WoI0VahKuUk.

51 **lost more than 500 million vists:** Sarah Whitten, "McDonald's shares soar as menu price increases fuel earnings beat," CNBC, May 2, 2018, www.cnbc.com/2018/04/30/mcdonalds-reports-first-quarter-earnings-2018.html.

53 **"something like All-Day Breakfast":** Daniel B. Kline, "The 1 Simple Thing That Saved McDonald's," *Motley Fool,* June 5, 2017, www.fool.com/investing/2017/06/05/the-1-simple-thing-that-saved-mcdonalds.aspx.

54 **"decisions being made today":** Stephanie Strom, "McDonald's C.E.O. on All Day Breakfast, Hourly Wages and Wall Street," *New York Times,* November 12, 2015, www.nytimes.com/2015/11/13/business/a-conversation-with-steve-easterbrook-of-mcdonalds.html?mtrref=www.google.com&gwh=094EA02D1CDDE3798DF5676F95D7E609&gwt=pay.

55 **"We continued to build":** Sarah Whitten, "McDonald's shares soar as menu price increases fuel earnings beat," CNBC, May 2, 2018, www.cnbc.com/2018/04/30/mcdonalds-reports-first-quarter-earnings-2018.html.

56 **"We don't need more customers":** Matt Egan, "Sears CEO: 'We Don't Need More Customers,'" *CNN Money,* May 11, 2017, http://money.cnn.com/2017/05/11/investing/sears-lampert-dont-need-more-customers/index.html.

58 **Sears even started Prodigy:** Tom Shea, "Big firms team up on videotex project," Infoworld, March 12, 1984, https://books.google.com/books?id=li4EAAAAMBAJ&pg=PA13#v=onepage&q&f=false.

58 **The once-iconic brand:** Lauren Thomas, "Sears shares jump after company reports a profit for holiday quarter, CNBC, March 14, 2018, www.sears-soars-after-reporting-lower-than-expected-full-in-comp-sales.html.

59 **"changed the game":** Ibid.

59 **"Skate to where the puck":** Jason Kirby, "CEOs: Stop Debasing Wayne Gretzky's 'I Skate to Where the Puck Is Going' Quote," CanadianBusiness.com, October 3, 2014, www.canadianbusiness.com/blogs-and-comment/stop-using-gretzky-where-the-puck-is-quote.

61 **Shop Your Way loyalty program:** Jim Tierney, "Can Sears' Shop Your Way Loyalty Program Keep Venerable Retailer Afloat in the Future?," Loyalty360, March 24, 2017, www.loyalty360.org/content-gallery/daily-news/can-sears-shop-your-way-loyalty-program-keep-vene.

62 **Nordstrom's ten million:** Glenn Taylor, "Can Department Stores Save Themselves in 2018?," RetailTouchPoints.com, January 4, 2018, www.retailtouchpoints.com/features/trend-watch/can-department-stores-save-themselves-in-2018.

NOTES

62   **following a pricing dispute:** Abha Bhattarai and Aaron Gregg, "Why Sears Ended a Century-Old Partnership with Whirlpool," *Washington Post*, October 24, 2017, www .washingtonpost.com/news/business/wp/2017/10/24/why-sears-ended-a-century-old -partnership-with-whirlpool/?utm_term=.e6b16580a7f8.

62   **the company is still #3:** Adam Levine-Weinberg, "Sears Just Stopped Carrying the No. 1 Appliance Brand," October 25, 2017, *Motley Fool*, www.fool.com/investing/2017/10/25/sears -just-stopped-carrying-no-1-appliance-brand.aspx.

62   **Sears struck a deal with Amazon:** Natalie Waters, "Sears and Amazon: the Best and Worst Retailers Team Up for a Second Time," *The Motley Fool*, December 30, 2017, www.fool.com/ investing/2017/12/30/sears-and-amazon-the-best-and-worst-retailers-team.aspx.

62   **Apple Watch wearers:** David Reid, "Apple Watch to Be Able to Control Whirlpool Appliances This Year," CNBC, January 8, 2018, cnbc.com/2018/01/08/apple-watch-to-be-able -to-control-whirlpool-appliances-this-year.html.

63   **its 2018 range of appliances:** Ibid.

63   **"We can't afford":** "History of the Search Catalog," Sears Archives, www.searsarchives.com/ catalogs/history.htm.

65   **Target claims as much as 70 percent:** Debbie Hauss, "1:1 with CIO McNamara: How Target Achieved 25% Digital Growth in 2017," RetailTouchPoints.com, January 12, 2018, www .retailtouchpoints.com/features/retail-success-stories/1-1-with-cio-mcnamara-how-target -achieved-25-digital-growth-in-2017.

65   **additional in-store purchase of $50:** "2018 Customer Engagement Awards," RetailTouch-Points.com, n.d., p. 6, www.retailtouchpoints.com/features/special-reports/2018-customer -engagement-awards.

PATH 3 MARKET ACCELERATION

70   **"China is going to be":** Krystal Hu, "One Quote from Jack Ma Sums Up a Huge Shift in China's Economy," Yahoo! Finance, June 22, 2017, https://finance.yahoo.com/news/one-quote -jack-ma-sums-huge-shift-chinas-economy-203255351.html.

70   **Global growth is projected:** *Global Economic Prospects: Broad-Based Upturn, but for How Long?* (Washington, DC: World Bank, 2018), www.worldbank.org/en/publication/global -economic-prospects.

70   **fastest-growing industries:** "The 10 Fastest-Growing Industries in the U.S.," SageWorks .com, July 24, 2017, www.sageworks.com/the-10-fastest/.

70   **All twenty-three economies:** Craig Turp, "Emerging Europe to Record Positive Growth Across the Board in 2018," EmergingEurope.com, November 7, 2017, http://emerging-europe .com/regions/emerging-europe-record-positive-growth-across-board-2018/.

70   **China now accounts for:** McKinsey Global Institute, "Digital China: Powering the Economy to Global Competitiveness," McKinsey & Company, December 2017, www.mckinsey .com/~/media/McKinsey/Global%20Themes/China/Digital%20China%20Powering%20 the%20economy%20to%20global%20competitiveness/MGI-Digital-China-Report -December-20-2017.ashx.

70   **sixty-three percent of respondents:** "Geographic Expansion," Frost & Sullivan, n.d., ww2 .frost.com/consulting/growth-processes/geographic-expansion/.

70   **By 2020, cross-border commerce:** "The 21st Century Spice Trade: A Guide to the Cross-Border E-Commerce Opportunity," DHL, December 2016, www.dhl.com/content/dam/downloads/ g0/press/publication/g0_dhl_express_cross_border_ecommerce_21st_century_spice_trade.pdf.

70   **In 2020, one out of five:** Ibid.

70   **China will continue:** "China Eclipses the US to Become the World's Largest Retail Market," eMarketer.com, August 18, 2016, www.emarketer.com/Article/China-Eclipses-US-Become -Worlds-Largest-Retail-Market/1014364.

71   **"Competition should not be for a share of the market":** The W. Edwards Deming Institute Blog, n.d., https://blog.deming.org/w-edwards-deming-quotes/large-list-of-quotes-by-w -edwards-deming/.

NOTES

74   **"Surround your disruptive core product":** Geoffrey A. Moore, *Crossing the Chasm* (New York: HarperBusiness, 2016).

74   **The global sports apparel market:** Priyanka Bisht, "Sports Apparel Market Is Estimated to Garner $184.6 Billion, Globally, by 2020," AlliedMarketResearch.com, press release, n.d., www.alliedmarketresearch.com/press-release/sports-apparel-market.html.

75   **"Great entrepreneurs take one product":** "Sailing into a Big, Blue Ocean of Opportunity," BNBranding.com, n.d., http://bnbranding.com/brandinsightblog/under-armour-marketing/.

76   **"For the first five years":** Ibid.

77   **international segment grew 47 percent:** "Under Armour (UAA) down 9.5% since earnings report: Can It Rebound?," Zacks Equity Research, March 15, 2018, www.zacks.com/stock/news/295762/under-armour-uaa-down-95-since-earnings-report-can-it-rebound.

77   **Retail partnerships were key:** Avi Salzman, "Under Armour's New Retail Strategy Is Winning Fans," Barrons.com, Barron's Next, May 31, 2017, www.barrons.com/articles/under-armours-new-retail-strategy-is-winning-fans-1496271018.

78   **"Make it electric":** David Pierce, "How Under Armour Plans to Turn Your Clothes into Gadgets," *Wired*, Gear, January 5, 2016, www.wired.com/2016/01/under-armour-healthbox/.

81   **"Forty-two percent of global respondents":** "Deeper Than Dollars: Global Perceptions About Premium Products," Nielsen.com, Insights, December 15, 2016, www.nielsen.com/us/en/insights/news/2016/deeper-than-dollars-global-perceptions-about-premium-products.html.

82   **"organic in nature":** *Baby Personal Care Market Analysis, Market Size, Application Analysis, Regional Outlook, Competitive Strategies, and Forecasts, 2016 to 2024*, Grand View Research, Market Research Report, October 2016, www.grandviewresearch.com/industry-analysis/baby-personal-care-market.

82   **parents have been spurning:** David Crow, "Shift to Organics Gives Johnson & Johnson the Babycare Blues," *Financial Times*, July 28, 2016, www.ft.com/content/f919110e-5379-11e6-9664-e0bdc13c3bef.

82   **losing market share:** Neil Howe, "Nothing's Too Good for My Baby," *Forbes*, Opinion, November 30, 2016, www.forbes.com/sites/neilhowe/2016/11/30/nothings-too-good-for-my-baby/#6bac86fa1ab6.

82   **in 2017 it experienced a flat year:** Serena Ng, "No Longer a Unicorn, Jessica Alba's Honest Co. Struggles to Grow," *Wall Street Journal*, January 5, 2018.

85   **Nick Vlahos, CEO of Honest:** John Kell, "Jessica Alba's Honest Co. to Sell Goods on Amazon.com," *Fortune*, June 15, 2017, http://fortune.com/2017/06/15/honest-co-jessica-alba-amazon/.

86   **For more than fifty million:** Gretchen Livingston, "More Than a Million Millennials Are Becoming Moms Each Year," Pew Research Center, FactTank, January 3, 2017, www.pewresearch.org/fact-tank/2017/01/03/more-than-a-million-millennials-are-becoming-moms-each-year/.

89   **"Our vision is to inspire":** "Mattel Unveils Plan to Reinvent Company and Deliver Enhanced and Sustainable Growth," Mattel Newsroom, June 14, 2017, https://news.mattel.com/news/mattel-unveils-plan-to-reinvent-company-and-deliver-enhanced-and-sustainable-growth.

89   **U.S. toy sales grew:** "Global and U.S. Toy Industry Sales Increase 1 percent in 2017," NPD.com, press release, January 25, 2018, www.npd.com/wps/portal/npd/us/news/press-releases/2018/toy-sales-globally-and-in-the-US-both-grow-by-1-percent-in-2017-reports-the-NPD-group/.

90   **The global market for toys:** Global Industry Analysts, Inc., "Innovation and New Product Launches Drive the Global Toys and Games Market," Strategyr.com, October 2017, www.strategyr.com/MarketResearch/Toys_and_Games_Market_Trends.asp.

90   **Specifically, the toy maker's:** "Mattel Unveils Plan to Reinvent Company and Deliver Enhanced and Sustainable Growth."

93   **have owned a Barbie:** Eliana Dockterman, "Barbie's Got a New Body," *Time*, January 28, 2016, http://time.com/barbie-new-body-cover-story/.

NOTES

94   **the loss of that contract:** John Kell, "Can Mattel Fill Gaping Hole Left by Loss of Disney Princesses?," *Fortune*, February 2, 2016, http://fortune.com/2016/02/02/mattel-disney-princesses-sales/.

PATH 4 PRODUCT EXPANSION

102   **"When we buy a product":** Clayton M. Christensen, Taddy Hall, Karen Dillon, and David S. Duncan, "Know Your Customers' 'Jobs to Be Done,'" *Harvard Business Review*, September 2016, https://hbr.org/2016/09/know-your-customers-jobs-to-be-done.

102   **Existing customers are 50 percent:** Khalid Saleh, "Customer Acquisition vs. Retention Costs—Statistics and Trends," Invesp, n.d., www.invespcro.com/blog/customer-acquisition-retention/.

102   **Sixty percent of global consumers:** "Global Consumers More Likely to Buy New Products from Familiar Brands," Nielsen.com, Press Room, January 22, 2013, www.nielsen.com/us/en/press-room/2013/global-consumers-more-likely-to-buy-new-products-from-familiar-b0.html.

102   **In the consumer products:** Richard Kestenbaum, "How the Beauty Industry Is Adapting to Change: The Business Plans," *Forbes*, June 20, 2017, www.forbes.com/sites/richardkestenbaum/2017/06/20/how-the-beauty-industry-is-adapting-to-change-the-business-plans/#6ce349d26007.

102   **By 2025, Thomson Reuters data:** Robert Rynd, "Go Global but What Are the Opportunities and Risks of Expanding into New Markets?," Thomson Reuters, Inside Financial & Risk, November 11, 2015, https://blogs.thomsonreuters.com/financial-risk/risk-management-compliance/go-global-but-what-are-the-opportunities-and-risks-of-expanding-into-new-markets/.

102   **One in three hundred products:** "New Product Development," Frost & Sullivan, n.d., https://ww2.frost.com/consulting/growth-processes/new-product-development/.

103   **"Don't find customers":** Seth Godin, "First, organize 1,000," Blogpost, December 23, 2009, http://sethgodin.typepad.com/seths_blog/2009/12/first-organize-1000.html.

104   **Forbes's Top Ten:** "The World's Most Innovative Companies," *Forbes*, n.d., https://www.forbes.com/innovative-companies/#75db2d541d65.

104   **World's Most Innovative Companies:** *Forbes* Staff, "Forbes Releases Seventh Annual List of the World's Most Innovative Companies," August 8, 2017, www.forbes.com/sites/forbespr/2017/08/08/forbes-releases-seventh-annual-list-of-the-worlds-most-innovative-companies/#745616884373.

106   **"[Millennials] create a community":** Richard Kestenbaum, "How the Beauty Industry Is Adapting to Change," *Forbes*, June 19, 2017, www.forbes.com/sites/richardkestenbaum/2017/06/19/how-the-beauty-industry-is-adapting-to-change/#4b04d06a3681.

106   **But independent brands:** Ibid.

106   **In the United States, "women are":** Fabrizio Freda, president and CEO of Estée Lauder, quoted in ibid.

107   **"Ever since I was probably fifteen":** "Kylie, the Entrepreneur," Shopify.com, n.d., https://www.shopify.com/kylie.

109   **"526 million posts that relate to the beauty industry":** "The Beauty Industry Faces a New Reality," Artémia, September 29, 2017, http://artemia.com/beauty-industry-faces-new-reality/.

109   **"Younger generations are":** Kestenbaum, "How the Beauty Industry Is Adapting to Change."

109   **#57 on the *Fast Company* list:** P. Claire Dodson, "How Kylie Jenner Built a Makeup Empire Out of Her Most Famous Asset," *Fast Company*, May 15, 2017, www.fastcompany.com/40413114/how-kylie-jenner-built-a-makeup-empire-out-of-her-most-famous-asset.

110   **"Spending zero dollars is":** Quoted in Kestenbaum, "How the Beauty Industry Is Adapting to Change."

110   **$1 billion mark by 2022:** Rachel Strugatz, "Kylie Jenner's Kylie Cosmetics on Way to Becoming $1B Brand," WWD, Beauty, August 9, 2017, http://wwd.com/beauty-industry-news/beauty-features/kylie-jenner-cosmetics-to-become-billion-dollar-brand-10959016.

NOTES

114 **"It's very important":** Josh Cable, "For John Deere, Customer Input Drives Product De-velopment," AmericanCity&County.com, Government Product News, October 27, 2008, americancityandcounty.com/news/john-deere-customer-input-drives-product -development.

117 **"OK, Houston, we've had":** Futurism Staff, "How Apollo 13 Avoided Disaster," Futurism, n.d., https://futurism.media/how-apollo-13-avoided-disaster.

119 **"Neither RedBox nor Netflix":** "Blockbuster CEO: Redbox, Netflix 'Not on Radar Screen' as Competition," Inside Redbox, December 11, 2008, www.insideredbox.com/blockbuster-ceo -redbox-netflix-not-on-radar-screen-as-competition.

120 **"We don't have any concern":** Mark Zoradi, quoted in February 2016 in "Foot in Mouth: 42 Quotes from Big Corporate Execs Who Laughed Off Disruption When It Hit," CBInsights, Research Briefs, February 2, 2018, www.cbinsights.com/research/big-compay-ceos-execs -disruption-quotes.

120 **Enron chose to terminate:** Anne Marie Squeo and Bruce Orwall, "Enron and Blockbuster Terminate Partnership for Video-on-Demand," *Wall Street Journal*, March 12, 2001, https:// www.wsj.com/articles/SB984181374790463655.

121 **Netflix today faces:** Brooke Barnes, "Disney Makes $52.4 Billion Deal for 21st Century Fox in Big Bet on Streaming," *New York Times*, DealBook, December 14, 2017, www.nytimes .com/2017/12/14/business/dealbook/disney-fox-deal.html.

123 **"Great companies are":** "Tesla Motors CEO Elon Musk: 'Great Companies Are Built on Great Products,'" Knowledge@Wharton podcast, May 13, 2009, http://knowledge.wharton .upenn.edu/article/tesla-motors-ceo-elon-musk-great-companies-are-built-on-great -products.

PATH 5 CUSTOMER AND PRODUCT DIVERSIFICATION

128 **"Taking an established American brand":** "Mondelēz International CEO Irene Rosenfeld on Strategy in the Global Snack Market," Yale School of Management, Recent News, May 1, 2014, http://som.yale.edu/news/2014/05/mondel%C4%93z-international-ceo-irene -rosenfeld-strategy-global-snack-market.

128 **Almost two-thirds:** "Looking to Achieve New Product Success?," Nielsen.com, June 2015, www.nielsen.com/content/dam/nielsenglobal/jp/docs/report/2015/Nielsen%20Global%20 New%20Product%20Innovation%20Report%20June%202015.pdf.

128 **Consumers want more new:** Ibid.

128 **value of global goods trade:** "What Are the Prospects for Global Trade Growth?," *Global Economy Watch*, October 2014, www.pwc.com/gx/en/issues/economy/global-economy-watch/ assets/pdfs/global-economy-watch-october-2014.pdf.

128 **Southeast Asian economies:** Ibid.

129 **"I believe the auto industry":** Joann Muller, "Davos 2016: GM Boss Sees a Revolution in Personal Mobility," *Forbes*, January18, 2016, www.forbes.com/sites/joannmuller/2016/01/18/ davos-2016-gm-boss-sees-a-revolution-in-personal-mobility/#52c59b8646bf.

131 **Amazon had to write down:** Taylor Soper, "Ouch: Amazon Takes $170M Write-Down on Fire Phone," GeekWire, October 23, 2014, www.geekwire.com/2014/amazon-takes-170m -loss-fire-phone/.

133 **"Companies are successful":** Bruce Rogers, "John Chambers on Market Transitions and Managing Change," *Forbes*, May 15, 2017, www.forbes.com/sites/brucerogers/2017/05/15/ john-chambers-on-market-transitions-and-managing-change/2/#2abc9f3c5a52.

136 **For many consumer entertainment:** Christopher A. H. Vollmer, "How to Make Entertain-ment and Media Businesses 'Fan'-tastic," *Strategy+Business* 87, Summer 2017, May 8, 2017, https://www.strategy-business.com/article/How-to-Make-Entertainment-and-Media -Businesses-Fan-tastic.

136 **Marvel took home:** Mike Sampson, "How Marvel Risked Everything to Go from Bankruptcy to Billions," ScreenCrush, April 23, 2016, http://screencrush.com/marvel-bankruptcy -billions/.

NOTES

138   **"the once unthinkable acquisition"**: Barnes, "Disney Makes $52.4 Billion Deal for 21st Century Fox in Big Bet on Streaming."

140   **"The price of inaction"**: Margaret Steen, "Meg Whitman: How We Grew eBay from 30 to 13,000 Employees," Stanford Graduate School of Business, Insights, May 1, 2006, www.gsb .stanford.edu/insights/meg-whitman-how-we-grew-ebay-30-13000-employees.

141   **By 2012, PayPal represented:** Will Ashworth, "Ebay-Paypal: A One-in-a-Million Deal," *InvestorPlace*, April 15, 2013, https://investorplace.com/2013/04/ebay-paypal-a-one-in-a -million-deal/#.Wiyo2UpKuUk.

141   **PayPal was once again:** Jonathan Chadwick, "eBay Takes Control over Online Payments by Ditching PayPal," ZDNet, February 2, 2018, www.zdnet.com/article/ebay-takes-control-over -online-payments-by-ditching-paypal/?utm_content=buffer7d6cc&utm_medium=social& utm_source=twitter.com&utm_campaign=buffer.

142   **By 2020, the global payments:** McKinsey Financial Services Practice, "Global Payments 2016: Strong Fundamentals Despite Uncertain Times," McKinsey & Company, September 2016, www.mckinsey.com/~/media/McKinsey/Industries/Financial%20Services/Our%20 Insights/A%20mixed%202015%20for%20the%20global%20payments%20industry/ Global-Payments-2016.ashx.

142   **"My goal is to":** "2016 Words of Wisdom: The CEO Edition," PYMNTS.com, December 26, 2016, www.pymnts.com/news/payments-innovation/2016/2016-words-of-wisdom-the-ceo -edition/.

142   **a suite of targeted products:** Dan Schulman, "PayPal's CEO on Creating Products for Underserved Markets," *Harvard Business Review*, December 2016, https://hbr.org/2016/12/ paypals-ceo-on-creating-products-for-underserved-markets.

143   **"Successful product launches":** "Consumers in Developing Countries Are More Likely to Be 'Early Adopters' of New Products," Nielsen.com, Press Room, June 23, 2015, www.nielsen .com/us/en/press-room/2015/consumers-in-developing-countries-are-more-likely-to-be-early -adopters-of-new-products.html.

145   **"Belief in oneself":** Attributed to Lydia Maria Child, original source unknown.

145   **"every second, seven new boxes":** James Delingpole, "When LEGO Lost Its Head—and How This Toy Story Got Its Happy Ending," *Mail Online*, December 18, 2009, www.dailymail .co.uk/home/moslive/article-1234465/When-LEGO-lost-head—toy-story-got-happy-ending .html.

145   **In 1999, LEGO decided to cut:** Alexandra Gibbs and Carolin Roth, "How LEGO Built Itself Back Together Again," CNBC, November 9, 2016, www.cnbc.com/2016/11/09/how-the -LEGO-group-built-itself-back-together-again.html.

146   **LEGO hit a growth stall:** Jacob Gronholt-Pedersen and Julie Astrid Thomsen, "LEGO to Cut 1,400 Staff as Decade-Long Sales Boom Ends," Reuters, Business News, September 5, 2017, www.reuters.com/article/us-LEGO-results/LEGO-to-cut-1400-staff-as-decade-long-sales -boom-ends-idUSKCN1BG0WK.

147   **"Suddenly the consumer":** Richard Milne, "LEGO Suffers First Drop in Revenues in a Decade," *Financial Times*, September 5, 2017, www.ft.com/content/d5e0b6b0-9211-11e7-a9e6 -11d2f0ebb7f0.

147   **LEGO has increased sales:** "LEGO Expands to Beat Supply Chain Bottlenecks," *Euronews*, June 9, 2016, http://www.euronews.com/2016/09/06/LEGO-expands-to-beat-supply-chain -bottlenecks.

148   **10 percent growth in sales:** "Global LEGO Group Sales Grew 10% in First Half of 2016," LEGO.com, LEGO Newsroom, September 6, 2016, www.LEGO.com/en-us/aboutus/news -room/2016/september/interim-result.

148   **"whether we will grow the next two years":** Jacob Gronhold-Pedersen and Julie Astrid Thomsen, "LEGO to cut 1,400 staff as decade-long sales boom ends," Reuters, September 5, 2017, https://www.reuters.com/article/us-LEGO-results/LEGO-to-cut-1400-staff-as-decade -long-sales-boom-ends-idUSKCN1BG0WK LEGO.

151   **Inge Thulin, president and CEO:** Michelle Caruso-Cabrera, "3M CEO: Research Is 'Driving This Company,'" CNBC.com, June 10, 2013, www.cnbc.com/id/100801531.

NOTES

151 **According to Harvard:** Kurt Schroeder, "Why So Many New Products Fail (and It's Not the Product)," *Business Journals*, March 14, 2017, www.bizjournals.com/bizjournals/how-to/marketing/2017/03/why-so-many-new-products-fail-and-it-s-not-the.html.

PATH 6 OPTIMIZE SALES

156 **"Work smarter . . . not harder,":** Attributed to Allan H. Mogensen.

156 **Sixty-four percent of consumers:** "Global Brand Simplicity Index 2017," Siegel+Gale, 2017, http://simplicityindex.com/.

156 **Only about 22 percent:** *Conversion Rate Optimization Report 2017*, Econsultancy.com, October 2017, https://econsultancy.com/reports/conversion-rate-optimization-report/.

156 **Forty-four percent of sales organizations:** Miller Heiman Group, *2017 CSO Insights Sales Enablement Optimization Report/Summary*, CSO Insights, 2016, 2017, www.csoinsights.com/wp-content/uploads/sites/5/2017/10/2017-SE-Executive-Summary.pdf.

156 **Over half of sales organizations:** Ibid.

156 **Sales teams spend an average:** Stefanie Jansen, "15 Sales Statistics That Prove Sales Is Changing," *Salesforce Blog*, November 17, 2017, www.salesforce.com/blog/2017/11/15-sales-statistics.html.

156 **Overall, 5 percent of shoppers:** Shelley Bransten, "How Salesforce Enabled Retailers to Power the Busiest Shopping Days of the Holiday Season," *Salesforce Blog*, November 29, 2017, www.salesforce.com/blog/2017/11/salesforce-powers-cyber-week.html.

156 **U.S. firms spend $15 billion:** "How to Predict Turnover on Your Sales Team," *Harvard Business Review*, July 2017, https://hbr.org/2017/07/how-to-predict-turnover-on-your-sales-team.

157 **"Pretend that every single":** Maribeth Kuzmeski, *The Connectors* (Hoboken, NJ: John Wiley, 2009), Kindle edition, chapter 5.

162 **"If I'm right":** Brian Stoffel, "America's 10th Best CEO Will Give You an Investing Edge," Motley Fool, March 29, 2013, www.fool.com/investing/general/2013/03/29/americas-10th-best-ceo-will-give-you-an-investing.aspx.

164 **CRM continues to be:** Louis Columbus, "Gartner Predicts CRM Will Be a $36B Market by 2017," *Forbes*, June 18, 2013, www.forbes.com/sites/louiscolumbus/2013/06/18/gartner-predicts-crm-will-be-a-36b-market-by-2017/#949be3a77e31.

166 **"How to energize":** Ken Krogue, "Behind the Cloud Part 4—The Sales Playbook," InsideSales.com, December 12, 2009, www.insidesales.com/insider/kens-notes/behind-the-cloud-part-4/.

166 **"there was an unrealized":** Marc Benioff, *Behind the Cloud* (San Francisco: Jossey-Bass, 2009), p. 73.

168 **"The ideal way to win a championship":** Phil Jackson, in Michael Benson, *Winning Words* (Lanham: Taylor Trade, 2008) p. 123.

170 **Walmart made its own foray:** Portia Crowe, "IT'S OFFICIAL: Walmart Is Buying Jet.com for $3 Billion," *Business Insider*, August 8, 2016, www.businessinsider.com/walmart-is-buying-jetcom-2016-8.

170 **"Across almost all categories":** Monica Watrous, "Wal-Mart Grocery Sales Surge in Latest Quarter," Food Business News, November 20, 2107, www.foodbusinessnews.net/articles/news_home/Financial-Performance/2017/11/Wal-Mart_grocery_sales_surge_i.aspx?ID=%7BA34B0D51-CBE8-4358-B3E3-5F9DD0B00533%7D&cck=1.

170 **managing two very distinct channels:** John Furth, "Amazon vs. Wal-Mart is shaping up to be a battle of mega-retailers," *New York Daily News*, August 30, 2017.

172 **McMillon announced a number:** "Walmart CEO McMillon Outlines Vision for 'Future of Shopping' at Annual Shareholders' Meeting," *Business Wire*, June 2, 2017, www.businesswire.com/news/home/20170602005650/en/Walmart-CEO-McMillon-Outlines-Vision-%E2%80%98Future-Shopping%E2%80%99.

172 **100 metropolitan areas by the end of 2018:** Phil Wahba, "Walmart Grocery Availabilty Delivery Grows to Some 40% of U.S. Households," *Fortune*, March 14, 2018, fortune.com/2018/03/14/walmart-grocery-3.

NOTES

173   **rose 50 percent in the United States alone:** Phil Wahba, "Walmart's U.S. Sales Blow Past Expectations Thanks to E-Commerce and Food," *Fortune*, November 16, 2017, http://fortune.com/2017/11/16/walmart-results-2/.

173   **Target acquired Shipt Inc.:** Matthew Boyle, "Target to Buy Shipt for $550 Million in Challenge to Amazon," *Bloomberg Business,* December 13, 2017, www.bloomberg.com/amp/news/articles/2017-12-13/target-to-buy-shipt-for-550-million-in-bet-on-same-day-delivery.

173   **A recent announcement by Alibaba:** Kesha Hannam, "Alibaba Is Spending $2.9 Billion to Challenge Walmart in China, *Fortune*, November 20, 2017, http://fortune.com/2017/11/20/alibaba-invests-chinas-sun-art/.

176   **world's second-largest bank:** Laura J. Keller and Katherine Chiglinsky, "Wells Fargo Eclipsed by JPMorgan as World's Most Valuable Bank," *Bloomberg*, September 13, 2016, www.bloomberg.com/news/articles/2016-09-13/wells-fargo-eclipsed-by-jpmorgan-as-world-s-most-valuable-bank.

176   **"Products" for the bank:** Bethany McLean, "How Wells Fargo's Cutthroat Corporate Culture Allegedly Drove Bankers to Fraud," *Vanity Fair*, Hive, May 31, 2017, www.vanityfair.com/news/2017/05/wells-fargo-corporate-culture-fraud.

176   **He had launched an initiative:** Ibid.

177   **biggest scandal in its history:** "The Hard Fall of Wells Fargo's Carrie Tolstedt," CBS MoneyWatch, April 11, 2017, www.cbsnews.com/news/the-hard-fall-of-wells-fargos-carrie-tolstedt/.

178   **aggressive sales targets:** Jana Kasperkevic, "Wells Fargo Eliminates Sales Quotas After Unauthorized Accounts Scandal, *Guardian*, Banking, September 13, 2016, www.theguardian.com/business/2016/sep/13/wells-fargo-eliminates-sales-quotas-unauthorized-accounts.

178   **3.5 million accounts:** Samantha Masunaga and James Rufus Koren, "Wells Fargo's Estimate for Unauthorized Accounts Jumps 67%, to 3.5 Million," *Los Angeles Times*, August 31, 2017, www.latimes.com/business/la-fi-wells-fargo-accounts-20170831-story.html.

180   **Ethics have become:** Mintel Press Team, "56% of Americans Stop Buying from Brands They Believe Are Unethical," Mintel.com, November 18, 2015, www.mintel.com/press-centre/social-and-lifestyle/56-of-americans-stop-buying-from-brands-they-believe-are-unethical.

PATH 7 CHURN (MINIMIZE DEFECTION)

186   **"The well-satisfied customer":** Attributed to J. C. Penney. Original source unknown.

186   **A 5 percent increase:** Alex Lawrence, "Five Customer Retention Tips for Entrepreneurs," *Forbes*, November 1, 2012, www.forbes.com/sites/alexlawrence/2012/11/01/five-customer-retention-tips-for-entrepreneurs/#3fd0e1a85e8d.

186   **Sixty-seven percent of consumers:** Vala Afshar, "50 Important Customer Experience Stats for Business Leaders," *Huffington Post, The Blog,* October 15, 2015, www.huffingtonpost.com/vala-afshar/50-important-customer-exp_b_8295772.html.

186   **Forty-two percent of companies:** Genesys, *3 Strategies to Improve the Customer Experience* (Daly City, CA: Genesys, 2014), www.genesys.com/resources/3Strategies_improve_CX_EB06022014_screen_(1).pdf.

186   **Retailers and publishers:** *Forbes* Staff, "Investing in Customer Retention Leads to Greatly Increased Market Share, Says Forbes Insights Study," *Forbes*, September 14, 2016, www.forbes.com/sites/forbespr/2016/09/14/investing-in-customer-retention-leads-to-significantly-increased-market-share-says-new-study/#78f28022472d.

186   **CMOs invested two-thirds:** Lizzy Foo Kune, James Meyers, "A Marketer's Guide to What Is—and Isn't—a Customer Data Platform," Gartner for Marketers, report, March 9, 2018.

187   **"Before going too wide":** Drew Neisser, "How Spotify Curated the Ultimate Playlist for Brand Growth," *Ad Age*, March 29, 2017, http://adage.com/article/cmo-strategy/spotify-curated-ultimate-playlist-brand-growth/308452/.

187   **"Customer churn rate is a metric":** Amy Gallo, "The Value of Keeping the Right Customers," *Harvard Business Review*, October 29, 2014, https://hbr.org/2014/10/the-value-of-keeping-the-right-customers.

NOTES

187 **"Companies typically track":** Allen Miller, Ben Vonwiller, and Peter Weed, "Grow fast or die slow: Focusing on customer success to drive growth," McKinsey & Company, https://www.mckinsey.com/industries/high-tech/our-insights/grow-fast-or-die-slow-focusing-on-customer-success-to-drive-growth.

188 **In April 2017:** Richard Kestenbaum, "Subscription Businesses Are Exploding with Growth," *Forbes*, August 10, 2017, www.forbes.com/sites/richardkestenbaum/2017/08/10/subscription-businesses-are-exploding-with-growth/#51961b5d6678.

188 **more than 80 percent of software vendors:** Christy Pettey, "Moving to a Software Subscription Model," Gartner.com, November 12, 2015, www.gartner.com/smarterwithgartner/moving-to-a-software-subscription-model/.

189 **lost 77 percent of its daily active users:** Cherie Hu, "Spotify's Churn Rate and Inactive Subscribers: Should the Music Industry be Concerned?," *Billboard*, March 26, 2018, www.billboard.com/articles/business/8258220/music-industry-spotify-churn-rate-inactive-subscribers.

190 **typical U.S. wireless carrier:** Dina Gerdeman, "A Smarter Way to Reduce Customer Churn," *Forbes*, Leadership, November 11, 2013, www.forbes.com/sites/hbsworkingknowledge/2013/11/11/a-smarter-way-to-reduce-customer-churn/#76ee339d2c0a.

190 **returning shoppers spend:** Sarabjit Singh Baveja, Sharad Rastogi, Chris Zook, Randall S. Hancock, and Julian Chu, *The Value of Online Customer Loyalty*, Bain & Company/Mainspring eStrategy Brief, April 1, 2000, www.bain.com/Images/Value_online_customer_loyalty_you_capture.pdf.

190 **companies that focus on retention:** *Forbes* Staff, "Investing in Customer Retention Leads to Greatly Increased Market Share, Says Forbes Insights Study."

190 **nearly 50 percent more likely:** Jason Grunberg, "A Forbes Insights Study: Linking Customer Retention with Profitable Growth," Sailthru, September 14, 2016, www.sailthru.com/marketing-blog/a-forbes-insights-study-linking-customer-retention-with-profitable-growth.

191 **"controlling it all the way":** Neisser, "How Spotify Curated the Ultimate Playlist for Brand Growth."

192 **"We don't think of":** Daniel Frankel, "Sling TV's Lynch: 'We Don't Think of People Leaving the Service as Churn,'" FierceCable.com, May 7, 2015, www.fiercecable.com/cable/sling-tv-s-lynch-we-don-t-think-people-leaving-service-as-churn.

192 **expected to show a growth rate:** "Digital Media Market Report," *Statista*, April 2018, www.statista.com/study/44526/digital-media-report/.

192 **As of January 2018:** "About: What Is Spotify?," Spotify.com, Press, n.d., https://press.spotify.com/us/about/.

192 **triple that of Apple's:** Micah Singleton, "Spotify Now Has 140 Million Active Users," The Verge.com, June 15, 2017, www.theverge.com/2017/6/15/15807826/spotify-140-million-active-users.

193 **Spotify's churn rate among premium subscribers:** Spotify Technology S.A. Registration Statement, United States Securities and Exchanges Commission, February 28, 2018, www.sec.gov.

193 **"You never get a":** Attributed to Will Rogers. Original source unknown.

195 **"Scaling Spotify's support":** Patrick Haughey, *How Spotify Keeps 99% of Its Customers Happy*, Voxpro.com, podcast, October 14, 2017, www.voxprogroup.com/customer-experience/how-spotify-keeps-99-of-its-customers-happy/.

196 **"Price is what you":** Benjamin Graham, as quoted by Warren Buffett, Berkshire Hathaway letter to shareholders, February 27, 2009, www.berkshirehathaway.com/letters/2008ltr.pdf.

196 **its conversion rate is:** Benjamin Brandall, "Freemium Conversion Rate: Why Spotify Destroys Dropbox by 667%," March 29, 2016, https://www.business2community.com/digital-marketing/freemium-conversion-rate-spotify-destroys-dropbox-667-01497671#cqiZvz54UaXJkGCx.97.

197 **help Spotify differentiate itself:** Tom Turula, "Spotify Will Now Sell Listeners Makeup Products Inspired by Popular Music Artists," *Business Insider*, November 13, 2017, www.businessinsider.com/spotify-to-sell-makeup-products-2017-11.

197   **as Spotify surpasses 170 million:** Anita Balakrishnan, "Spotify stock plunges after reporting earnings for the first time," CNBC, May 2, 2018, www.cnbc.com/2018/05/02/spotify-earnings-q1-2018.html.

197   **Controlling Churn for Spotify:** Sanjeev Sularia, "iTunes, Spotify, Kindle: Reinventing How You Spend," *Brand Quarterly,* December 19, 2017, www.brandquarterly.com/itunes-spotify-kindle-reinventing-spend.

197   **Fifty-three percent of consumers:** Kimberlee Morrison, "Consumers Want Personalization in Exchange for Their Data (Infographic)," *Adweek,* October 21, 2016, www.adweek.com/digital/consumers-want-personalization-in-exchange-for-their-data-infographic/.

199   **Netflix was one of:** Thomas Franck, "Buy Netflix Before Earnings Because Subscriber Growth Will Top Street: UBS," CNBC, October 4, 2017, www.cnbc.com/2017/10/04/buy-netflix-before-earnings-because-subscriber-growth-will-top-street-ubs.html.

199   **ratchet up marketing spending:** Todd Spangler, "Netflix Blasts Past Q4 Subscriber-Growth Expectations, Shares Soar to All-Time High," *Variety,* January 22, 2018, http://variety.com/2018/digital/news/netflix-q4-2017-earnings-stock-1202672341.

199   **At the beginning of 2017:** Marketwired, "Parks Associates: 19% of U.S. Broadband Households Cancelled an OTT Video Service in the Past 12 Months," Yahoo! Finance, February 1, 2017, https://finance.yahoo.com/news/parks-associates-19-u-broadband-140000232.html.

200   **more than 50 percent of U.S. OTT subscription:** "More Than One-Half of OTT-Subscribing Households Pay for Multiple OTT Video Services," ParksAssociates.com, November 30, 2017, www.parksassociates.com/blog/article/pr-11302017.

200   **subscribing to five or more services:** Ibid.

201   **"Netflix plans to spend":** Nick Statt, "Netflix Plans to Spend $8 Billion to Make Its Library 50 Percent Original by 2018," TheVerge.com, October 16, 2017, www.theverge.com/2017/10/16/16486436/netflix-original-content-8-billion-dollars-anime-films.

201   **nearly 50 percent of the content:** Jessica Rawden, "Netflix Is Adding More Originals but There's a Definite Downside for Users," CinemaBlend.com, n.d., www.cinemablend.com/television/1605310/netflix-is-adding-more-originals-but-theres-a-definite-downside-for-users.

201   **Netflix was the top earning:** Sarah Perez, "Netflix Was 2017's Top Non-Game App by Revenue," *TechCrunch,* January 12, 2018, https://techcrunch.com/2018/01/12/netflix-was-2017s-top-non-game-app-by-revenue/.

202   **Netflix Q1 2018 results:** Tim Mulligan, "Netflix Q1 2018 results: Hiking Prices or Fighting Churn?," Midia Research, April 18, 2018, www.midiaresearch.com/blog/netflix-q1-2018-results-hiking-prices-or-fighting-churn/.

203   **profit of roughly 50 percent on DVD:** Michael Liedtke, "Netflix's Shrinking DVD Service Faces Uncertain Future," Associated Press, January 19, 2017, https://www.apnews.com/7bdf66b8c20d4f6889eb825b33f72780/Netflix's-shrinking-DVD-service-faces-uncertain-future.

205   **"Consumer preferences for food":** Abigail Stevenson, "Campbell Soup CEO: Stunning Disruption in the Ecosystem of Food," CNBC, "Mad Money with Jim Cramer," July 21, 2016, https://www.cnbc.com/2016/07/21/campbell-soup-ceo-stunning-disruption-in-the-ecosystem-of-food.html.

205   **Home-delivered "meal kits":** Bob Goldin and Barry Friends, "Meal Kits: Are They a Real Threat to Foodservice, Retail or Both?," *Pentallect POV,* June 27, 2017, http://pentallect.com/wp-content/uploads/2017/06/Pentallct-POV-Meal-Kits.pdf.

205   **multitrillion-dollar food industry:** Ibid.

206   **class-action "stock drop" lawsuit:** Katie Roof, "Blue Apron Hit with Multiple Class Action Lawsuits," *TechCrunch,* August 21, 2017, https://techcrunch.com/2017/08/21/blue-apron-hit-with-class-action-lawsuit-from-shareholders.

207   **According to an analysis:** Daniel McCarthy, "A Detailed Look at Blue Apron's Challenging Unit Economics," LinkedIn Article, June 27, 2017, https://www.linkedin.com/pulse/detailed-look-blue-aprons-challenging-unit-economics-daniel-mccarthy.

207   **for Q4 2017, it reported:** Blue April Holdings, Inc. Reports First Quarter 2018 Results," BusinessWire, May 3, 2018. www.businesswire.com/news/home/20180503005277/en/Blue-Apron-Holdings-Inc.Reports-Quarter-2018-Results.

NOTES

208 **"Our initial indications":** "Blue Apron Holdings' (APRN) CEO Matt Salzberg on Q3 2017 Results—Earnings Call Transcript," SeekingAlpha.com, November 2, 2017, https://seeking alpha.com/article/4119692-blue-apron-holdings-aprn-ceo-matt-salzberg-q3-2017-results -earnings-call-transcript.

211 **"bitterness of poor quality":** Attributed to Aldo Gucci. Original source unknown.

212 **retaining existing customers:** Khalid Saleh, "Customer Acquisition vs. Retention Costs— Statistics and Trends," Invesp, n.d., www.invespcro.com/blog/customer-acquisition-retention.

PATH 8 PARTNERSHIPS

216 **"Partnership is the way":** Attributed to Alanis Morissette. Unknown source.

216 **Forty-eight percent of global CEOs:** "Joint Ventures and Strategic Alliances: Examining the Keys to Success," PwC.com, 2016, www.pwc.com/us/en/deals/publications/joint-ventures -strategic-alliances.html.

216 **Two-thirds of CEOs:** *Now or Never: 2016 Global CEO Outlook,* KPMG.com, June 2016, https://home.kpmg.com/content/dam/kpmg/pdf/2016/07/2016_Global_CEO_Outlook_ Final.pdf?logActivity=true.

216 **Eighty-five percent of business owners:** *Grow from the Right Intro: A Report on the Strategic Value of Business Alliances and Compatible Partner Matching,* Powerlinx, BPI Network, and CMO Council, September 2014, www.powerlinx.com/blog/grow-from-right-intro -strategic-partnerships/.

216 **Michael Dell launched PC's Limited:** "About Dell: Our History," Dell.com, www.dell.com/ learn/us/en/uscorp1/our-history.

217 **Dell found itself:** "Direct the World Over: Dell Fiscal 2006 in Review," Zonebourse.com, n.d., www.zonebourse.com/DELL-TECHNOLOGIES-31257688/pdf/73012/Dell%20 Technologies_Rapport-institutionnel.pdf.

217 **"If you are not partnering":** *Challenge or Be Challenged: How to Succeed in Today's Business Environment, Forbes,* Insights, in association with Gap International, 2017, https://i.forbesimg .com/forbesinsights/gap_international/ChallengeOrBeChallenged.pdf, 8.

217 **Gateway closed all 188 stores:** Jamie Holguin, "Gateway Closing Stores," CBS News, April 2, 2004, www.cbsnews.com/news/gateway-closing-stores/.

218 **$43 billion under the newly formed DELL-EMC partner program:** Lynn Haber, "Dell EMC Shores Up Partner Program for 2018," February 7, 2018, *Channel Futures,* www .channelfutures.com/channel-futures/dell-emc-shores-partner-program-2018.

221 **"Partners have been":** Mark Haranas, "Cisco CEO Chuck Robbins: The '5 Key Elements' of Cisco's Digital and Channel Strategy," CRN.com, November 1, 2017, www.crn.com/ slide-shows/networking/300094906/cisco-ceo-chuck-robbins-the-5-key-elements-of-ciscos -digital-and-channel-strategy.htm.

222 **Cisco Systems discontinued:** Mark Reilly, "How Flip's Demise Got GoPro on Best Buy Shelves," *Minneapolis/St. Paul Business Journal,* June 20, 2013, Bizjournals.com, www .bizjournals.com/twincities/morning_roundup/2013/06/how-flips-demise-got-gopro-on -best.html.

222 **GoPro became one of:** R. D. Greengold, "How Best Buy's Success Could Be a Blessing for GoPro," *Motley Fool,* September 9, 2015, www.fool.com/investing/general/2015/09/09/ how-best-buys-success-could-be-a-blessing-for-gopr.aspx.

223 **"We've always felt":** Christopher Heine, "Red Bull and GoPro Team Up to Create More High-Flying Videos," *Adweek,* May 24, 2016, www.adweek.com/digital/red-bull-and-gopro -team-create-more-high-flying-videos-171648/.

223 **"As partners, Red Bull":** "GoPro and Red Bull Form Exclusive Global Partnership," GoPro. com, The Inside Line, May 24, 2016, https://gopro.com/news/gopro-and-red-bull-form -exclusive-global-partnership.

224 **According to Statista:** "Most Popular YouTube Brand Channels as of October 2017, Ranked by Total Number of Video Views (in Billions)," Statista.com, n.d., www.statista.com/ statistics/277765/most-popular-youtube-brand-channels-ranked-by-views.

NOTES

224 **On its fourth-quarter 2017:** "GoPro Announces Fourth Quarter and Full Year 2017 Results," PR Newswire, Cision, February 1, 2018, www.prnewswire.com/news-releases/gopro -announces-fourth-quarter-and-full-year-2017-results-300592276.html.

224 **GoPro has made partnerships:** Leo Sun, "Do Any of GoPro Inc's Recent Partnerships Matter?," *Motley Fool,* March 2, 2016, www.fool.com/investing/general/2016/03/02/do-any-of -gopro-incs-recent-partnerships-matter.aspx.

224 **"We view this as":** Adam Rogers, "What Do Analysts Expect from GoPro in 2Q16?," Market Realist, July 15, 2016, http://marketrealist.com/2016/07/gopros-major-partnerships-2q16.

227 **"It is literally true":** Attributed to Napoleon Hill. Original source unknown.

227 **Airline Deregulation Act:** David Morris, "Airline Deregulation: A Triumph of Ideology over Evidence," *Huffington Post,* The Blog, December 13, 2013, updated April 19, 2017, www .huffingtonpost.com/david-morris/airline-deregulation-ideology-over-evidence_b_4399150 .html.

227 **Civil Aeronautics Board (CAB) set fares:** Ibid.

228 **largest domestic U.S. carrier:** Madhu Unnikrishnan, "A Law That Changed the Airline I ndustry Beyond Recognition (1978)," Aviation Week Network, June 4, 2015, http:// aviationweek.com/blog/law-changed-airline-industry-beyond-recognition-1978.

229 **number of air passengers tripled:** Jeffrey M. Jones, "Airline Satisfaction Remains High," Gallup, December 13, 2007, http://news.gallup.com/poll/103237/airline-satisfaction -remains-high.aspx?version=print.

229 **expects 7.2 billion passengers:** "IATA Forecasts Passenger Demand to Double over 20 Years."

229 **The International Air Transport:** "IATA Forecasts Passenger Demand to Double over 20 Years," IATA Pressroom, press release, October 18, 2016, www.iata.org/pressroom/pr/ Pages/2016-10-18-02.aspx.

229 **Airline ticket prices have fallen:** Derek Thompson, "How Airline Ticket Prices Fell 50% in 30 Years (and Why Nobody Noticed)," *Atlantic,* February 28, 2013, www.theatlantic.com/ business/archive/2013/02/how-airline-ticket-prices-fell-50-in-30-years-and-why-nobody -noticed/273506/.

230 **frequent flyer programs:** Julian Mark Kheel, "Do Loyalty Programs Make More Money for the Airlines Than Flying?," ThePointsGuy.com, March 31, 2017, https://thepointsguy .com/2017/03/do-loyalty-programs-make-money/.

230 **leverage the partnership:** Hugo Martin, "Frequent Flier Programs Generate Profits for Airlines and Frustration for Travelers," *Los Angeles Times,* September 15, 2017, www.latimes .com/business/la-fi-frequent-flier-programs-20170914-story.html.

231 **"Our partnership with American Express":** Ibid.

231 **Best Airline Alliance:** "Skytrax World Airline Awards," WorldAirlineAwards.com, n.d., www .worldairlineawards.com/Awards/worlds_best_airline_alliance.html.

233 **"It doesn't matter":** Kelsey Murray, "Mark Cuban Says It Doesn't Matter if You Fail, You Just Have to Be Right Once," ThriveGlobal.com, June 5, 2017, https://journal.thriveglobal .com/mark-cuban-says-it-doesnt-matter-if-you-fail-you-just-have-to-be-right-once -e19b32b4de0c.

236 **commission rates for iTunes affiliates:** James Vincent, "Apple Clarifies Commission Cuts for iTunes Affiliates," TheVerge.com, May 8, 2017, www.theverge.com/2017/5/8/15577104/ itunes-affiliate-program-commission-rate-changes.

237 **"A strong relationship with":** Donald V. Fites, "Make Your Dealers Your Partners," *Harvard Business Review,* March–April 1996, https://hbr.org/1996/03/make-your-dealers-your -partners.

PATH 9 CO-OPETITION

242 **"No one can succeed":** Thomas L. Friedman, "Collaborate vs. Collaborate," *New York Times,* January 12, 2013, www.nytimes.com/2013/01/13/opinion/sunday/friedman-collaborate -vs-collaborate.html.

NOTES

242 **Creating partnerships or:** *Now or Never: 2016 Global CEO Outlook*, KPMG.com, June 2016, https://home.kpmg.com/content/dam/kpmg/pdf/2016/07/2016_Global_CEO_Outlook_Final.pdf?logActivity=true.

242 **Eighty-five percent of CEOs:** *Architects of a Better World: Building the Post-2015 Business Engagement Architecture*, UN Global Compact–Accenture CEO Study on Sustainability, September 2013, https://acuns.org/wp-content/uploads/2013/10/ARCHITECTS-OF-A-BETTER-WORLD.pdf.

243 **"While the law":** Andrew Carnegie, *The Gospel of Wealth*.

246 **"In order to advance":** "Fiat Chrysler to Aid in the Development of World-Leading Autonomous Driving Platform," BusinessChief.com, August 17, 2017, http://europe.businesschief.com/technology/1402/Fiat-Chrysler-to-aid-in-the-development-of-world-leading-autonomous-driving-platform.

247 **"The companies are talking":** Dean Takahashi, "Fiat Chrysler Joins Intel and BMW to Develop Self-Driving Cars," VentureBeat.com, August 16, 2017, https://venturebeat.com/2017/08/16/fiat-chrysler-joins-intel-and-bmw-to-develop-self-driving-cars.

248 **"The two factors":** Ibid.

248 **According to A. T. Kearney:** Michael Romer, Steffen Gaenzle, and Christian Weiss, *How Automakers Can Survive the Self-Driving Era*, ATKearney.com, 2016, www.atkearney.com/automotive/article?/a/how-automakers-can-survive-the-self-driving-era.

249 **"The future of transportation":** Phil LeBeau, "Fiat Chrysler Joins BMW and Intel to Develop Self-Driving Cars," *CNBC*, August 16, 2017, www.cnbc.com/2017/08/15/fiat-chrysler-joins-bmw-and-intel-to-develop-self-driving-cars.html.

251 **"the most powerful alliance in tech history":** Aaron Tilley, "The End of Wintel: How the Most Powerful Alliance in Tech History is Falling Apart," *Forbes*, March 10, 2017, https://www.forbes.com/sites/aarontilley/2017/03/10/microsoft-intel-divorce/.

251 **"Wintel is a computer trade industry term":** Wintel definition, TechTarget, http://searchwindowsserver.techtarget.com/definition/Wintel.

252 **Gates proposed to acquire:** Alice Kreit and Jessica Wanke, "Timeline: Bill Gates. From Geek to Gazillionaire to Do-Gooder," NPR, www.npr.org/news/graphics/2008/june/bill_gates/gates_timeline_04.html.

253 **The great lesson of the Wintel story:** Ajay Shah, "Windows + Intel = Wintel?," Mayin.org, 1998, www.mayin.org/ajayshah/MEDIA/1998/wintel.html.

256 **"Cisco and EMC":** "Cisco and EMC, Together with VMware, Form Coalition to Accelerate Pervasive Data Center Virtualization and Private Cloud Infrastructures," Cisco.com, Newsroom, November 3, 2009, https://newsroom.cisco.com/press-release-content?type=webcontent&articleId=5211915.

258 **Cisco's CEO at the time, John Chambers, remarked:** Steve Kaplan, "Customers Embracing Vblocks, but VCE Sales Harmony a Work in Progress," BytheBell.com, October 19, 2010, http://bythebell.com/2010/10/customers-embracing-vblocks-but-vce-sales-harmony-a-work-in-progress.html.

261 **"the partners' strategic goals":** Gary Hamel, Yves Doz, and C.K. Prahalad, "Collaborate with Your Competitors—and Win," *Harvard Business Review*, Jan-Feb 1989 issue, https://hbr.org/1989/01/collaborate-with-your-competitors-and-win.

PATH 10 UNCONVENTIONAL STRATEGIES

264 **"Swim upstream":** Sam Walton with John Huey, *Sam Walton, Made in America: My Story* (New York: Bantam, 2012), p. 317.

264 **Seventy-nine percent of consumers:** Mathew Sweezey, "The Future of Marketing: Five Marketing Megatrends for 2018," MarketingProfs, November 29, 2017, www.marketingprofs.com/articles/2017/33206/the-future-of-marketing-five-marketing-megatrends-for-2018.

264 **Eighty-one percent of business executives:** *The Business Case for Purpose: A Harvard Business Review Analytic Services Report*, sponsored by EY Beacon Institute, 2015, www.ey.com/gl/en/issues/ey-beacon-institute-the-business-case-for-purpose.

264 **Sixty-six percent of consumers:** "Consumer-Goods' Brands That Demonstrate Commitment to Sustainability Outperform Those That Don't", Nielsen, http://www.nielsen.com/us/en/press-room/2015/consumer-goods-brands-that-demonstrate-commitment-to-sustainability-outperform.html.

264 **Social capital is achieving a newfound status:** Dimple Agarwal et. al., "The rise of the social enterprise," Deloitte Insights, March 28, 2018, www2.deloitte.com/insights/us/en/focus/human-capital-trends.html.

265 **Sixty-four percent won't take a job:** "Half of Employees Won't Work for Companies That Don't Have Strong CSR Commitments," Sustainable Brands, June 1, 2016, www.sustainablebrands.com/news_and_views/organizational_change/sustainable_brands/half_employees_wont_work_companies_don%E2%80%99t_hav.

265 **"If you want to grow":** Jillian D'Onfro, "15 quotes that show the strange, relentless genius of billionaire Alibaba founder Jack Ma," *Business Insider*, July 1, 2016.

266 **"A desire for purpose":** Patrick Struebi, "Are We Becoming More Socially Responsible?," WEForum.com, October 2, 2015, www.weforum.org/agenda/2015/10/are-we-becoming-more-socially-responsible.

267 **Apple's most memorable ad campaigns:** Adam Lashinsky, "Apple's Tim Cook Leads Different," *Fortune*, March 26, 2015, http://fortune.com/2015/03/26/tim-cook/.

268 **"There's all this incredible energy":** Robert Safian, "Salesforce's Marc Benioff on the Power of Values," *Fast Company*, April 17, 2017, www.fastcompany.com/40397514/salesforces-marc-benioff-on-the-power-of-values.

268 **"My goals for":** "Building a Company with Heart," Salesforce.com, www.salesforce.com/company/ventures/pledge1.

269 **Salesforce was ranked #1:** Andrew Nusca, "These are *Fortune*," 100 Best Companies to Work For in 2018," *Fortune*, February 22, 2018, fortune.com/2018/02/22/best-companies-to-work-for-2018/.

270 **"What we said was":** Andy Boynton, "Unilever's Paul Polman: CEOs Can't Be 'Slaves' to Shareholders," *Forbes*, July 20, 2015, www.forbes.com/sites/andyboynton/2015/07/20/unilevers-paul-polman-ceos-cant-be-slaves-to-shareholders/2/#60b8ff3b6f06.

270 **"I also made it very clear":** Boynton, "Unilever's Paul Polman: CEOs Can't Be 'Slaves' to Shareholders."

270 **BlackRock's chief executive:** Alicia McElhaney, "Larry Fink to CEOs: Contribute to Society or Lose BlackRock's Investment," *Institutional Investor*, January 16, 2018, www.institutionalinvestor.com/article/b16j67x4y04cvx/larry-fink-to-ceos-contribute-to-society-or-lose-blackrock%E2%80%99s-investment.

272 **"Goals are only wishes":** Melinda Gates, at the World Economic Forum 2016, "Progress towards Parity" panel, January 22, 2016, https://www.weforum.org/events/world-economic-forum-annual-meeting-2016/sessions/progress-towards-parity.

275 **"Make TOMS a movement again":** Blake Mycoskie, "The Founder of TOMS on Reimagining the Company's Mission," *Harvard Business Review*, Jan-Feb 2016 issue, https://hbr.org/2016/01/the-founder-of-TOMS-on-reimagining-the-companys-mission.

275 **TOMS's concept of "one-for-one":** Shawn Donnelly, "16 Brands That Use the TOMS Model of One-for-One Giving," RealClear Life, n.d., www.realclearlife.com/books/16-brands-use-TOMS-model-one-one-giving.

277 **"Being an inspiration":** Leigh Buchanan, "What's Next for TOMS, the $400 Million For-Profit Built on Karmic Capital," *Inc.*, n.d., www.inc.com/magazine/201605/leigh-buchanan/TOMS-founder-blake-mycoskie-social-entrepreneurship.html.

279 **"We have to execute":** Quoted in Gary Burnison, *No Fear of Failure* (San Francisco: Jossey-Bass, 2011), p. 34.

279 **"Eighty-one percent of millennials":** Sarah Landrum, "Millennials Driving Brands to Practice Socially Responsible Marketing," *Forbes*, March 17, 2017, www.forbes.com/sites/sarahlandrum/2017/03/17/millennials-driving-brands-to-practice-socially-responsible-marketing/#1ae315c24990.

NOTES

279 **"Eighty-three percent of junior staff"**: Sweezey, "The Future of Marketing: Five Marketing Megatrends for 2018."

280 **millennials are looking for brands:** *The 2006 Cone Millennial Cause Study*, Cone, Inc., 2006, http://www.centerforgiving.org/Portals/0/2006%20Cone%20Millennial%20Cause%20Study .pdf.

280 **2017 "Change the World" list:** "Change the World," *Fortune*, n.d., http://fortune.com/ change-the-world/.

281 **"Giveback is a unique feature":** "About Lemonade," Lemonade Inc., n.d., www.lemonade .com/faq#service.

282 **Lemonade has raised a total of $180 million:** Paul Sawers, "Lemonade Raises $120 Million from SoftBank, Others to Take Its Chatbot-Based Insurance Service Global," VentureBeat .com, December 19, 2017, https://venturebeat.com/2017/12/19/lemonade-raises-120-million -from-softbank-others-to-take-its-chatbot-based-insurance-service-global.

283 **in August 2017, Lemonade Insurance:** John Peters, *The Lemonade Insurance Underwriting Report—Almost a Year In*, Lemonade Inc., August 30, 2017, www.lemonade.com/blog/ lemonade-h1-underwriting-report-2017/.

283 **at Lemonade, a woman is 50 percent more likely:** Yael Wissner-Levy, "Why Do Women Love Lemonade More?," Lemonade Inc., July 23, 2017, updated March 2018, www.lemonade .com/blog/women-love-lemonade/.

284 **"We love our customers":** Peters, *The Lemonade Insurance Underwriting Report—Almost a Year In*, www.lemonade.com/blog/lemonade-h1-underwriting-report-2017.

285 **prides itself on its transparency:** Daniel Schreiber, "The Lemonade Transparency Chronicles," Lemonade Inc., January 10, 2017, www.lemonade.com/blog/lemonade-transparency -chronicles/.

285 **Its customers are:** Shai Wininger, "Lemonade's Year in Review, 2017," Lemonade Inc., January 17, 2018, www.lemonade.com/blog/lemonade-review-2017.

286 **"Purpose is that sense":** Mark Zuckerberg's Commencement Address at Harvard," *Harvard Gazette*, May 25, 2017, https://news.harvard.edu/gazette/story/2017/05/mark-zuckerbergs -speech-as-written-for-harvards-class-of-2017.

287 **"The origin of Grameen Bank":** "History of Grameen Bank", Grameen Research, http:// grameenresearch.org/history-of-grameen-bank/.

287 **The Grameen Bank Project:** "History of Grameen Bank of Bangladesh," Grameen Bank, www.grameen-info.org/history/.

287 **Grameen pioneered micro-loans:** Evaristus Mainsah, Schuyler R. Heuer, Aprajita Kalra, and Qiulin Zhang, "Grameen Bank: Taking Capitalism to the Poor" (paper written for "Emerging Financial Markets" course at Columbia Business School, New York, fall 2003), www0.gsb.columbia.edu/mygsb/faculty/research/pubfiles/848/Grameen_Bank_v04.pdf.

291 **"When you sacrifice":** Kara Swisher, "Arianna Huffington Has Raised Another $30 Million for Thrive Global at a $120 Million Valuation," Recode.net, November 29, 2017, www .recode.net/2017/11/29/16714392/arianna-huffington-30-million-thrive-global-120 -million-valuation.

291 **"Mission-driven" companies:** Josh Bersin, "Becoming Irresistible: A New Model for Employee Engagement," Deloitte, Insights, *Deloitte Review* 16, January 26, 2015, www2.deloitte .com/insights/us/en/deloitte-review/issue-16/employee-engagement-strategies.html.

291 **Companies with highly engaged workforces:** Susan Sorenson, "How Employee Engagement Drives Growth," Gallup, *Business Journal*, June 20, 2013, http://news.gallup.com/ businessjournal/163130/employee-engagement-drives-growth.aspx.

292 **"We stand on the brink":** Klaus Schwab, "The Fourth Industrial Revolution: What It Means, How to Respond," WEForum.org, January 14, 2016, www.weforum.org/agenda/2016/01/the -fourth-industrial-revolution-what-it-means-and-how-to-respond.

295 **"Not everything that can be counted":** William Bruce Cameron, *Informal Sociology: A Casual Introduction to Sociological Thinking* (New York: Random House, 1963).

297 **"Success is where":** Attributed to Bobby Unser. Original source unknown.

NOTES

298 **"Execution is not just":** Larry Bossidy and Ram Charan, *Execution: The Discipline of Getting Things Done* (New York: Crown Business, 2002), p. 6.

301 **"When we do something":** Shelby Skrhak, "Daniel Pink on Why Time of Day Matters," Success.com, January 11, 2018, www.success.com/podcast/daniel-pink-on-why-time-of-day -matters.

AMAZON CASE STUDY: STAYING IN DAY ONE

302 **"If we have a good quarter":** Daniel Lyons, "Why Bezos Was Surprised by the Kindle's Success," *Newsweek*, December 20, 2009, www.newsweek.com/why-bezos-was-surprised -kindles-success-75509.

305 **Amazon's U.S. customers read:** Sanjeev Sularia, "iTunes, Spotify, Kindle: Reinventing How You Spend," *Brand Quarterly*, December 19, 2017, www.brandquarterly.com/itunes-spotify -kindle-reinventing-spend.

306 **'International Shopping' experience:** "Amazon launches the International Shopping Experience in the Amazon Shopping App," *Business Wire*, April 17, 2018.

307 **"Jeff, what does Day 2 look like?":** *Bezos*, "2016 Letter to Shareholders."

330

NOTES

INDEX

INDEX